# ELIZA LYNN LINTON

*By the same author*

THE TOPS OF THE MULBERRY TREES
(ed.) THE PRIME MINISTERS

# *Eliza Lynn Linton*
## The Girl of the Period

A Biography
by
HERBERT VAN THAL

London
GEORGE ALLEN & UNWIN
Boston      Sydney

*Dedicated to John Bright-Holmes*

First published in 1979

This book is copyright under the Berne Convention. All rights are reserved. Apart from any fair dealing for the purpose of private study, research, criticism or review, as permitted under the Copyright Act, 1956, no part of this publication may be reproduced, stored in a retrieval system, or transmitted, in any form or by any means, electronic, electrical, chemical, mechanical, optical, photocopying, recording or otherwise, without the prior permission of the copyright owner. Enquiries should be sent to the publishers at the undermentioned address:

GEORGE ALLEN & UNWIN LTD
40 Museum Street, London WC1A 1LU

© Herbert van Thal, 1979

**British Library Cataloguing in Publication Data**

Van Thal, Herbert
   Eliza Lynn Linton.
   1. Linton, Elizabeth Lynn – Biography
   2. Authors, English – 19th century – Biography
823'.8   PR4889.L5Z/   78-41056

ISBN 0-04-920057-7

Typeset in 11 on 12 point Baskerville by Bedford Typesetters Ltd
and printed in Great Britain
by Unwin Brothers, Old Woking, Surrey

## Contents

| | | |
|---|---|---|
| *Author's Acknowledgements* | | *page* viii |
| Introduction | | 1 |
| 1 | Eliza's birth and parents | 3 |
| 2 | Gadshill | 15 |
| 3 | Quest for a career | 20 |
| 4 | Occultism | 34 |
| 5 | Correspondent in Paris | 40 |
| 6 | Marriage to W. J. Linton | 48 |
| 7 | Life without Linton | 67 |
| 8 | The *Saturday Review* | 72 |
| 9 | *Sowing the Wind* (1867) | 95 |
| 10 | Beatrice Sichel and A. W. Benn | 102 |
| 11 | Mrs Tweedie and Henry James | 117 |
| 12 | Return to Italy | 129 |
| 13 | *The Autobiography of Christopher Kirkland* | 142 |
| 14 | A letter from Herbert Spencer | 155 |
| 15 | The *Fortnightly Review* | 169 |
| 16 | *Was He Wrong?* | 178 |
| 17 | Beatrice Harraden | 191 |
| 18 | *In Haste and at Leisure* | 199 |
| 19 | Malvern | 203 |
| 20 | The last year | 215 |
| List of Eliza Lynn Linton's Works | | 229 |
| References | | 232 |
| Bibliography | | 240 |

## Author's Acknowledgements

Three people play a most important part in this biography of Mrs Lynn Linton, to whom I am considerably indebted: Malcolm Barnes, for his editing of the manuscript which was originally twice this length; Mrs D. L. Mackay, for her deciphering and typing of the manuscript; and Miss Nancy Anderson, whose thesis on Eliza was a masterly and valuable piece of work.

I also wish to thank the following: Raymond M. Bennett of Rutgers University; Elizabeth Carter; Dr Donald Coggan, Archbishop of Canterbury; Professor Leon Edel; Dr Richard Hitchcock, University of Exeter; Geoffrey T. Large; D. C. Rose; Dr F. B. Smith, Australian National University; Lord Soper.

'Let us hope there is an Olympus for forgotten authors'
*George Eliot to Thomas Adolphus Trollope*

# Introduction

Eliza Lynn Linton (1822–90) was the first woman to be paid a salary on a famous daily newspaper, whilst her first novel, *Azeth the Egyptian* (1846), was published when she was twenty-four. From the days when she left the bleak and lonely rectory in Cumberland where she was born and came to London, she was soon absorbed in a circle of famous contemporaries, beginning when Walter Savage Landor praised her second novel, *Amymone* (1848). Subsequently she met Dickens, Herbert Spencer, George Eliot, Swinburne, Frank Harris, Rider Haggard, Sir Walter Besant, Henry James and countless other eminent Victorians.

She was renowned for her journalism, and in particular, her contributions to the *Saturday Review*. Here she became concerned with the position of the modern woman. The article on 'The Girl of the Period' (1868) created a furore. She accused the modern girl of being 'loud and rampant', with 'false red hair and painted skin, talking slang as glibly as a man, and by preference leading the conversation to doubtful subjects'. The article was reprinted in a New York journal, and the phrase 'The Girl of the Period' became taken up by *Punch* and other papers of the day. Everyone wondered who the writer was, since it appeared anonymously.

On 24 March 1858 she had married the engraver William Linton. She was thirty-six and he ten years older and the father of a number of children by his first wife. When his wife had died Eliza had considerable sympathy with his plight, but their temperaments were completely incompatible and they subsequently parted, although they never divorced.

Eliza recounted a certain amount about herself in a very strange novel, *The Autobiography of Christopher Kirkland*. She writes of herself as a male, and one suspects that she would have liked to have been born of the opposite sex. When she

*Eliza Lynn Linton*

submitted the manuscript to her publisher she wrote: 'I could not publish my own autobiography without some such veil as this of changed sex and personation. How could I speak of my husband and my long agony of futile love unless behind a screen which takes off the sting of boldness and self-exposure?' Apart from her views upon her own sex there is much modernity in her religious views and her novels have a great readability and verve.

On her death Swinburne wrote to a relative (on 28 July 1898): 'Perhaps you may know that I have lost another dear and honoured friend in Mrs Lynn Linton. It was a great shock and grief to me to see her death announced in the newspapers – I did not even know that she had been ill. She was not only one of the most brilliant and gifted, but one of the kindest and most generous of women. She *would* give me some priceless manuscript relics of Landor – her spiritual father, whose best and truest friend she was. I never knew any one more nobly upright and unselfish and loyal and true. No one ever will.'

# I
# Eliza's birth and parents

The Brontës were not the only writers who suffered the rigours of upbringing in a remote country vicarage. Crosthwaite vicarage in Cumberland was just as remote a place as Haworth; moreover, it was equally lacking in comfort. It was there that on 10 February 1822 Elizabeth Lynn was born.

Her father, the Reverend James Lynn, had been educated at Rochester Grammar School, whence he went to Wadham College, Oxford, where he took his degree, and was ordained at Horsham, Sussex. He next became curate to the parish church at Maidstone and then canon at Rochester, where in addition he held the offices of chaplain to the garrison at Chatham and to the *Argonaut* hospital ship. In 1804 he was appointed to the perpetual curacy of Strood, and seven years later combined this same appointment with Sebergham. He married in 1805 Charlotte Alicia, the daughter of Samuel Goodenough, Dean of Rochester and botanist to Queen Charlotte, who subsequently became Bishop of Carlisle. Lynn resigned his curacy at Strood in 1814, and through the influence of his father-in-law, the Bishop, was appointed Vicar of Caldbeck in Cumberland, adding in 1820 the living of Crosthwaite. Miss Goodenough was very young when the Reverend James Lynn married her, and obviously had little experience of life; nor was she to have, other than bearing her husband twelve children and dying a few months after the birth of the last child, Elizabeth. Much later in life James married again, by which time his children had grown up. Eliza, as she always called herself rather than Elizabeth, was for the first two years of life brought up by her eldest sister, and then by other elder brothers and sisters, her father finding

3

*Eliza Lynn Linton*

looking after, let alone educating, twelve children all too much for him. As Eliza later wrote:

> My poor dear father! The loss of my beautiful mother, and a year after her death, that of his eldest daughter [Charlotte Elizabeth], who seems to have been one of those sweet mother-sisters sometimes found as the eldest of the family, had tried him almost beyond his strength. His life henceforth was a mingled web of passion and tears – now irritated and now despairing – with ever that pathetic prostration at the foot of the Cross, where he sought to lay down his burden of sorrow and to take up instead resignation to the will of God – where he sought peace he never found.[1]

Time had softened her opinions of her father, for life with him at the rectory had been far from easy. The Bishop of Carlisle had tried to assist his son-in-law and made suggestions as to how he might help financially, but Lynn was unresponsive to these, whereupon the Bishop had said to him in exasperation, 'In the name of heaven what do you mean to do for your children?' To which the cleric replied: 'Sit in my study, my lord, smoke my pipe, and commit them to the care of Providence.'[2]

And so the children were left mainly to their own devices by their grossly overburdened father, who, though a classical scholar, found it impossible to impart his considerable learning to them. On top of his parochial duties, the family became rather beyond his control. Eliza records: 'He was a good classical scholar and a sound historian; and though his mathematics did not go very deep, they were better than our ignorance. But he was both too impatient and too indolent to be able to teach, and I doubt if the experiment would have answered had he tried it.'[3]

The result was that, after her eldest sister left home to marry, the eldest son was made responsible for the younger brothers, while Eliza and the sister next to her in age were left totally without education: '... there reigned among us the most disastrous system of tyranny exercised by those unfledged viceroys of Providence over their subordinates...'. Eventually James Narborough, George Goodenough and Arthur Thomas,

*Eliza's birth and parents*

the three eldest sons, went to college, while the next, Samuel, chose the sea. The youngest, Edmund, had died young. Eliza assessed her father as,

> Tory in politics and a democrat in action, defying his diocesan and believing in his divine ordination; contemptuous of the people as a political factor, but kind and familiar in personal intercourse with the poor; clever, well-read and somewhat vain of his knowledge, but void of ambition and indifferent to the name in literature which he might undoubtedly have won with a little industry; not liberal as a home provider, but largely generous in the parish.

The Reverend James Lynn's attitude to life is hardly surprising, for his parish was sparsely populated and rambling. There was only one school between the two livings;[4] on the other hand there were seventeen public houses and jerry-shops, and 'the man who did not get drunk would have been the black swan which the white ones would have soon pecked to death'. No one, however, tried to experiment with sobriety. There was no sense of public decency, no idea of civic order and as little of private morality. 'The parish-constable would have thought twice before taking up a crony for any offence short of murder; and then he would have left the door of the lock-up ajar!'[5] Marriage only became a necessity when a child was imminent and then it was nearly always performed at Gretna Green. Drunkenness was a daily pastime rounded off by 'murry-neets' – dances in barns where the men got drunk, the women fuddled. There were regular Saturday-night fights at which the curate would have to attend, and even Lynn himself had on occasions to marry a couple because the child of the liaison was on the point of arrival.

When Mrs Lynn was alive she could not afford the time for village affairs, for she herself was everlastingly encumbered with childbirth and otherwise trying to run her household; but at least the tithes were lucrative:

> Our place used to overflow with produce at tithing-times. At Easter, eggs came in by the hundred, and at 'sheering-time' wool by the cartload. Everything else was in like

*Eliza Lynn Linton*

quantity. The tithers' supper made a supreme holiday for us young ones. Easter was celebrated by hodgepodge, plum pudding and a glass of punch to follow, and sometimes a cracked fiddle was put into requisition.

The Lynns' maids took the opportunity to dance with the men, threesome and foursome jigs 'where the women held their aprons ("brats" as we called them) by the two corners and flourished them thumbs upward with clumsy coquetry as they jigged'.[6]

Communication with the outside world was only possible from Crosthwaite, where the coach ran twice a week to London and took three days and two nights. A letter would cost thirteen and a half pence, and as there were no envelopes peeping Toms had a grand time of it. Excitement for the women came with the arrival of the itinerant pedlars, who were generally Swiss–Italians. They sold jewelry, shawls and trinkets of all descriptions, and endeavoured to obtain extortionate prices for their wares. Tramps abounded and expected to be 'put-up' at the Rectory. They were known locally as 'gaberlunzies' and looked for a 'bed' in the outhouse, supper at the kitchen door, and sixpence or a shilling at the parting in the morning.[7]

Not only were there tramps to deal with, but the village idiots, who would sit and grimace at all who passed by them. Poachers and smugglers were numerous and to these could be added the local Burkes and Hares, who would often scare those who dared venture out at night.

The Church, itself a fine old Norman structure 'was choked with barbarisms' ... and had long lost its beautiful frescoes, the walls had been whitewashed, and the stained windows replaced by pieces of plain glass. The congregation sat in all directions and went to sleep in the corners comfortably. The choir was composed of a few young men and women who practised among themselves as they liked, and sometimes essayed elaborate anthems which resulted in vocal caricatures. The orchestra was a flageolet, on which the

*Eliza's birth and parents*

clerk, as the official leader and bandmaster, gave the keynote; and at the feet of the choir, in the dark at the west end, the High-School boys and girls sat on benches which now and then tipped up or overturned, played marbles, had free fights, laughed aloud, and were dragged out by the hair, kicking and yelling, when their conduct was too obstreperous for even the lax reverence of the rest to bear.[8]

Visitors at the rectory were rare; there were only two families in the whole district who kept up any pretence of some standard of living. 'We never or rarely gave parties, but on the occasions we did, the ladies would tuck up their skirts and the men turn up their trousers, and walk gaily through the snow in winter, and the dust in summer, lighted by lanthorns when there was no moon, and wearing wooden-soled clogs shod with iron when the roads were "clarty".'[9]

The Lynns' own way of living was extremely simple. 'The servants wore short woollen petticoats; cotton bedgowns and blue-checked aprons; huge caps with flapping borders and flying strings; and thick-soled shoes, with which they wore out the carpets and made a hideous clatter on the bare boards,' while 'the gardener . . . had been a soldier, and . . . in memory of his past glory, always wore a scarlet waistcoat on Sundays'. They had a hayfield, a farmyard, and two cows, 'Cushie' and 'Hornie', which 'in the summer evenings we used to go with the cook to bring home from the field to the milking-byre. I think I could replace every dock and ragwort and plot of nettles and mayweed in that ragged bit of pasture-land, sloping down to the little brook where the minnows were.'[10] Food consisted of porridge, night and morning; for dinner meat was served only twice a week.

On the 'banyan days' we had large tureens full of milky messes of exquisite savour, or enormous paste puddings – 'roly-polys' – of fruit, jam, or undecorated suet. It was simple fare, but it made a stalwart, vigorous set of boys and girls; and out of the whole dozen, only two were relatively undersized and only one was delicate. The rest averaged six feet for the men and the full medium height for the women.[11]

*Eliza Lynn Linton*

On the few occasions when there were visitors there was often disaster; thus, when Mrs Hemans visited them, the Vicar's daughters, in order to show their domesticity, darned their 'dirty' linen in her presence, which so shocked the good lady that she fled from the room.

As she grew older Eliza realised that the spartan and unintellectual life of the rectory was stultifying her. Education was left to the elder children, who were responsible for the younger.

> Hence ... a tyranny from which there was no redress, however great the wrong. It was no use to appeal to my father. Had he sided with the complainant, things would have been worse in the end, and there would then have been revenge and retaliation to add to the original count. It was better to take things as they came, or to fight it out for one's self. And there was always some one still younger to whom it could be passed on. ... Add to this a still more disastrous system of favouritism, and the knowledge that no justice was to be expected from my father downwards.[12]

So it was Eliza, the youngest, who received the brunt of most of the ructions. She was not by any means unattractive, but she was very short-sighted, tall with a beautiful skin. She was totally unafraid of being flogged, which she was, and often unfairly, as well being confined to a dark closet under the stairs. She recalled in later life how on one occasion she was sent by the elder children to steal some apples and by means of a garden rake achieved her object; unfortunately the rake fell upon her and cut her head. Her nurse strapped up the wound, but the matter was reported to her father, and she suffered the penalty. Moreover, she frequently suffered from the bullying of an elder brother, whom she called by a nickname that he disliked, which led him to attack her unmercifully; but in the end her brother Arthur came to her aid, and it was to him that she then became devoted. Such an upbringing was to make her into a very self-contained young woman. Though outwardly hard, she was full of charity and thoughtfulness.

One day a baby was brought into the house and Mr Lynn

*Eliza's birth and parents*

came upon Eliza nursing it. 'Well, Eliza,' he exclaimed with surprise, 'I never knew you were so much of a woman.'[13] This remark of her father she found derisory.

Her sister Lucy was two years older than herself; all their lives they were close to one another. Lucy was an accomplished pianist, and if she had been given the training might have become professional. She subsequently married the Reverend Augustus Gedge. She had always been a delicate girl, and it was a nursery tradition that when she was born she was the exact length of a pound of butter, was put into a quart pot and dressed in her eldest sister's doll's clothes.[14] Lucy's disposition was far more equable than Eliza's. She was the adored one, and was very pretty.

Arthur, when he was twenty, went to fight for the Poles. He was taken prisoner by the Russians and was ordered to be hanged. The rope was actually round his neck when the Russian officer was so struck by Arthur's looks that he ordered his life to be spared. Arthur was subsequently imprisoned, but was released three years later. On his return home his family did not recognise him and thought him to be a tramp.

Eliza was then eleven and was overtaken by a passion for reading. She came to know many books by heart, including *Little Henry and His Bearer*, *William and the Woodman*, *Sandford and Merton*, *Paul and Virginia*, *Evenings at Home*, *The Arabian Nights*, *Tales of the Castle*, *Tales of the Genii*, *Robinson Crusoe*, *Pilgrim's Progress*, Edgeworth's *Moral Tales*, and *Elizabeth and the Exiles of Siberia*, not forgetting Fox's *Book of Martyrs*, and *The History of All Religions*. Between eleven and seventeen years of age she taught herself French, Italian, German and Spanish. She also had some knowledge of Greek, Latin and Hebrew. By the time she had reached seventeen she was a handsome young woman, though gawky and still short-sighted and with no care for her personal appearance, and, like so many young people, was burning with 'causes'. She became a zealot and a staunch republican. She refused to look in her mirror, and denied herself the pleasure of sleeping in her own bed, using the bare floor instead. On one occasion, to show her disregard for bodily pain, she dug out an aching tooth with a penknife. As to her religious beliefs, in order to purge herself of any sins that she thought she had committed she prayed often and

9

*Eliza Lynn Linton*

fervently. For a while she went through all the priggish religious attitudes. She was one of God's personal brides and was prepared never to sin again. However, the phase passed.

It was obvious that if Eliza, at that time in a highly emotional state, had been befriended by someone who understood her, or if she had had her mother to turn to, she would have been less of the outcast that she felt herself to be.

> I was snubbed by my father, whom I constantly worried and often angered, roughly handled by my brothers, whose authority I defied when they came home for their vacations from college; sent to Coventry by my sisters whom I revolted by my violence and affronted by my impertinence; . . . If our dear Mother had lived, things would have been different.[15]

It was only too natural that Eliza was sick at heart at seeing her formative years slipping by when she should have been enjoying the far wider education for which she yearned, but her father never gave a thought to the matter. Eliza also realised that her acute short-sightedness would undoubtedly affect her future, and she turned more and more towards literature. She had not read Gibbon for nothing. Long arguments began with her father. They were poles apart. He, a peaceful man, liked to be left alone to smoke his pipe. On the other hand he could rise to considerable wrath if argued with by his unruly youngest daughter. On one occasion tempers became so heated that her father knocked her down for her 'republican' impertinence.

Eliza, despite her difficulties, tells of an incident at Hallowe'en which shows the strength of her imagination at this time:

> My sisters and I were melting lead, roasting nuts, and wasting eggs – whereby the white drawn up by the heat of the hand through water might determine the future – when I was dared to that supreme trial: to go upstairs into my bedroom, lock the door, and, with the candle set on the dressing-table, deliberately pare and eat an apple, looking at myself in the glass all the while. I would in those days have accepted any challenge offered me – to go into a lion's

den, if need be – this bit of fantastical bravery was easy enough! . . . Jauntily and defiantly I bounded up the stairs, locked the door, pared and began to eat my apple, with my eyes fixed on the glass. And there, suddenly out of the semi-darkness – the eyes looking into mine – peered a face over my shoulder; a dark, mocking, sinister face, which I could draw now as I saw it then – how many years ago! . . . Long after this I had in my ears the sound of rushing wings. They were so loud that I used to wake from my sleep with the noise of large wings about my bed. And with these there were mingled whisperings and voices; but no intelligible words ever came to me, though I made no doubt they were the same voices as those who haunted Christian when passing through the Valley of the Shadow.[16]

Apart from her religious feelings, Eliza became increasingly concerned about her future. Reading Ovid's *Metamorphoses* under a hedge in a meadow led her to much reasoning upon the foundations of the Christian religion. The analogies between the stories in the Old Testament and those of Greek mythology were a subject to which she gave considerable thought. She was further concerned regarding the virgin birth of Christ. She needed to clarify her mind, and she needed to discuss these matters, which she could not do with her father, who would have been enraged at her even daring to question him on such dogmas. Fortunately, she was able to open her mind to the Reverend Myers, who had lately been appointed incumbent of the neighbouring parish of St Johns. He was, Eliza tells us:

> A Coleridgean, able to reconcile Faith with Reason by the higher way of the Understanding . . . He was a 'made' as opposed to an instructive and national man; one who held art to be superior to nature, and the intellect a greater thing than emotion. Of the ancients, Plato . . . of the moderns, Goethe and Coleridge were his '*dii majores*'; and the schools of Sappho and Pindar, Schiller and Byron he abhorred.[17]

It was he who introduced her to the works of Coleridge and made her read them, as well as Wordsworth and Carlyle. He was a follower of Maurice. She found him deaf to any of her

*Eliza Lynn Linton*

own arguments. He allowed for no questions regarding the impregnability of his faith.

Notwithstanding Myers, the young Eliza was steeping herself in the mystics of the past, in the arts of astrology and alchemy, and in witchcraft, which culminated in the publication in 1861 of her book of *Witch Stories*[18] which were to shock the public with their realism. She introduced herself to the theories of the Rosicrucians, and years later was present at Home's manifestations, which never convinced her. The supernatural powers of such men as Cornelius Agrippa and Albertius Magnus she took to be 'undeniable'. She questioned the virgin birth, and whether Christ was God or man.

> There were certain beings in the character and doings of Christ . . . which seemed to me simply and purely human; His wholesale denunciations of the Pharisees and Sadducees; His cursing the fig-tree for its natural and normal barrenness; His sending the devils into a herd of swine, so that the innocent brutes were all drowned, while the devils were presumably not damaged, being of the nature of immortal spirits; and a few more of these elementary difficulties over which all inquiries stumble. And as for the effects of Christianity on society divorced from civilization, surely these have been more than beneficent! Religious zeal has only added another and still more pungent ingredient to the fierce compound of the natural man, by adding fanaticism to cruelty. It has made of a peaceful paradise a reeking hell in South America, devastated the Low Countries; set Catholics to shoot down Huguenots; Episcopalians to massacre Covenanters, and all dominant sects to destroy all nascent ones; it has deluged the earth with blood wherever the Cross has been raised and the Beatitudes have been preached in the name of the Prince of Peace and God of Love.[19]

With this, and a great deal more, she confronted the austere Reverend Myers, admitting to having no logical method in her questionings. She told him:

> If Christ were God – that is, Omniscient as well as Omnipotent – why did He not teach things that could be tested

*Eliza's birth and parents*

by man and proved by experiment, rather than those which are assertions only? Why for instance, instead of telling us about Lazarus in heaven, leaning on Abraham's bosom and separated by a great gulf from Dives in hell, did He not give us a form of political government whereby men might have been made with equal justice to all? Why did He not tell us that the earth is not the centre of our system, and that our system itself is not the all-important part of creation we have imagined it to be? Galileo would not then have been subjected to the Inquisition, and Giordano Bruno would not have been burned.[20]

She questioned and questioned.

It was, however, at this critical time in her life that she experienced a new and deep relationship. A strange couple came to stay at Crosthwaite. The husband was homosexual while the wife, who was part-Polish and delicate, had equally strong leanings towards her own sex. The husband was exquisitely groomed, well scented, and would prance about with his innumerable small dogs, considering himself a poet of substance. Eliza describes the wife as 'the most exquisite creature under heaven – a woman more like an impersonate poem, or embodied music, or a spirit half-transparently incarnate . . . with a cream and white skin, and dark eyes full of inconceivable pathos and a kind of far-away spiritualized listening look . . .'.[21] She spoke four languages, with a slight accent, she loved music and was very well read. At first these two people, presumably well-off, were well received by Lynn; however, as time went on he found little in common with them, though there is no doubt that Eliza worshipped the ground upon which the lady trod. Eliza was attracted to her physically; what is more she had at last found someone with whom she could discuss her literary ambitions: 'All thoughts which I had to elaborate for myself, seemed crude, uninformed, unbeautiful; without life or artistry – all but my love of Liberty, and that I think must come from the formation of my brain from birth. I had been such a rude clod up to now. . . .' She dreamed of this woman night after night:

. . . but never as an ordinary woman – always with a halo of

> divinity about her which took her out of the ranks of common humanity and lifted her heaven-high above the rest. ... I used to want to kneel to her, to kiss the hem of her garment, to make myself her footstool, her slave, so that I could be of use to her. I would have liked to have spent my life in ministering to her, as if she had been a living goddess in a temple and I her whole servitor. ... She was the divine part of humanity; the incarnation of all its beauty; the last expression of all its poetry and purity and inner wisdom. She was the Seraph of the hierarchy; ... for her sake I loved the meanest creature that belonged to her; and to meet and speak to one of the servants of the house, to caress one of the dogs in her absence, made me comparatively content. That 'rose and pot' – how true all real poetry is!

Not content to see her by day alone, Eliza would secretly leave the house by night and, hiding among the laurels, would look up at the woman's window, to be rewarded when she came to her balcony. On one such night they met.

> I did not speak, nor did she. It was like an enchanted spell which words would have broken; and we walked in the dark alleys of the shrubbery in a silence that was at once divine in its blessedness and painful in its vagueness, and more like a dream than a fact. I did not know what it meant, and yet I dared not break it; and she did not. We went into a small summer-house at the end of the garden, and sat there hand in hand, till the morning broke. Then the faint flush on the mountain-top and the first stirring of the birds told us it was time to part. 'See how I have trusted you!' she said, as she stood up to go. She lay both her hands on my shoulders, then drew my face forward and kissed me as she had done once before, on the forehead and the eyes. 'Your consecration', she said, 'the seal of our eternal oneness.' Overpowered by an emotion so powerful as to be physical pain, I knelt on the ground at her feet; and I think for a moment I died.[22]

She nearly did, for the emotion of it all caused her to be laid low with a violent fever, and when she had recovered the mysterious lady and her husband had disappeared.

2
# Gadshill

There were happier times. Eliza's father had purchased a house which he had coveted since boyhood. This was Gadshill near Rochester. It had been empty for some time whilst he endeavoured to obtain permission from his Bishop to move from the Keswick vicarage. Eventually he was granted a five years' leave of absence and the whole family took up residence in Kent. Eliza was nine years old at the time, but her account of the life she led there was vividly described in an article in the *Fortnightly Review* in 1885.[1]

> Gad's Hill House had been 'hoc erat in votis' to my father a generation before Charles Dickens fell in love with the place. Each man in his boyhood had had the same wish to become the possessor of this charming house with its pleasant shrubbery across the road and fine old-fashioned gardens to the side; and each had vowed to himself that he would, if he could, buy it out and out when time grew riper and money more plentiful. My father, as the older man, accomplished his desire first in the order of time. When he died and his property had to be sold, Charles Dickens, hearing that Gad's Hill House was in the market, made an anonymous offer for it under cover of his friend and mine, Henry Wills, not caring to appear as the purchaser in the first instance, for fear that we should ask more on account of his name. As I was the only daughter left unmarried at the time of my father's death, he had appointed me in his will executrix and trustee, together with a brother and our family solicitor; it was literally I who sold Gad's Hill House to Charles Dickens . . . We had a small triumph when we

*Eliza Lynn Linton*

came to details. The modest sum we asked for ornamental timber was disputed and the case referred to arbitration. The arbitrator gave us nearly as much again as we had asked, namely, seven-eighths instead of four.*

The century was very little past the first quarter when we Lynns lived at Gad's Hill House. My father had kept the place empty for some years, hoping always for that permission to remove which, after some difficulty and much importunity, Bishop Percy at last granted. Then we quitted the lake and mountains and pleasant vicarage of lovely Keswick on a five years' leave of absence, and my father's dearest wish was fulfilled. . . .

Gad's Hill House stands a little way back from the road. The grand highway between London and Dover, not to speak of between Gravesend and Rochester, it was as gay as an approach to a metropolis. Ninety-two public coaches and pleasure vans used to pass in the day, not counting the private carriages of the grandees posting luxuriously to Dover for Paris and the grand tour. Soldiers marching or riding to or from Chatham and Gravesend to embark for India, or on their return journey home; ships' companies paid off that morning, and cruising past the gates, shouting and singing and comporting themselves in a generally terrifying manner, being for the most part half-seas over and a trifle beyond; gipsies and travelling tinkers; sturdy beggars with stumps and crutches; Savoyards with white mice and organ-men with a wonderful wax doll, two-headed and superbly dressed, in front of their machines; chimney-sweepers, with a couple of shivering little half-naked climbing boys carrying the bags and brushes; and costermongers, whose small flat carts were drawn by big dogs, were also among the accidents and circumstances of the time. And many a saucy salute, as well as less exhilarating request, came from the road to the room where a group of girls might always be seen on the seats of the open windows.

* Dickens purchased Gad's Hill Place on 14 March 1856 and he paid £1,790 for it. Dickens had considerable alterations and repairs done to the house and did not take possession of it until 1857.

## Gadshill

'The Falstaff'* which stands opposite the kitchen garden, was a certain kind of protection to us; and if we had had occasion to ring the big alarm bell, which swung in the cupola, it would have sent us over a stalwart potman or two to look into matters touching our safety. But if it saved us from Point and Pistol, Bardolph and the ragged crew in general, it brought up officers from the garrison at Chatham to shoot pigeons in our field at the back of the house, and make eyes at the older girls from the bow window at the inn. . . .

Old Mr Weller was a real person, and we knew him. He was 'Old Chumley' in the flesh, and drove the stage daily from Rochester to London and back again. Once when my father was in town, the sister next to me needing the overlooking of Sir James Clark, she and I were sent up to London under the care of Old Chumley. We were put inside at our own gates, and the good-natured, red-faced fellow came regularly to the door whenever we stopped to change horses or to water them, to ask the little misses if they wanted anything, and how they found themselves? In the coach with us were a couple of bold, giggling, overdressed girls, with a certain 'Enery on the top. They were the 'Arry and 'Arriets of the day. I yet remember the childish disdain with which we, the little misses of twelve and thirteen, received the overtures of these bold-faced jigs, as Robin would have called them – our amazement at their familiarity to 'Enery, to whom one, evidently his own particular she, gave her parasol through the window, telling him not to 'spoil his complexion', and our disgust at his cockney accent chaffing them back from the roof of the coach.

When they left, a horrid old woman got in. She smelt of gin, had a black reticule on her arm, wore a gay bonnet with dirty flowers and called us 'dear' and 'ducky'. She asked us very many intimate questions, and specially wanted to know why we were going to London, and where. My

---

\* Dickens was proud of the fact that his house had Shakespearean connotations and had a plaque on a wall indoors bearing the words 'This house, Gad's Hill Place, stands on the summit of Shakespeare's Gadshill, ever memorable for its association with Sir John Falstaff in his noble fancy.'

*Eliza Lynn Linton*

sister – a beautiful staid little maiden of the Fra Angelico type, golden-haired, with natural ringlets to her waist, blue eyes under finely arched brows, a complexion like a monthly rose, and a childish figure of perfect promise – and I – a shy, robust savage – were but ungrateful ground under the questionable tillage of this old wretch. It was with serious dignity that my sweet little sister put by her inconvenient questions. For myself, I was too shy to answer at all.

During this visit my father took us to the theatre, and we saw Liston as Paul Pry. The applause that broke out when a man, queerly dressed in a green coat, striped trousers, white curly-brimmed hat, and long-fingered gloves came on, was a marvel to me. I do not remember understanding the play at the time, but it came back to me in after years when Wright took Liston's part, and reproduced some of the old lines. I knew more of what was going on at Gravesend, when we went to hear Herr von Joel, and he filled the place with the songs of birds, almost as good as the real thing. . . .

During our stay at Gad's Hill, I, of course, was too young to go into society, but my elder sisters were not. As we had neither nursery nor schoolroom, and lived all in a bunch together, the gossip of the place used to be discussed before us little pitchers, who were conveniently assumed to neither hear nor heed. Society then, all over the kingdom, was desperately exclusive, and to be 'not born' was as certain ostracism as it is now in a German court. The old-established families, with ancestors and traditions, would have nothing to do with the *nouveaux riches* who dated from yesterday, and indeed, riches without ancestry were cause for contempt rather than claims to respect. The society at Rochester followed the national rule, and a family, which afterwards became one of the most influential in the place, was then denied entrance into the *huis clos* of the local aristocracy, for all its frantic efforts to force the gates. It was rich, it was respectable, it was well educated, but it was 'not born'; and the great ladies who curtsied to each other and made no unfriendly comments whatever, went astray, turned shoulders as cold as ice to those others whose descendants are now among the recognised local leaders. . . .

The *Satirist* then held the heedless world in terror. It had

18

## Gadshill

a correspondent at Rochester, and I distinctly remember the consternation among the girl friends of my elder sisters when they called one day at the house and spoke of a paragraph about some young ladies at Rochester who had been seen hiding behind a wall near the barracks. They all seemed possessed with a horrible dread, and one said: 'No one is safe; it may be our turn next.' All the same, not a few of the Rochester girls of that time were notoriously 'wild'; now they would be called 'fast'; and things went on in the green tree which I imagine some of them, now in the dry, must remember with a little astonishment and more regret. . . .

The woods of the grand hall of our neighbourhood – beautiful Cobham Woods – were among our favourite hunting-grounds. So was the Park, where we were more than once frightened by the deer and half-wild cattle objecting to our presence and forcing us to beat a speedy retreat; specially by one of evil kind, whether gnu, yak, or bison, I cannot now determine. I only remember that it was something outlandish and ferocious, and that we used to fly for our lives when we espied it stamping under the trees in the distance. The aviary, where the emus, gold and silver pheasants, and other gorgeous creatures strutted in the sun and showed off their splendid plumage, was an endless source of delight. And how full the woods were of wild flowers and rare mosses!

. . . During the five years that we were at Gad's Hill House, I do not remember seeing one man of note, save my then King of Men – the political Agamemnon, Daniel O'Connell. He came to Rochester on an electioneering expedition; and we went to a friend's house in Strood to give him the window-welcome proper to a half-triumphant procession. I gave him my young heart as well; and even to this day I cannot see him in what were probably his true proportions.

# 3
# Quest for a career

The affair of the Polish lady caused a revolution in Eliza's mind. It increased her determination to seek a career, for she knew that if she remained at the rectory she would achieve nothing. She was thinking along two lines, of becoming either an artist or a writer. However, she quickly dismissed the notion of taking up art, because of her short-sightedness. But writing was another matter. She started by writing a short poem which she proposed to use as a test of the publishers' response to the quality of her work.

At this time she was reading two magazines: Ainsworth's *Miscellany* and Douglas Jerrold's *Shilling Magazine*, while her father subscribed to 'Maga', by which name *Blackwood's Magazine* was then known. She felt, however, that her poem did not have the necessary quality for *Blackwood's* and decided to offer it to Ainsworth's. She wrote them a 'girlish' accompanying letter full of entreaty and fervour, pleading with the editor to consider her work favourably. To her joy the poem was accepted and she was paid two guineas, receiving a letter of encouragement 'assuring you of success if you would persevere'.

She was over the first hurdle, and now she was determined to go to London to pursue her career. But the next step was more difficult by far – that of obtaining her father's consent, for she knew he would never approve of 'scribbling' as an occupation for a daughter of his, and was bound to remind her of the fact that she was the granddaughter of a bishop. As she had feared, when she approached him, he said, 'I thought, with your fine ideas, you had more ambition than to make yourself a mere newspaper hack, a mere Grub Street poet.

*Quest for a career*

Do you think you can do nothing better for yourself than write poems for Warren's blacking, or scratch up Bow Street for dinner?' She replied, 'I do not intend to write poems for Warren's blacking, nor to scratch up Bow Street details for dinner.'
'There is no good talking to such an obstinate young puppy as you,' her father concluded. 'If you go to London, as you propose, you go without my consent – do you hear? – and the curse of God rests on disobedient children to the end of their lives. . . .'[1]

Hardly a helpful interview. 'I reasoned the thing out in my own way, and came to the conclusion that, although self-sacrifice for the good of others is absolute and imperative, the sacrifice of a real vocation for one's good and simply because of the arbitrary opposition of a parent, is not.'[2]

Yet how was it to be achieved? Fortunately for her, at this crucial juncture in her life the family solicitor, William Loaden, arrived at the house. He took a liking to her and, as his opinions were very much respected by her father, matters progressed. Mr Loaden saw in her characteristics which should be encouraged and felt she could make a name for herself; that she was wasting her time at the vicarage; she would be better employed in studying at the British Museum. He told her that he would help her and look after her in London. She showed him what she had written and he gave his candid advice. As a result, the vicar gave way and agreed to allow her sufficient money to live in London for a year. 'After that,' he said, 'you sink or swim on your own account.'

It was in 1845 at the age of twenty-three that Eliza Lynn settled in London. Mr Loaden found a room for her in a small boarding-house at 35 Montagu Place, which was conveniently close to the British Museum, where she went daily, gathering the material for her projected novel.

I improved my knowledge of classical times and circumstances, and blessed Becker and Winckelmann; and I lost myself in the mazes of comparative mythology and Higgins's *Anacalypsis* . . .[3] I was never weary of that badly-lighted, ill-ventilated and queerly tenanted old room, with its legendary fleas and uncleansed corners. The first to come and the last

21

*Eliza Lynn Linton*

to leave, and always surrounded by a pile of books, of which number brought down on my young head many a good-natured sarcasm from the attendants, I soon became known to the officials and habitues, whom my youth interested and my enthusiasm amused.[4]

She was even observed, and soon to be befriended, by the principal, Mr Antonio Panizzi (later Sir Antonio), who was responsible for founding the British Museum reading room and library. He it was who told her she should not make a personal friend of one of the attendants who so carefully looked after her. 'You are a lady', said Panizzi, 'and he is only a servant. Make him keep his place and you maintain your position. These familiarities with low people always end badly.' Then he bent his head; 'You are very young,' he continued, 'and you think you can revolutionize society. You will find that you cannot; and that if you knock your head against stone walls you will only make it ache and alter nothing.'[5] Eliza did not approve of his admonitions, though she enjoyed talking with him; nevertheless she continued on friendly relations with the attendant and accepted an invitation to meet his wife in their small suburban home in Stoke Newington.

Thus she worked steadily, just making ends meet, and never asked her father or the Loadens for any further money. She was happy at her boarding-house, which was kept by a Mrs Brown, known to the inmates as 'Aunt Brownie'.

She had a heart as soft as swansdown, and as large as an elephant's. She was totally unfit for any undertaking in which she had to resist encroachments and defend her own rights. Anyone could talk her over. She was influenced by her affections more than by her interests; and where she took a liking she would sacrifice her gains to please the favoured him or her by extra liberalities.[6]

Eliza observed the fellow boarders carefully and duly recorded her observations of them.

... the house was a queer experience to me. The tremendous love-affairs which budded and blossomed, but never set into the permanent fruit of matrimony; the friendships that began, continued, and then suddenly one day went pouf! in the smoke of a blazing quarrel; the fights of the old ladies for the footstools, the favourite easy-chair, the best place by the fire, and the stratagems and wiles put in force for victory and prior possession. . . . And what extraordinary people came and went like shadows, or stayed as if they were coeval with the foundations of the house, and as little to be moved as these![7]

Her first effort in fiction was called *Azeth the Egyptian*. She had been working on it in the British Museum, studying the works of Gardner Wilkinson, Rossellini, and numerous other hierologists. It had taken her a year to write and she came to an arrangement with the somewhat roguish publisher, T. C. Newby, to publish it at a cost of fifty pounds. William Loaden advanced her the money, which she duly repaid. Her joy was to come, for *The Times* reviewed it favourably. It was certainly a momentous day for her, and she records it thus: 'I remember the sunset as I went up Oxford Street, to what was not yet Marble Arch. For I could not rest in the house. I could not go home for dinner. I felt compelled to walk as if for ever . . . to damp down the glad fever in my veins I could only breathe out in the open.'[8]

*Azeth the Egyptian* is today unreadable; it is verbose and is stuffed with undigested 'British Museum learning' and with many of the ideas that were buzzing through its author's youthful head. It is the story of an Egyptian god who is banished from the skies and sent to live on earth to expiate his sensual 'sins'; they are eventually purged and he is allowed to return to his heavenly abode. In her later years Eliza herself saw the book as a youthful *jeu d'esprit*, and when, in 1894, she was being interviewed by Mrs Alec Tweedie she told her that she did not dare re-read the book because she would feel so ashamed. Yet she had at least begun a literary career, and she knew that there was no turning back.

She had been in London for the stipulated year, and she dutifully returned home, but naturally enough life at the rectory was constricted. She was working on another historical novel, *Amymone*, set in the age of Pericles, which she tactfully dedicated to her father. She submitted it to one of London's leading publishers, George Bentley, who accepted it and paid her a hundred pounds. This novel attracted the attention of Walter Savage Landor, who was addicted to novels with a classical background, and he gave it a good review in *The Examiner*. J. T. Delane, editor of *The Times*, was also impressed.

Her father gave her thirty pounds with which to live in London for a further year. But it was quite clear that Eliza would be unable to subsist in London by writing historical novels only, so she was now determined to try her hand at journalism. She wrote an article on 'Aborigenes', no doubt mugged up in the British Museum, and sent it to the *Morning Chronicle*. Her choice of newspaper was wise, for the editor was John Douglas Cook, a remarkable man. When very young, Cook had been sent to India but did not get on with his employers, so that, according to his own account, he walked halfway home. When he at last arrived in London he found himself destitute, but he immediately set to and tried his hand at writing an article which he sent to *The Times*: it was accepted. He became acquainted with John Walter, manager of *The Times*, and it was while he was helping Walter to be elected as Tory MP for Nottingham that he met Lord Lincoln, a member of Peel's administration. Much later some of Lincoln's friends, having bought the *Morning Chronicle*, appointed Cook as its editor. During the first twenty years of the nineteenth century it had been 'not only the greatest of Whig journals then in existence, but the leading journal of Great Britain'.[9] Cook showed real ability, though he spent money freely.

When Cook read Eliza's article, he asked her to come to see him. She was naturally excited and awaited her appointment with trepidation.

> I was punctual to the moment, and with a beating heart but very high head went swinging up the narrow dingy court into which the 'editor's entrance' gave; and then up the still dingier stairs to a room whence I could not see the street for dirt which made the windows as opaque as ground glass. Here I was told to wait till Mr Cook could see me. In about half an hour the messenger returned and ushered

me into the awful presence.... A tall, cleanly shaved, powerfully built man, with a smooth head of scanty red hair; a mobile face instinct with passion; fiery, reddish hazel eyes; a look of supreme command; an air of ever-vibrating impatience and irascibility, and an abrupt but not unkindly manner, standing with his back to the fireplace, made half a step forward and held out his hand to me as I went into the room. 'So! you are the little girl who has written that queer book, and want to be one of the press-gang, are you?' he said, half smiling, and speaking in a jerky and unprepared manner, both singular and reassuring. I took him in his humour and smiled too. 'Yes, I am the woman,' I said. 'Woman, you call yourself? I call you a whippersnapper.'

Obviously Cook enjoyed 'terrorising her'. Yet his sense of humour and his kindness to the obviously frightened girl, won the day. But he was a hard task-master and told her to give him a report on the Parliamentary Commission upon the conditions of mines relative to the 'Truck System'. He gave her three and a half hours in which to write it and not one minute longer. She did it and her paper pleased Cook immensely.

This was a remarkable achievement. She became the first woman paid writer on a newspaper, but she was not the first woman journalist, as she has often been erroneously called. Harriet Martineau, Caroline Norton and Mrs Grote had all written for newspapers previously. The only occasions when she 'sailed near the wind' were when she expressed her 'republican' views too strongly, and for the time being she escaped the irascibility of the editor. On one occasion she witnessed a journalist who had offended Cook having a heavy bottle of ink thrown at him; luckily it missed the man but made a sharp dent upon the edge of the wall, which was blackened by the streaming ink.

Eliza was now able to afford her own sitting-room at Mrs Brown's, for she was earning twenty guineas a month from the newspaper. Between August 1849 and February 1851 she wrote no fewer than eighty articles and thirty-six reviews. But her position with the *Morning Chronicle* was not to last. Severe criticism of her work began and her articles were rejected. 'I was too energetic to be demoralised by my first failure; and

## Eliza Lynn Linton

my fall in no-wise maimed the hope and resolve which are the best pioneers of certainty.' Then came the day when Cook shook his fist in her face. And that was the end. She packed up and left.

In the meantime Eliza began to move within a large circle of notabilities. In 1847 she went to Devizes, where she stayed with the eccentric Dr Brabant, who, like Dr Bartolo, considered himself something of a 'ladies' man'. Brabant, who had taken his medical degree in Edinburgh in 1821, had numbered among his patients Thomas Moore and Samuel Taylor Coleridge. In 1843 he had taken a fancy to the then Mary Ann (or Marian) Evans, later known as George Eliot, and had asked her to stay with him. She had 'been captivated by him', Mary Ann had written to her friend Caroline Hennell, who was always known as Cara. 'I am in a little heaven here, Dr Brabant being its archangel . . . time would fail me to tell you of all his charming qualities. We read and walk and talk together, and I am never weary of his company.' But this idyllic situation did not last long, for the doctor's wife, who was blind, sensed that her husband and Mary Ann were too friendly and demanded that she should leave.

Eliza always maintained that Brabant was the original of Casaubon in *Middlemarch*, but there are other and different opinions. It was, however, while staying with Brabant that she met Landor:

> I was in the shop of Mr Empson,* a noted aesthete in those days, when there came in an old man, still sturdy, vigorous, upright, alert. He was dressed in brown, and his whole style was one of noticeable negligence. His clothes were unbrushed and shabby; his shirt-front was coarse and plain, like a night-shirt; a frayed and not over-clean blue neck-tie, carelessly knotted was awry; his shoes were full of bumps and bosses like an apple pie; and the contrast between him and Dr Brabant, who was always spruce and trim, and well got up and well preserved, was exceedingly striking. But the face beneath the somewhat shapeless hat was not one to be passed unremarked even in a crowd. The keen eyes; the lofty brow; the thin, close-set lips, with the sweetest smile

* In Bath.

*Quest for a career*

that ever man had to correct the first impression of sternness, and to soften the undoubted resolution of the whole of the lower jaw; the look of thought and power that shone in his eyes and rested like a written word on his face; and, with all the shabbiness of the outward man, the dignity, the superiority, the self-respect of his bearing and its wonderful courtesy to women, made him noticeable, even to those who did not know who he was.

When he came in, Dr Brabant presented me to him. As it happened, I knew his *Imaginary Conversations* almost by heart . . . When, therefore, I heard his name all my heart broke out with a kind of jubilant reverence – that kind of loving awe with which any follower would greet his chief, any worshipper would come into the presence of his God; and what I felt I showed. . . .

We made friends on the spot; I soon became his daughter. He never called me anything else, and never wrote to me as anything but his 'dear daughter', and never signed himself even 'W.S.L.', but always 'Father' and the friendship that began then continued without a break to the last day of his conscious life. I loved him with my whole heart and soul. I was mortally afraid of his quick temper, which I soon understood, and was careful never to cross.[10]

It was a remarkable friendship between two highly attuned temperaments, yet understandable. Landor loved women who were attractive and gracious, and his best side flourished when anyone took the trouble to try to understand him, for he was a generous man though he could ill afford it, yet those he loved he would go to any lengths to help. As with Rose Paynter, his friendship with Eliza never faltered. As Eliza had never been on a cosy relationship with her father, she yearned for the sympathy which Landor provided. She went to stay with him every year:

> . . . sometimes twice in the year . . . and I remember certain things which came into the ordering of our lives as one remembers songs and sunsets and beautiful places. One was his evening reading of Milton – which was the same kind of thing as a noble voluntary on a magnificent organ. An-

other was our daily walk in the park, and our talks when we rested on the benches perhaps near some children whom he passionately loved, perhaps near a lilac bush, which was one of his favourite flowers.[11]

Landor put himself out for Eliza; he disliked crowds, and parties, but he enjoyed taking her to the Assembly Rooms, to which they went in sedan chairs. She had only one ball dress – black lace over a black skirt, and in order to vary it she would alter the trimmings, from ivy leaves, to roses, or scarlet berries. She had also to put up with his adoration for Pomero, his yapping Pomeranian dog, which he was always losing: '. . . he would go out and scour all Bath for him; then he would offer rewards – wild rewards – a hundred pounds – his whole fortune – if anyone would bring him back alive.'

Eliza was not oblivious of his faults. 'He was irascible and inconsiderate – rash in speech and action, and dogged in his resolve not to hear reason, and not to see where he had been to blame. But a nobler more loving, more lofty nature never took on itself human form than his.'[12] She was deeply upset when he was forced to leave England forever after his foolish impetuosity over the Yescombe case.[13] She would have given so much to have succoured him in his last lonely days in Florence. She was with him when the deaths occurred in 1848 of his two old friends, Sir Samuel Meyrick and Lady Nugent. Their demise was a reminder of his own advanced age, for he was then seventy-four. 'I could not sleep last night,' he said to Eliza and flung across the table what are probably some of his best known lines:

> I strove with none, for none was worth my strife:
> Nature I loved, and next to Nature, Art:
> I warmed both hands before the fire of Life;
> It sinks; and I am ready to depart.

'I remember the tears coming into my eyes,' Eliza recorded, 'when I said how beautiful and pathetic I thought it. He smiled in his sweet, half-sad way – not that boisterous laugh which was like the bursting forth of a volcano, but the quiet and gentle smile, which was perhaps his truer self and his greatest charm.'

On his seventy-fourth birthday Landor had unexpected visitors. Charles Dickens and John Forster arrived: 'This was my first introduction to both these men. I found Dickens charming, and Forster pompous, heavy and ungenial. Dickens was bright and gay and winsome, and while treating Mr Landor with the respect of a younger man for an elder allowed his wit to play about him, bright and harmless as summer lightning . . .' Eliza remarked. '. . . Forster was saturnine and cynical. He was the "harbiterary gent" of the cabman's rank, and one of the most jealous of men.'[14] Forster had no time for Eliza, and this is reflected in his subsequent biography of Landor, in which he made scant reference to her. She never forgot this. Forster's *Life of Landor* was published in 1869, and Dickens subsequently asked her if she would review it for *All the Year Round*, not realising how Eliza disliked Forster. Of course she was delighted and began her review, 'The Life of Walter Savage Landor has yet to be written.' At this time Dickens was still friendly with Forster, and on reading this venomous notice he was not a little embarrassed, and wrote to Eliza on Saturday 19 June 1869:

> Although your article on our old friend is an interesting piece of personal remembrance, it does not satisfy my desire as a review of Forster's book. It could hardly be otherwise than painful to Forster that I, one of his oldest literary friends, and certainly of all others his most intimate and confidential, should insert in these pages an account of Landor – or touch on the subject – without a word of commendation of a biography that has cost, to my knowledge, a world of care and trouble. I find from your letter to my son that you do not think well of the said book. Admitting that the life was to be written at all I *do*. And it is because I think well of it, and wish highly to commend it on what I deem to be its deserts, that I am staggered and stopped short by your paper, and fear I must turn to and write another in its stead.

Eliza's reply to Dickens is not extant, but Dickens did write to her again to the effect that he was perfectly prepared to pay for the article.

*Eliza Lynn Linton*

She wrote a further article on the book in the *North British Review*, and yet another on Landor was contributed in August 1869 to a journal called *Broadway*. At a dinner given by Charles Shirley Brooks (later editor of *Punch*) at which Lord Houghton was present, Brooks asked Lord Houghton whether he had seen Eliza's notice of the book, to which he replied, 'It is the neatest thing I know. She has taken the skin off him so – so,' he added, making a movement as if tearing strips along his arm.[15]

Having left the *Morning Chronicle*, Eliza began work on her third novel, *Realities*, which, on account of its realism, was to attract some rough handling by the critics. By now she was aware that her 'historical' novels had received only very limited attention, and she turned to the contemporary style, which, as with all her novels, contained a certain amount about herself.

For a short time Eliza became a boarder with the publisher John Chapman, the 'Raffaele Bookseller' as he was then called, who was living at Clapton.[16] Chapman had been born on 21 June 1821 at Ruddington, near Nottingham.[17] He was a handsome man and so resembled Byron that his friends would refer to him by that name. He had an original speculative mind, eager to welcome phrenology or co-operatives, or any new idea that promised to improve the lot of mankind. Chapman met many of the advanced figures of his day. He had studied medicine at St Bartholomew's and in Paris. On 27 June 1843, when he was twenty-two, he married Susanna Brewitt, the daughter of a Nottingham lace manufacturer, and his father-in-law made a handsome settlement upon her. They bought a house in Clapton, where they not only entertained but took in boarders. Chapman forsook medicine and decided to become a publisher and author; his literary ambitions were considerable and his mind was filled with literary projects, which expanded as did his household. The house in the Strand to which he eventually moved was also large enough to accommodate boarders, but Eliza did not accompany the Chapman family to the Strand establishment. But when she had finished *Realities* she gave it to Chapman and he agreed to publish it.

In March 1850, when Mary Ann Evans left Geneva for

London, she wrote to her friend Cara Hennell asking her to inquire upon Chapman's charges for lodgers, as she was seriously considering living in London. In October of that year Chapman published Mackay's *The Progress of the Intellect as Exemplified in the Religious Development of the Greeks and the Hebrews*, and having met Marian Evans, as Mary Ann was now calling herself, whom he greatly admired, he asked her if she would care to review the book for the *Westminster Review*, which journal he published and subsequently, in May 1851, purchased. Marian was only too delighted to have some serious literary work to undertake, and completed the article in November. It appeared in the issue of January 1851. It was then that Chapman persuaded her to stay in his house.

Eliza and Marian first met at one of Chapman's Friday night parties. Marian reported to Cara,* 'She [Eliza] says she was "never so attracted to a woman before as to me" – I am "such a lovable person".' She added, 'I have enjoyed my visit very much, and am to come again in January.' Her mind was made up. If Eliza Lynn could write books, so could she. She would live in London and earn her living by the pen.[18]

She returned to the Strand on 8 January 1851. Chapman was by now deeply attracted to her. When Eliza recorded her first impressions of Marian they were by no means cordial, though time was to show her deep respect for Marian's work. However, after this first meeting she wrote:

> Confession is good for the soul, they say; and I will candidly confess my short-sighted prejudices with respect to this – to be – celebrated person. These were her undeveloped as well as her insurgent days. She was known to be learned, industrious, thoughtful, noteworthy; but she was not yet the Great Genius of her age, nor a philosopher bracketed with Plato and Kant, nor was her personality held to be superior to the law of the land, nor was she recognised as a conventional gentlewoman; in those days, indeed, she was emphatically not that!
> She was essentially under-bred and provincial; and I, in the swaddling-clothes of early education and possession as I was, saw more of the provincial than the genius, and

* Later Mrs Charles Bray.

was repelled by the unformed manner rather than attracted by the learning. She held her hands and arms kangaroo fashion; was badly dressed; had an unwashed, unbrushed, unkempt look altogether; and she assumed a tone of superiority over me which I was not then aware was warranted by her undoubted leadership. From first to last she put up my mental bristles, so that I rejected then and there what might have become a close acquaintance had I not been so blind, and so much influenced by her want of conventional graces.[19]

When the proofs of Eliza's novel *Realities* appeared, it would seem that only then did Chapman read the book carefully for the first time. He was deeply concerned over certain passages, being of the opinion that they were far too outspoken for him to publish. He decided to ask Marian for her opinion. She concurred with him, and they both reported to Eliza that the book could not be published in its original form. The offending passages should be excised. Eliza was extremely annoyed and consulted her lawyer, who urged her to find another publisher.

This was the end of Eliza's relationship with Chapman. It might be thought that Eliza could hardly have wanted to see Marian again, for she was aware of her considerable influence with Chapman; in fact, it was not until 1855 that the two women met again. Marian had gone to Germany with George Henry Lewes, the journalist and author; on returning to London they lived together at 8 Victoria Grove Terrace, Bayswater, where Eliza was invited to visit them. Of this visit she records:

> There was none of the pretence of a sanctioned union which came afterwards – none of the somewhat pretentious assumption of superior morality which was born of her success. She was frank, genial, natural, and brimful of happiness. The consciousness that she had finally made her choice and cast the die which determined her fate, gave her a nobility of expression and a grandeur of bearing which she had not had when I first knew her. Then my heart warmed to her with mingled love and admiration, and I paid her the homage she deserved.[20]

## Quest for a career

Eliza was not completely unqualified in her praise. It was a case of one astute woman assessing another; presumably the other was making her own assessment too. Yet Eliza never deviated in her beliefs. She considered that Marian in later life lived an unreal existence in her endeavour to harmonise two irreconcilables – to be at once conventional and insurgent.

She was always the goddess on her pedestal – gracious in her condescension – with sweet strains of sympathetic recognition for all who came to her – ever ready to listen to her worshippers – ever ready to reply, to encourage, to clear from confusion minds befogged by unassimilated learning, and generous in importing her own. But never, for instance, did she forget her self-created Self – never did she throw aside the trappings of the airs of the benign Sibyl. Her soft, low voice was pitched in one level and monotonous key, and her deliberation of speech was a trifle irritating to the eager whose flint was already fired. Her gestures were as measured as her words; her attitudes as restrained as her tones.

*Realities*, dedicated to Walter Savage Landor was published by Sanders & Otley in 1851, but, as already mentioned, it had a bad reception, which naturally depressed Eliza, so that it was with a certain amount of joy that she accepted the invitation of the Loadens to accompany them to the Continent. She was away for three months and kept a diary of her travels in France, Germany, Switzerland and Italy, from which she returned on 28 October 1852.

# 4
# Occultism

Eliza now had to consider her position as a novelist; she had achieved neither fame nor fortune. It is true that she had accomplished a good deal, but it was her personality, not her writing, that had so far dominated her situation, inasmuch as her circle of friends was certainly becoming prestigious. Among those whom she met was Leigh Hunt's son, Thornton, who at this time was contributing to the *Spectator*, and helping his friend, George Lewes, to establish *The Leader*, for which paper Eliza was soon to be correspondent in Paris.

She had also met one with whom she had fallen in love, and whom she called 'Brother Edward'. They corresponded all their lives but could never marry because he was a staunch Catholic and she an agnostic and they would not alter their convictions.*

Others who came within her orbit were William Smith, known to all as 'Thorndale', Dr Hodgson, Charles Bray, Edward Piggott, Froude – 'one of our best, if most prejudiced historians, master of style and eloquent Devil's Advocate' – and Mrs Gaskell 'with her beautiful white arms bare to the shoulder, and as destitute of bracelets as were her hands of gloves'.[1] She was also introduced to Carlyle and Emerson, whom she first met at the same gathering, where neither spoke to the other, though both had their own coterie of admirers. To her the sycophancy was sickening. But it was at Mrs Milner Gibson's parties that she was to meet so many notabilities. This lady was the wife of the President of the Board of Trade, he had entered Parliament in Lord John Russell's ministry in 1846. He was a man of both ability and courage. He and his

* This correspondence seems to have disappeared.

*Occultism*

wife held open house, especially to exiled patriots. Although Mrs Milner Gibson was a devout Catholic, she was the first woman publicly to embrace spiritualism and hold séances. There was a genuine instinct of hospitality, an innate good feeling; the pleasure that arises from giving pleasure to others, the happiness of seeing those around her happy, were the sole end and aim of the lady who presided over the miscellaneous company that used to meet together in the corner house of Wilton Crescent.

Among the many people Eliza met at the Gibson home were Louis Blanc, the French socialist historian; Mazzini, the Italian patriot and writer; Sir Alexander Cockburn, the judge; Thackeray; Monckton Milnes; the painters Landseer, Leighton and Leech; the actor Charles Kean; the singer Mrs Sartoris; the conductor Charles Hallé; and other literary or artistic people, together with a troop of Irishmen and Radical Members of Parliament. These gatherings were not a matter of small-talk, ices and lemonade: a substantial supper was a feature of the evening, and the foreigners had a pleasant way of rushing down directly food was served and sweeping the table clean.

Soon Mrs Milner Gibson's parties and social evenings were to be revolutionised by the appearance of medium Daniel Dunglas Home, of Edinburgh birth, who had just arrived from America where he had been living since boyhood. He claimed to be the illegitimate son of the tenth Earl. Among Home's first visitors had been Edward Bulwer-Lytton, who invited him to hold séances at the Lytton house in Park Lane. Such interest was shown in his manifestations that he was summoned to Knebworth. His moving and gliding 'furniture' and even his levitations were found to be sufficiently important 'spiritual manifestations', he declared, 'to be identical with the best-attested phenomena in witchcraft in all ages and in every country under the sun; and they would have been explained long ago if wise men had been about their proper business'. Opinion, however, was acutely divided. Curiosity and excitement about 'something new' accounted for much, and Home was taken up by society and many crowned heads.

As far as Mr Milner Gibson was concerned, he was acutely embarrassed by his wife's enthusiasm and he quickly decided

35

*Eliza Lynn Linton*

that he had no desire to attend the séances in his own home or anywhere else for that matter. Eliza, at this time in her life, was far from uninterested in the spirit world, but she was not to be hoodwinked. After witnessing one of Home's séances, she commented:

> Mr Hume* was in his usual place at the end of the chain of experimenters, where the circular table touched the jamb of the window, leaving a free space between him and Mademoiselle, the governess, who always sat opposite to him. Our hostess was always on his left hand. The room was almost pitch-dark – lighted only from the distant lamp in the mews, which this window faced. Suddenly Mr Hume left his seat and came over to where I was sitting. He leaned over my chair and spoke to my neighbour and me, saying that the spirits were preparing something . . .

The usual movements of furniture took place while Home's convert, a gentleman called Smith who had come from Peckham, instead of Home, made ecstatic appeals as if 'praying to the Lord'. Home purported to have levitated himself and in doing so had scratched the ceiling. A search was made for any dislodged pieces. Eliza considered it was all a hoax.

Having been drawn into Home's circle, it was not unnatural that Eliza was cajoled by other followers, or dupes, as Eliza realistically called them, to believe in their 'supernatural powers'. Thus, one Robert Bell

> . . . expatiated warmly on the supernatural power which enabled a pencil to lie – on a clinging velvet cloth – without rolling off when the table was tilted to a certain angle. I tried the experiment at home, and found that by careful manipulation I could tilt my own table at an even more acute angle than the medium had done, and that neither the pencil nor the glasses would fall.[2]
> 
> When I said this to Robert Bell he was exceedingly angry, and what had been a very pleasant friendship came to an abrupt and sudden end.[3]

---

\* Eliza spells his name 'Hume', which is the correct pronunciation of this Scottish family name.

*Occultism*

Then there was Dr John Ashburner[4] who also wished to convert her. At his house she saw

> ... the medium who writhed like a demoniac when the spirits were writing in red letters on his large white fine-skinned arm a name that should carry conviction to the soul of the unbeliever. This man had two tricks – that of this skin-writing, which was soon found out; and that of reading with the tips of his fingers the names written on small pieces of paper, folded up into pellets and flung into a heap on the table. This sleight-of-hand was respectable; but I caught the trick, and told Dr Ashburner what I had seen. The dear old man did not believe me and he did believe Mr Foster, the medium, even after he found out that he had been to prison for felony.[5]

Thus, she says, she could fill a volume of such accounts of spiritualistic frauds, suspicions and impostures. 'I have never seen anything whatever that might not have been done by trick and collusion, and I have seen almost all the mediums.' It was not as if she had not an open mind on the subject.

> I was yearning to believe – to be forced by irrefutable proofs to accept one undoubted authority, which would have ended for ever certain gnawing pains. These proofs never came. On the contrary, with every séance at which I assisted came increased certainty of imposture. And yet, now, at the end of it all, though I have never seen a medium who was not a patent trickster, I believe that there is an uncatalogued and perhaps developed human force, which makes what the Americans call a magnetic man, and which is the substratum of truth underlying the falsehoods of spiritualism, the deceptions of hysteria, and the romances of religious fervour. We have not said the final word yet on the development of man; and this uncatalogued force may be one of the chief factors in the sum of future progress.[6]

Of course she was not alone in her views. On 16 September 1860 Dickens had written to her from Gad's Hill:

37

*Eliza Lynn Linton*

Pray do not suppose that I sent you that very unspiritual magazine for any other purpose than to keep you *au courant* to the subject. It has not in the least disturbed my equanimity. I hold personal inquiry on my part into these proceedings to be out of the question for two reasons. Firstly, because the conditions under which such inquiries take place – as I know in the recent case of two friends of mine with whom I discussed them – are preposterously wanting in the commonest securities against deceit or mistake. Secondly, because the people lie so very hard, both concerning what did take place and what impression it made at the time on the inquirer. Mr Hume or Home (I rather think he has gone by both names) I take the liberty of regarding as an imposter, if he appeared on his own behalf in any controversy with me, I should take the liberty of letting him know publicly why. But be assured that if he were demonstrated a humbug in every microscopic cell of his skin and globule of his blood, the disciples would still believe and worship.

Not unnaturally, Home's fame was greatly helped by women. One of the first was Elizabeth Barrett Browning, who remarked in Florence, when Home was there, that 'When people gather round a table now it isn't to play whist.' She went with Robert to a séance at Ealing, and Robert was sceptical. As far as Eliza was concerned, she was always sceptical about spiritualism and its attendant phenomena. In 1899 Layard[7] wrote on the subject to Eliza's old friend A. P. Sinnett, who replied:

> I myself constantly talked to her of such matters, endeavouring to convey to her the assurance I had myself reached, that trustworthy knowledge was to be obtained concerning other states of human consciousness besides this (of the physical plane), with which we are all familiar. The attitude of mind in which I generally found her was one of keen interest in the views I held (or the knowledge which I conceived myself to possess), coupled with what she used to describe as an ever-present terror lest she should be led into believing something which in spite of all appearances might not be true. This apprehension was emphasised in her mind by the consciousness, of which she often spoke to me,

that in her youth she had been susceptible in a high degree to mesmeric influence . . .

In the same letter he added:

> During her residence at Queen Anne's Mansions, Mrs Linton had one specially bad illness in which she all but died. After her recovery she told me that at the worst crisis of the illness, when those around her thought she was actually dying, or had died, she remembered floating away as it seemed to her in space, borne as a child might be borne in the arms of some great motherly creature, and bathed in a sense of wonderful peace, contentment, and happiness. And, curiously enough, that during this period the thought crossed her mind, Mr Sinnett ought to know of this. Remembering this thought, she said she felt it a duty to tell me of what had occurred or seemed to occur.[8]

# 5
# Correspondent in Paris

Among those Eliza met in London at this time were the novelist Harrison Ainsworth, with whom she had dinner at his house at Kensal Green, and whom she found very handsome, and the dramatist Douglas Jerrold. Although keen, witty and sarcastic, Jerrold was very kind-hearted. She also attended the Sunday-evening gatherings at the Thornton Hunts. She was introduced there to Miss Julia Pardoe, the novelist, 'who took the substance for the shadow, and spent on society the proceeds which she should have husbanded for old age, to find, when too late, that fashion is about the worst bank in which you can invest . . .'. She adds:

> Once I was taken to see Miss Jane Porter [novelist], then living in a little street in Bayswater. She was in her bedroom, dressed in black, and I think she wore a white cap underneath a long black scarf over head. I was considerably awed by her presence and manner, and I felt as if I had been in one of Mrs Radcliffe's rooms. She was an eerie, ghastly old lady, and she had that stagey and stately manner of the old school which impresses young people so painfully – impresses and crushes them.
> Then there was that pretty little wife of the QC, with her trim little figure, childish shoulders, youthful manners, and plain featured daughters – whom she suppressed. She was one of my social-godmothers, and stood sponsor for me in more houses than one. She took me, inter alia, to Sir Charles Babbage's [English mathematician], telling me on the way that he admitted to his evening parties only pretty women

and distinguished men. The compliment was two-edged, and pleased both her and me alike.¹

Now, however, Eliza was in need of work, so she accepted at a small salary, barely enough to live on, the post of correspondent in Paris for *The Leader*.

I shared the apartment of a fellow country-woman a few years older than myself. Her French mother and Irish father were dead – the latter quite lately – and her sole inheritance was the lease of this apartment for the five years it had to run. We lived a rough kind of life; but at our age roughnesses did not count. An old woman used to come in the morning to *faire le ménage* for the day; after which we were left to ourselves.²

*The Leader* was the brainchild of Thornton Hunt, who envisaged a lively paper, selling mainly to a middle-class, free-thinking, reformist public.³ W. J. Linton (the engraver whom Eliza was subsequently to marry), George Henry Lewes and W. E. Foster (afterwards Secretary for Ireland) took shares in the venture, as well as John Minter Morgan, a wealthy former Owenite and collaborator with Larken in village settlement schemes. But the principal shareholder was the Reverend Edmund Larken, a friend of Hunt, and a 'Christian socialist' of the school of Frederick Maurice, the theologian, and Charles Kingsley. Larken was well off because he had married a daughter of Lord Monson, and his rectory was pleasantly situated in his father-in-law's estate at Burton, three miles from Lincoln. It was Linton's intention that *The Leader* should be an international journal like *The National* and the Paris *Réforme*. But Mr Linton's participation in *The Leader* was short-lived, for he did not see eye to eye with Hunt or Lewes; he thought their direction of the paper was capricious, and like Leigh Hunt's Irishman's pig 'up all manner of streets'.⁴ Nevertheless, the first number of *The Leader* appeared on 30 March 1850.

Eliza found living in Paris hard going financially, and she was grateful for a gift of five pounds from her friend W. H. Wills, who was the assistant editor of *Household Words*, to

*Eliza Lynn Linton*

which she was now contributing regularly. Dickens commented: 'She is good for anything, and thoroughly reliable.' Writing to Wills on 16 June 1853, she remarked:

> ... I would rather stay here on £100 a year than live in London on five. I have a canary that I hang amongst my flowers, roses and mignonette, and carnations and 'Laurier' rose (I don't remember the English name), which, for want of a flower stand, I place on one of my boxes. My room is tiled, beautifully clean, and as slippery as glass. My curtains are ragged and patched crimson cotton; my bed is a small sofa covered with canvas; I have a glass about three inches square, which gives me a wen on one side of my face; and I am up *au quatrième*. We are both very poor, my pretty hostess and myself, and we make 'treats' of a few radishes or a dish of peas or asparagus. We live very plainly, and study economy in everything – but I am so happy, so happy! It is a life I love. I always hated the stiff, heavy, expensive English mode, when all one's money went in board and lodging. I want my books and a few old favourite ornaments I have got in London – a 'Sabrina' and a gold basket and a case of birds – I want an easy-chair, for I have not got one – and a new bonnet! – and I should be perfectly satisfied. But I am ten years younger than I was last winter, and have almost forgotten how to shed tears – which has generally been rather a favourite occupation of mine. All, all that I want now is just enough to go on with. I had only provision for two weeks more, when now your £5 have made me, oh, happier than our poor little queen is![5]

It was not long before she met a variety of people. Among them were the Mohls. Julius von Mohl (1800–76) was a distinguished orientalist who had married an accomplished Englishwoman, Mary Clarke (1793–1883). Eliza said of Julius:

> He was a very dungeon of learning – I use the word intentionally – for, like a dungeon, for the most part he kept his treasures under lock and key, away from the daily light, and only at stated times made a grand goal-delivery in his books. Still, he was gentle and human, and knew when to

*Correspondent in Paris*

unbend; and though he did not take the initiative, he gave me valuable advice when I asked for it, and such information as I wanted, and in all things treated me like a rational being – though I must have been to him terribly embryonic and inchoate.[6]

Not everybody was so agreeable. Eliza met Fanny Kemble, the actress, and an immediate hostility sprang up between them. 'The deep voice and stage-stateliness of manner, the assumption of supremacy and really cruel strength of this lady, crushed me flat,' Eliza wrote later. On the other side of the coin, Henrietta Cockran recorded of Eliza:

> I dislike gush, and I distrusted her purring caressing manner. Though I am fond of cats she reminded me too much of that animal's scratching propensity. I was afraid of her claws, for I had quickly detected that she had claws. I often heard her make bitter remarks in a soft but intense tone of voice. Sometimes I thought she resembled a bird of prey – a vulture.
>
> She had protruding pale blue eyes shining through large gold-rimmed spectacles; her lips were thin; her nostrils quivered when she spoke. She had pretty golden wavy hair. I believe many people fought shy of her because of the novels she had written – *Realities* and *Aspasia* [sic].[7]

There was no love lost either between Eliza and Elizabeth Barrett Browning. Eliza wrote:

> When she talked to me she used to look at me through the dropping curtains of her long ringlets as if she would have read my secret soul. I used to feel as if I were on a moral dissecting-table, while she probed my thoughts and touched speculative tracts which probably seemed to her hopelessly wrong and corrupt. She did not show that she disliked nor distrusted me, but something about me must have jarred her highly strung, sensitive nature.[8]

Apart from people, Eliza enjoyed her Paris. She went to Mabille, then in its glory, to La Closerie des Lilas which had just opened, and to the Bals de l'Opéra.

43

*Eliza Lynn Linton*

The students and grisettes who danced the can-can and did extraordinary steps at these places, seem to me to have been different from the men and women who haunt the public dancing-halls today. The fun and frolic, if decidedly fast and more than 'risqué' was more spontaneous, less professional, less commercial and calculated than now, and the whole style of thing was simpler. It was all the difference between grisette and the cocotte – the student of the Quartier Latin and the petit *crevé* of the Boulevard Italien.[9]

One of Eliza's closest friends was a certain Madame de Clairvaux, a Parisienne born and bred who introduced her to a variety of people and places. Madame de Clairvaux told Eliza she was concerned about her friend, Madame de Niemand, who had kept her lover for six weeks in the loft of her country house while her husband was absent, though her child and sister were at home. 'It was very difficult', she related, 'to find him food and see that he had fresh air and exercise,' and how she had to go foraging in the kitchen after all the servants had gone to bed, and the embarrassment in the mornings when the cook would report the disappearance of food. There were nocturnal walks in the woods and once they were fired upon by robbers.

In many ways Eliza's experience of life was broadened in the scenes she saw enacted around her. She went for a short stay in a *pension* at Tours where she met a M. and Mme de Blainville and a M. and Mme Saint-Georges. She soon discovered that Mme Saint-Georges had been the mistress of M. de Blainville, before he had married the present Mme de Blainville for the sake of her money. His ardour for Mme Saint-Georges, however, had not cooled although hers for him had.

It was emphatically diamond cut diamond with M. de Blainville and Madame Saint-Georges; a game at chess with lives and hearts for pawns and queens, a duel *à outrance*, where rapiers were none the less deadly at the points for being covered with velvet at the hilts. Madame Saint-Georges had transferred her affections from her old lover, whose marriage she had never forgiven, to a handsome young fellow in the neighbourhood, to whom such an adventure was a godsend. M. de Blainville, suspecting what was going on, set his wits to work to prove what he feared. He had the light tread and the supple spring of a panther, and no one ever knew where he was nor where he might not appear when least expected. He used to say that he was going away for the whole day, but he would conceal himself in the branches of a tree which served as a kind of watchtower whence he could see all that went on; and night and day he stole about the house and grounds, noiselessly, untiringly, watching with the vigilance of jealousy for the moment of conviction. I lived on the ground floor; and I slept with my windows open; safe against intruders by strong iron stanchions and bars. Often at the dead of night I used to be awakened by M. de Blainville suddenly calling me by my name; and during the morning, as I sat there doing my work, a shadow would fall across my paper, and I would look up to see those dark gleaming eyes shining from beneath the broad sombrero as M. de Blainville said to me curtly 'Good-day', and passed on satisfied that I at least was innocently employed.

At last he was rewarded. During one of his nocturnal prowls, when he was believed to be in Paris and had hidden all day in the woods, he saw a rope-ladder hanging from a certain window, not too high for a courageous man's leap. Up this ladder he crept like a cat, and sprang lightly into the room. There was a woman's smothered cry; a dumb struggle between two men; then a bold leap into the dark; and Madame Saint-Georges had lost the game.[10]

Others whom she met, if in less dramatic circumstances, were painters, poets and statesmen, whose fame now had dwindled, but the one man she grew to like and respect most at that time was William Rathbone Greg, an essayist. He had in 1842 won the prize offered by the Anti-Corn Law League for his essay 'Agriculture and the Corn Laws'; his reputation was further enhanced when he published *The Creed of Christendom* (1851). Greg was an ardent philanthropist, who appealed to Eliza for his 'epicurean fastidiousness', since his desire was to see public affairs controlled by an enlightened oligarchy.

*Eliza Lynn Linton*

He was ten years older than Eliza and they had considerable mutual respect.

Eliza spent almost two years in Paris and returned to England in 1854. Distinct changes were now beginning to manifest themselves in her attitudes. As a self-educated woman, she was at that time never quite sure of herself. Earning money by the pen was no easier then than it is now. How was she going to make her mark? As a novelist she was as yet unknown, and the world of journalism was a decidedly male one. She was determined to be independent, nevertheless, so she set to and wrote an article on Mary Wollstonecraft for *The English Republic*. Because of her attitude as a feminist, expressed in her *Vindication of the Rights of Woman* (1792), Mary Wollstonecraft had hardly been held up as a woman of esteem. She considered women had been treated as the servile creatures of men and, as she had lived with a man and borne his child, her book was scarcely proper reading for Victorian matrons. Yet in her essay Eliza asserted that there was no woman 'stronger, more independent, or more noble than she', and that the book was one of the boldest and bravest ever published. Yet Eliza never returned to the subject, nor did she in later life ever refer to Mary Wollstonecraft again.

When her next article appeared, it was for Dickens's *Household Words*. It had some pertinent things to say, but her approach towards her sex was hesitant. It was titled 'Rights and Wrongs of Women',[11] and in it she advocated that a woman's place was in her home. When one thinks of the fearlessness of her article upon Mary Wollstonecraft, her new attitude comes as rather a shock:

> Homes deserted, children – the most solemn responsibility of all – given to a stranger's hand; modesty, unselfishness, patience, obedience, endurance, all that has made angels of humanity must be trampled underfoot, while the Emancipated Woman walks proudly forward to the goal of the glittering honours of public life, her true honours lying crushed beneath her, unnoticed.

She did, however, stress that

*Correspondent in Paris*

Women have grave legal and social wrongs, but will this absurd advocacy of exaggeration remedy them? The laws which deny the individuality of a wife, under the shallow pretence of a legal lie; which award different punishments for the same vice; the laws which class women with infants and idiots, and which recognise principles they neither extend nor act upon; these are the real and substantial Wrongs of Women, which will not however be amended by making them commanders in the navy or judges on the bench.

In short, what Eliza was now saying was that women could have greater influence in the home, helping their husbands, educating their children, than carving out careers for themselves. 'Let women have their rights, in Heaven's name, but do not thrust them into places which they cannot fill, and give them functions they cannot perform – except to their own disadvantage...'.

# 6

# Marriage to W. J. Linton

It is scarcely conceivable that Eliza Lynn would marry a commonplace man. Nevertheless, her eventual choice could not have been more disastrous either from her point of view or the man's, yet at first they seemed ideally suited. They were both advanced thinkers and both republicans; both hotheaded in their outlook on life and both with kind dispositions. But in domestic compatibility they were irreconcilable.

Eliza hated disorder – especially domestic disorder. She was now thirty-six years old, no longer a young woman, practically middle-aged for those years, and the reason which may have led to this ill-arranged marriage was her love of children, especially girls. Now she had met a man whom she thought needed her help and sympathy, William James Linton, but her views and strong demands were, as we shall see, disastrous to them both.

William James Linton was born on 7 December 1812 and until he was five years old lived in Ireland's Row, off the Mile End Road, near by Charrington's Brewery. He went to school in Stratford and from an early age was a voracious reader, particularly enjoying the works of Walter Scott. 'After a serious illness,' he records, 'I read in bed some of Scott's novels, one of the volumes of *Rob Roy* in manuscript, page after page written out by Mr Crick, the librarian of the Stratford Circulating Library.'[1]

His interest in engraving began with collecting State Lottery Bills. In 1828 he was apprenticed to George Wilmot Bonner (1796–1836), the wood-engraver, who was a nephew and pupil of Robert Branston (1778–1827), the effective founder of the London School of Engraving. Linton lived with the

Bonner family in Kennington for the next six years and found Bonner a good master, 'making his pupils learn and do everything connected with their work, even to sawing up a boxwood leg and plaining [sic] and smoothing the rounds of wood to fit them to receive the drawings. For these we might also sometimes have to make the sketches and draw them on the wood for our own engraving. It was good artistic training.[2]

Meanwhile his radical tendencies were growing; these, he maintained, were inherited from his father and were furthered by a fellow engraver from Stockton-on-Tees, to whom he was devoted and from whom he learned much. This man, whose name is not revealed, but is thought to be Sumner Jones, brother of Ebenezer Jones the poet, was described by Linton as '. . . almost womanly in his delicacy of aspect and gentleness of manner.' He was organist at two City churches, and the readings piquantly took place at lunch time between services. But it was the man's steadfast revolt and eventual break from his orthodox, bigoted family which impressed Linton most; he found in his friend's example a rationalisation of his own estrangement from his mother. Linton remained lovingly grateful to his preceptor and kept sacred their brief relationship until his death.

By 1837 the number of Linton's friends considerably widened when he met the poet Thomas Wade (1805-75). Wade lived in Great Quebec Street, Montagu Square, with his two sisters and widowed mother. He had published a volume of poems, *Mundi et Cordis Carmina*, which Linton had admired, and had also written a play, *The Jew of Aragon*, in which both Charles and Fanny Kemble had appeared. Wade, however, made no money from his literary efforts and eventually went broke, so he betook himself to Jersey, then a debtor's paradise, where he found a job editing a weekly newspaper. He died quite soon afterwards, leaving his literary effects to Buxton Forman. Among those who went to Wade's parties was Hengist Horne,[*] whom Linton considered had qualities of writing 'more vigorous in character than anything that had been written since Elizabethan days', though he admitted he was a very uneven

---

[*] Richard Henry or Hengist Horne, 1803-84, advocated establishment of the Society of Literature (1833), edited the *Monthly Repository* (1836-7); his most famous poems were *Cosmo de Medici* (1837) and *Orion* (1843).

*Eliza Lynn Linton*

writer. Others whom he was to meet were Douglas Jerrold, who was soon to find fame as editor of *Punch*, and W. J. Fox, the famous Unitarian preacher, whose house at No. 5 Craven Hill, Bayswater, he was to visit and there meet many others, including Browning, Dr Southwood Smith, one of Bentham's executors, and physician to the Jewish and Fever hospitals.

Linton had meanwhile fallen in love with Wade's sister, Laura, a highly attractive woman, though shy and unobtrusive, who liked singing and had a good voice. To Linton she was 'an ideal, accessible to merit' – an ideal, despite his beliefs in sex equality, with a distinctive feminine subordinate role. Her passivity warmed his confidence in his own talents: 'I am vain enough', he told her 'of my own intellect — too proud to bow to that of any . . . but whatever superiority of intellect may be mine . . . is more balanced by your heart's purest noble feelings.'[3]

In 1836 she was twenty-seven, three years older than he. There was no enthusiasm for the match either by the Wades nor the Lintons. Linton had no prospects nor did he have any money to support a wife. The Wades, however, were in no financial position to lay down the law, and although Mrs Linton did not approve of Laura, her main objection being her 'religious beliefs', they were married at St John's Church in Paddington on 21 October 1837. It was to end tragically. Six months later Laura was dead from consumption.

Linton, completely desolate, wrote some poignant poems on her death and immersed himself in his work and ideals. On his way to work he used to pass a bookshop in the City Road, where he would often browse. The shop was owned by a remarkable character, James Watson, whose life Linton was subsequently to write. Watson was a quiet and unobtrusive man, and one can quite understand how he came to be one of Linton's closest friends – his characteristics and ideals were so very much in accord with his own.

In 1822 Watson had journeyed from Leeds to London to run Richard Carlile's shop after Carlile's wife had been gaoled for selling an issue of the periodical *The Republican*, published by her husband, which justified tyrannicide. He was already serving a prison sentence for subversive writings.* Further prison sentences were passed upon his sister, for selling a copy

---

\* Richard Carlile (1790–1843), English reformer and freethinker.

of Carlile's *Appendix to Paine's Theological Works*, and on five of his shop assistants charged with 'blasphemy', upon information laid by the Constitutional Association and Society for the Suppression of Vice. Watson helped to install in the shop an invention to protect the remaining assistants from identification.[4] Watson himself ran into trouble in 1834 when he sold copies of Hetherington's unstamped paper, *The Conservative*.

Watson first became Linton's publisher when on 5 January 1839 he launched his periodical *The National*, although it was to last for only six numbers. Linton, who had always been imbued with the influence of Shelley, devoted much of the first number to anti-clerical and anti-authoritarian ideals. There was praise for Robespierre and advocation of the abolition of the death penalty, a lifelong desire; but the journal was a financial failure and June 1839 saw the last issue.

The most important of all Linton's friends was Henry Hetherington. Born in 1792, he was a printer and an atheist and strongly demonstrative in his contempt of the Stamp Duty that was then imposed on newspapers. For his defiance of the act he was sent to prison. In 1831 he launched a paper, *The Poor Man's Guardian*, which survived for four years despite endless prosecutions. Its *raison d'être* was the abolition of the 'taxes on knowledge' which made newspapers a luxury the poor could not hope to enjoy. The newspaper tax had been steadily rising. It began in 1712 with a penny per copy, rose to $1\frac{1}{2}$d in 1756, 2d in 1789, $2\frac{1}{2}$d in 1795, $3\frac{1}{2}$d in 1804 and 4d in 1815. In 1836 a reduction of a penny took place. The tax was not finally removed until 1855. '*The Poor Man's Guardian* was pugnacious and provocative.'[5]

Hetherington was imprisoned twice in connection with his paper, but he finally forced a trial before Lord Lyndhurst and a special jury, with the result that it was declared to be 'a strictly legal publication'. Hetherington was one of the great leaders of the Chartist movement, and his was one of the thirty-three names of those who established the Working Men's Association on 26 June 1836. Two years later the People's Charter was published and was accepted at large public meetings in Glasgow and Birmingham, and in Palace Yard, Westminster. Linton was present at the London meeting, where he heard Ebenezer Elliott, the 'Corn-Law Rhymer', metaphorically foam at the mouth. On the following day the Anti-Corn-Law League was formed. The result showed in the following year when 1,228,000 signatures were obtained and were placed in the hands of that enormously popular MP for Birmingham, Thomas Attwood. The petition was rejected by the Commons by 235 votes to 46.

Linton was now thoroughly immersed in the Chartist movement and was also at this time contributing to the *Illustrated London News*, so he was able to afford to give more and more attention to the activities of the Chartists. Of Hetherington he wrote:

> He was a leader of men, a ready and effective speaker, plain, pathetic, humorous, or sarcastic, as the occasion required; a bold thinker and a good organiser, prompt, energetic, earnest, and devoted. As a printer, publisher, and a news-agent, he might have become a rich man, but his time was only too ungrudgingly given to the public service, which he would not neglect even when his attention to it might be at the risk of his own business . . .

In 1841 Linton edited for him one of his unstamped papers, the *Odd Fellow*, which he had started in 1839, and so entitled because it chronicled the proceedings of the 'Oddfellows' at that time, which subsequently became a benefit society. It was a weekly with the usual very small circulation. Linton contributed a weekly leading political article, much verse and criticisms of books and plays.

> It also included a poem by Longfellow, probably the poet's first appearance in the English press, and an early sign of Linton's lifelong interest in American verse. Under his editorship the paper had a split personality; its staple, fiery news snippets were crowded around Linton's earnest editorials, while vulgar quips were commingled with the editor's high-minded verses.[7]

Exactly when Linton decided to live with his deceased wife's sister, Emily Wade, is not clear. By law he was not able to marry her. In order to do so, it was suggested that they went

*Marriage to W. J. Linton*

to Boulogne to have the ceremony performed, but no marriage is recorded either at Somerset House or at Boulogne.[8] In May 1839 Emily gave birth to the first of his family, a son who was always known as 'Willie'. They were very low financially, and Emily had written to her brother for aid. Wade too was 'broke', but he sent them his sole remaining five pounds.

An improvement in Linton's affairs came when, in the autumn of 1842, he became a partner of John Orrin Smith; Smith was a pioneer craftsman in wood-engraving who became famous for his important developments in the art of engraving. They called the firm Smith & Linton. Among the engraved work they undertook were the illustrations for Bell's *Life in London* and Chatto's *History and Art* (1848), but their principal commission was the engravings they made for the *Illustrated London News*.

The Lintons were now able to afford to leave Woodford, and they moved to Judd Street, Brunswick Square. Linton had become friendly with the artist, Thomas Sibson (1817–44), a strange, lonely man, who was consumptive. Linton suggested to him that they should produce an illustrated history of England. It was to be written as a people's history, Sibson to contribute the illustrations while Linton would write the text. But Sibson decided to go to Germany for further study and unfortunately was forced to return on account of his wretched health. Linton nursed him on his return to England and when he was a little better Sibson went to Malta, only to die there shortly after arrival. The projected history was never written.

Nothing remained static for long in Linton's life, for in the autumn of 1843 John Orrin Smith died and Linton was left supporting Smith's widow and four children besides his own family. So it was back to Woodford. The next major step in Linton's life was his friendship with Mazzini, to whom he became attracted in 1844. Mazzini, exiled from Italy as a rebel against Austrian power, had landed in England in January 1837, the only country where there was no price upon his head. His early years in this country were spent in extreme poverty, but he made some staunch friends, among them Dr Bowring, who, at the first public meeting of Mazzini's People's International League, took the chair. Another friend was a Mrs Fletcher, a Yorkshire woman married to a Scottish professor, who helped him to get acquainted with the British Museum Library. Linton met Mazzini through Joseph Toynbee, an eminent aurist who had then recently been elected a Fellow of the Royal Society. He was the son of Arnold Toynbee, the founder of Toynbee Hall. Toynbee had been drawn to Mazzini's cause through the scandal that ensued when the Home Secretary, Sir James Graham, authorised the opening of Mazzini's correspondence and the communication of the contents to the Austrian Ambassador to London, Baron Phillip von Neumann. Graham had long been distrusted by Chartists on account of his undemocratic views. Resulting from their meeting, Linton was introduced by Mazzini to two other famous exiles, both Polish – Stanislas Worcell and Karl Stolzman. Linton, who had been corresponding with Mazzini, discovered that his own letters were being opened and tampered with.

> At first we were only aware of letters being delayed; and only by accident found out that they were opened and resealed. [At that time it was still the custom to seal letters with wax.] Then we learned the method: which was to take an impression of the seal, then carefully break it, and afterwards, first slightly heating the surface of the wax, to press the counterfeit stamp precisely as it had been done before so that there was no alteration of position, nor outward appearance of any kind to show that the seal had been tampered with. But they could not prevent the breakage of a hair or a slip of paper placed under the seal as a means of detection; and the heating of the wax was only on the surface just enough to take the new impression, leaving the main underbody of the seal broken. This I discovered by happening to keep a letter loose in my pocket for a couple of days, when the surface-joined seal sundered and revealed the procedure. We also obtained exact information from a subordinate in the post office.[9]

Linton reported the whole matter to Thomas Duncombe, who was the radical member for Finsbury. 'At first he would not believe me, but when convinced, gave himself up heartily to the exposure, and brought the matter up in the Commons.'[10]

*Marriage to W. J. Linton*

After a considerable debate a Select Committee was formed both in the Commons and in the Lords, by Lord Radnor, to investigate the whole affair. Public opinion ran high, and *Punch* caricatured Graham as 'Paul Pry at the Post Office'. The government was much shamed, especially when it was revealed that the Prime Minister, Lord Aberdeen, had himself been passing over the contents of the letters to the Austrian Ambassador.

The 'letter' business brought Mazzini and Linton still closer together, and their discussions resulted in the founding of the People's International League, officially brought into being at a public meeting held on 28 April 1847 at the Crown and Anchor Tavern in the Strand. The three main principles agreed upon were: (1) to enlighten the British public as to the political condition and relations of foreign countries; (2) to embody and to manifest an efficient public opinion in favour of the right of every people to self-government and the maintenance of their own nationality; (3) to promote a good understanding between the peoples of all countries.

Linton had observed that at that time in England even the best informed paper, the *Spectator*, found its columns closed to much that was happening in Europe. Mazzini first sent his draft views to Linton, who copied them out himself for general submission; he was appointed Honorary Secretary of the League, and the offices were registered at his house at 85 Hatton Garden. After the official business had been discussed at the meetings, Mazzini and Linton would drink rum and water and walk through the night.

In 1848 Linton went to France with Mazzini and shared lodgings with him in Paris for more than a week. During this time he met George Sand, who agreed to authorise him to translate her works into English, but this project did not materialise. He also met while in Paris a man who had deeply influenced his ideals. This was the Abbé Lamennais, who edited his own daily paper, *Le Peuple Constituant*, which purported to 'teach the true principles of republicanism . . .':

I had a cordial reception from the old Abbé,* a small,

---

* He, of course, remembered and knew Linton, who had translated his *De l'esclavage moderne* (1839).

*Eliza Lynn Linton*

spare, worn man, physically weak, and poorly circumstanced, who was editing his paper in the one bare room in which he lived in the rue Jacob; in spite of his age and weakness, fervent and energetic, a man truly of the stuff of which heroes and saints are made, if ever there was one.[11]

On returning from Paris he hoped to revive Chartist ideals with the publication of a weekly paper of his own, called *The Cause of the People*. He edited this jointly with G. J. Holyoake, the social reformer, although he claimed Holyoake did nothing. Holyoake was the last person imprisoned in England on a charge of atheism. *The Cause of the People* was published in the Isle of Man, which island, along with the Channel Islands, were exempt from the invidious paper tax. It lasted nine weeks.

Linton also met, about this time, Charles Gavin Duffy (later Sir Charles), the Irish nationalist, who was to publish in 1892 his *Conversations with Carlyle*. Duffy later asked Linton to join him on the editorial staff of the Dublin *Nation*, but Linton refused on two grounds. He did not wish to be tied down, and he differed on points with the Irish party. Linton strongly advocated 'the right of the Irish people to the whole land of Ireland', while his close association with Mazzini, who was naturally anti-papal, led to disagreement. Nevertheless, he wrote much verse for that paper under the pseudonym of 'Spartacus'.

In May 1849 Linton, who now had a large family – for in that month Emily gave birth to a son, Edmund, which was his fourth child since there was besides Willie a daughter, Emily, and another son, Lancelot – went to live in the Lake District, for which he had formed an enthusiasm on a walking tour in 1846. He was now heavily in debt and his work for the *Illustrated London News* had dwindled to nothing. He took a house some sixteen miles outside Whitehaven in Cumberland.

However, he soon returned to London. Thornton Hunt and George Henry Lewes had launched their weekly paper, *The Leader*, and had asked Linton to join them. Linton's idea of the paper was to establish it as an organ for the European Republicans. 'I would do what has never been done – i.e. organize a trustworthy correspondence everywhere ... This we should manage in connection with the League of democrats throughout Europe.' Daily he bombarded Thornton Hunt with ideas until that rather amiable man began to quail before him.

In January 1850, after having told everybody how to run the paper, he went to Switzerland to consult Mazzini. It was at Lausanne that he finally found him:

> My hotel was opposite to where the diligence stopped. I breakfasted and when daylight came sauntered through the streets. Presently my glance rested on another saunterer, whom I guessed to be an Italian. I accosted him, got into some sort of half-understood conversation with him, and at last won so much of his confidence as to learn where I might hear of Mazzini.

He spent a week with Mazzini, who gave him letters of introduction to correspondents and tracts that he wanted distributed in Paris. On his return home, via Paris, he saw Lamennais as well as Alexander Herzen, the Russian political thinker, to whom he had been given a letter of introduction by Mazzini. Both agreed to write for *The Leader*.

In order to earn a little money, Linton engraved a hundred stagey illustrations for an anonymous translation of the tales of Heinrich Zschokke, the German playwright, and persuaded a small London publisher to issue the book. The tales sold well and the proceeds must have formed Linton's main source of income. Probably most of the family expenses were met by Emily Wade. He also turned to another standby: writing children's stories and illustrated alphabets. The tales themselves are dankly moral, but exquisitely illustrated with flower and landscape vignettes.[12]

But isolation from the political scene was soon to irk his restive spirit. The fact that he never made enough money to live on and follow up his ideas, Emily's ill health, the burden of four small children who were being brought up in complete disorder without proper schooling, were millstones around his neck, although he was not a man to worry about his domestic circumstances unduly. In June he composed a memorial against the British Government's refusal to intervene on behalf of Mazzini's Roman Republic, and forwarded it to Colonel

Perronet Thompson, the ardent supporter of women's suffrage. Emily Wade, incensed by Linton's feelings, wrote to her friend Ellen Watson: 'His continual brooding over the World's Wrongs affects his temper and *outward manner* but . . . I know how *very* very great and good the inmost soul is.'[13]

The *Leader*'s first number appeared in March 1850. Hunt was principal editor, James Ballantyne, Scottish artist and writer, contributed articles on English affairs and Linton on foreign. But once again things were not to go smoothly for long and Linton found that Hunt was not going to allow him to have entirely his own way as to the policy of the paper. Furthermore, Lewes's sympathies were not with the Republican party. Ballantyne became so dissatisfied with Linton that he demanded his contributions should consist solely of illustrated material. The final split occurred over a sum of twenty-five pounds expenses allowed to Linton, which were considered to have been misspent.

Linton's next activity was to write a series of articles on republican principles, being an exposition of the views and doctrines of Mazzini, for a journal called *The Red Republican*, edited by his friend George Julian Harvey. But Linton was never content to write for long for a paper other than his own, and very shortly he produced a monthly, *The English Republic*. His ideals were even more 'left' than those of our contemporary socialists. This monthly journal appeared during four years, from January 1851 until April 1855, was printed in Leeds, and circulated with another paper called the *Present Age*. When *Present Age* collapsed, Linton asked his old friend Watson to distribute it in London. In all, a circulation of three hundred copies was achieved. Linton gave away a large number of copies, and Landor presented the Reform Club with his copy! Linton's friend Joseph Cowen paid the bills for paper and printing.[14] One of the outstanding contributions to the paper that Linton received was from Herzen, 'Russian People and Their Socialism', which Linton translated from the French.

Quite obviously, Linton's sweeping aim to turn the country into a socialist republic, to disestablish the Church, to abolish the House of Lords and to rid the country of capitalism did not augur well for his hope of a large circulation, but the paper did bring Linton's name to the forefront of the National

*Marriage to W. J. Linton*

Chartist movement. He stood for the Chartist executive in the late 1850s but was beaten into fifteenth place.[15]

With the failure of his *English Republic*, Linton again returned to politics; his main objective now was to find supporters for the Society of Friends of Italy, which had been founded in 1851. He returned at this time to the Lake District and found a large and dilapidated house there called Brantwood. 'The manorial right', Linton tells us,[16] 'had fallen to the Buccleughs at the time of the dissolution of the monasteries, and to the Duke of Buccleugh, my portion of the land being copyhold, I paid a yearly fine of one shilling and three halfpence, to have my title recorded in the manorial books, when, after a year's tenancy, I was enabled by the help of mortgage-money to buy the estate, – a fairly large house and ten acres of copse-wood steeply rising up the fell.'

He made several friends in the district, among them the two Miss Romneys, granddaughters of the artist, Harriet Martineau, the authoress, William Bridges Adams, Joseph Cowen, William Bell Scott, the painter, and Dr Leitch of Keswick, 'who would come thirty miles to give his unfee'd services'. It was Dr Leitch who on one of his visits told Linton about a certain Miss Lynn who was an ardent radical, a writer, a novelist, and someone whom he ought to meet. So she was invited to visit him. 'We were all captivated by her appearance, a tall stately, handsome young woman.'[17] She was asked to write for *The English Republic*, and her first contribution was her essay on Mary Wollstonecraft. 'My object', wrote Linton,[18] 'in publishing *The English Republic* was to explain Republican Principles, to record Republican Progress, and to establish a Republican Party in England.' But, as with so many journals that Linton had given birth to and edited, he never obtained sufficient backing, or the political slant was too far to the left. It is true that his republican ideas were closely linked with Chartist feelings, but a paper published in a remote part of England was unlikely to achieve commercial success even with Chartist blessings.

In 1855 *The English Republic* ceased publication and Linton immediately launched a new paper, an artistic journal, *Pen and Pencil*, and this enterprise lasted but a year. Misfortune continued to plague him, with the death of Emily in December

*Eliza Lynn Linton*

1856. Eliza Lynn, who had been a friend indeed, nursing Emily during her illness and looking after his children, now took Linton and the two youngest girls to Hastings, believing that the sea air would do them all good. The youngest girl of Linton's family, which had reached seven in number, was called Eliza (or Elizabeth) and Eliza Lynn had grown very devoted to this child, but she died a year later. Eliza was now much concerned about Linton himself, and she gave considerable thought to his predicament and the grim future before him. She had stayed at Brantwood and recorded her first impressions:

> I felt as if I had got into a new world – one with which my experiences on this old earth of ours had no point in common, and were of no use as guide or glossary. Playing in the neglected, untrimmed garden, where never tree nor bush were lopped or pruned, and where the long grass was starred with dandelions and daisies as better flowers than man could cultivate, was a troop of little children, none of whom was more beautiful than another. They were all dressed exactly alike – in long blouses of that coarse blue flannel with which housemaids scrub floors; and all had precisely the same kind of hats – the girls distinguished from the boys only by a somewhat broader band of faded ribbon. Nazarenes, even to the eldest boy of fourteen, they wore their hair as nature ordained, in long loose locks to their shoulders. It was difficult to distinguish the sex in this queer epicene costume, which left it doubtful whether they were girls bloomerised or boys in feminine tunics; for the only differences were – cloth trousers for the boys, cotton for the girls, and the respective width of the hat ribbon aforesaid. But they were as lovely as angels, and picturesque as so many Italian studies; so that amazement lost itself in admiration, and one forgave the unfitness of things for the sake of their beauty.

Indeed, the poor children suffered much from the local youngsters, who would mock them unmercifully.

> The house itself was found and furnished on the same lines. There were no carpets, but there were rare pictures and first

## Marriage to W. J. Linton

proofs unframed; casts of noble cinque-cento work, darkened with dust; superb shells; and all the precious lumber of an artist's home, crowded on shelves of rough-hewn, unvarnished deal set against the unpapered whitewashed wall. There were not enough chairs for the family, and empty packing cases eked out the deficiency. For their food, meat was a luxury, wine as rare as Olympian nectar, and sweetmeats were forbidden as the analogues of vicious luxury. Milk bread, vegetables and oatmeal, with treacle as the universal sweetener, were the food-stuffs by which the Lintons believed they should rear a family consecrated to the regeneration of society. The boys were to be great artists or divine poets. The girls were to be preachers or prophetesses. One or two might be told off as mothers to keep up the supply of the Chosen. But for my part their sphere of activity would be the world, not the home – their care humanity, not the family.[19]

As for Linton himself, 'No one who knew him in those early days could fail to love and reverence him. No matter how little you sympathised with his methods, you could not do other than respect and admire his personality.'[20] Eliza admired his noble presence, and respected the fact that his socialism was his religion. He told her that he expected a social revolution; he hoped the time was ripe for war to cease and that a new social justice was at hand.

In the meantime Eliza herself became ill, so much so that she did not think she would recover. When at last she was well enough, she resumed responsibility for the Linton family. She was earning very little herself, so that her own resources were strained. 'I was Philistine enough to feel that the saint is less useful than the housekeeper, and that Mary's part is not always the most profitable.'[21] She realised how distraught the Lintons were, how lost they were going to be without Emily, that kindly woman who had tried so hard to keep their home together.

They clung to me like children and I was glad to put all my resources at their disposal. Strength and energy – time and money – I poured all into their hands, and thought nothing lost which gained them ease. I was deeply interested in them. They had fascinated me by their very strangeness, linked as this was to so much goodness and so much beauty; and feeling myself to be of use to them seemed to compensate me . . .[22]

Eliza had been with Emily when she died and Emily had said to her: 'I leave them to you my dear friend. I have always held that God sent you to us for our good, and I die quite happy, sure that you will accept your charge and fulfil its obligations.'[23] Linton and Eliza were married at St Pancras Church on 24 March 1858. She revealed quite frankly that 'I was in that frame of mind which made benevolence my greatest solace and my only happiness. I had the desire to sacrifice myself for the well-being of others, feeling in this self-sacrifice my purest balm. I had given up my love for truth: – now I wanted to give myself as an offering to God. . .'[24]

It is obvious that this was no love-match. How could it be? Eliza was a very fastidious woman, but she had reached full maturity and longed to be loved. She had loved both a woman and a man, and these affairs had been failures. She had appealed to Landor, begging his advice, and he had written to her:

Dear Eliza: If you had not asked my opinion, I wd. never have given it. You are now bound by honor, the holiest of sacraments, to complete an engagement which was formed inconsiderately. I know Mr Linton to be a man of intellect and worth; I hope he is Good tempered. These are three qualities without which you would be wretched. I hear he has five children; he may expect five more at least. What a prospect for those parents who already are poor; and are destitute of such friends as are a furtherance to fortune. I look forward with anxiety to your future . . . I could have wished that Mr L had overcome his passion for you. Such victories, tho' arduous, are practicable, and conscience well rewards them. I would share my wealth with the woman I loved, but I would not invite her to share my poverty. Fly rather – die rather.[25]

*Marriage to W. J. Linton*

It is surprising that she did not act on Landor's advice, knowing the regard that she had for him and how much she had in the past revered his opinions.

Eliza's father had died in 1856, leaving Eliza, the only unmarried daughter, a mere £1,500 in addition to the house Gadshill. If Eliza married, the income was to be divided equally between herself and two other married beneficiaries. The house, Gadshill, had been sold to Charles Dickens in March 1856 for £1,790, but Eliza was entitled to only a third share in the proceeds. She was, therefore, scarcely a wealthy woman. Eliza and the family stayed on at Hastings for a while, and then she took a house at 27 Leinster Square, Bayswater. She asked her husband for a list of all his debts so that she could estimate what she could spend on furnishing and decorating the house. Linton considered spending money on such matters a mistake – it would be better to give it to humanity. Eliza, one imagines, took little notice of her husband's protestations; she wanted a house in town where she could entertain. Furthermore, she insisted that the children be properly dressed and the boys sent to school, while a governess should be employed to give the girls proper tuition at home. Linton was amused at the idea of the girls studying, but apparently took it good-naturedly enough, interfering in neither the appointment of the governess nor her curriculum. Eliza wrote:

> All the things in the house, and the house itself, being new and fresh, the radical defects of my husband's character as a master were not at first visible. Though I objected to the children amusing themselves by carving fancy arabesques on the sideboard, playing at ball in the drawing-room, slitting up the oilcloth, and the like, things went on with peaceful serenity, and for the first two months we 'stood on velvet'. Also, the sense of security from poverty, of rest from strain, of a stable background and a strong arm on which to lean, won Mr Linton to a certain amount of domesticity, and made many things in his new life comforting and joyful. Then he liked me in a way that had charm of novelty. He looked up to me as more practical than himself, and as having a surer judgment in worldly matters; and for a time

he laid aside his own and accepted my responsibility, which was like taking a breath on an uphill climb.[26]

As a professional, Eliza was full of verve and enthusiasm for her husband's work and would arrive at his office in a fast hansom cab. Harvey Orrin Smith, who was the son of Linton's partner, remembered that

... she always wore spectacles, was nearly handsome, and had a dashing way with her that was distinctly attractive. Linton, a thorough Bohemian, was quite fascinated by her fine ladyism.

I remember her saying that she would gladly renounce any intellectual gifts to which she might claim, for the compelling power of great physical beauty. Later in life she once said to me, 'Oh, Harvey! how sad a thing it is when, by the process of time, a woman feels that she is losing her personal charm.' Linton and his new wife were very fond; she called him 'Manny', and all went well for some while.

The real trouble began over the fact that Linton was by no means content to devote his life to pursuing his considerable accomplishments as an engraver. He was a political reformer, an idealist who was determined to put world matters right as he saw them. Their social lives were therefore poles apart. Their friends just did not mix.

Mr Linton soon began absolutely to disregard the times and rules without which no home-life can go on with comfort or decency. For an eight o'clock breakfast he would come down at ten; for a six o'clock dinner he would appear at eight; and he took it as unloving – not disrespectful, but unkind – if we sat down without him. This was disastrous for us all. For my own work it was ruinous; for the children destructive both to their health and education. But remonstrance made matters worse, and the only way in which I could touch my husband was by a tender kind of coaxing flattery – beseeching him to do of his own free, grand, loving heart, that which was the absolute obligation of his plain duty. And I ask, how is married life possible under such conditions?[27]

The marriage gradually broke up. The Leinster Square house had to be given up and the Lintons moved to Gang Moor House on Hampstead Heath, not far from Jack Straw's Castle. But their temperaments were incompatible. There is little doubt that he did greatly admire her, but there was no physical side to their marriage whatsoever. They were both strong characters, each too far set in their ways to alter their mode of life. 'I see now', Eliza wrote later, 'that my marriage had no real element of stability in it. Unless Linton or I could have radically changed, we must have made shipwreck in one of the many rocks ahead. And though we struck fast on that of my worldliness, others had to come.'[28]

The situation was very severely aggravated when in September 1858 Linton invited a Polish refugee, called Anton Zabicki, to stay at the house. They excluded her from their society upon the premise that they wanted to experiment in chemistry and photography. In actuality, they prised open Eliza's desk and stole two passports belonging to her as well as 'letters from eminent political men which had come to her in the way of business'. When she accused them of the theft Linton's 'passionate indignation was so intense as very nearly to make an end of everything'. Finally, Linton admitted to the act. Apparently Zabicki was intending to return secretly to Poland, disguised as a naturalised Englishman, and needed a passport to travel to Prussia.

By 1862 most of Eliza's savings were gone: 'My pride is broken,' she wrote, 'and I do not like the dirty meanly furnished lodgings that we have like our beautiful London house.' But despite her unhappiness she was a model stepmother, devoting herself to the children.

They all returned to Leinster Square until the lease expired in 1863. In May of that year they went together to the Lake District and wrote their only joint book, *The Lake Country* (1864). By the spring of the following year they had separated: Linton went to Brantwood, while Eliza took rooms in Russell Square. After his return to Brantwood, Linton's work as an engraver declined rapidly. Eliza did visit him, but he was now determined to go to America and begin a new life.

Linton was certainly happier in the States than he had been in England, and he published a great deal. But for one brief visit to England he remained there to the day of his death. His eldest son Willie remained in England to look after his affairs. For a while Eliza took care of his two daughters, Margaret and Ellen, but as soon as Linton found them accommodation they joined him.

7

# Life without Linton

On her last visit to Brantwood Eliza had written to a Mrs Moir, a close friend:

What to tell you of myself, dear love? – Nothing pleasant, nothing gracious. And is there any value in querulous complaints? I could fill this sheet with them, but I doubt if your true woman's heart would love me as much after as you do before! It sounds so harsh, so unwomanly, for a wife not to feel perfect happiness in the husband's society – and especially after such a long separation – and especially again when the husband loves personally as mine loves me; but I am not happy here, and never shall be now as one of the Linton family. The real main cord is broken, and all the little threads that bind us together now are of worth only because of their number, but not one has the strength of a hair; the Love, the Home, the Motherhood, the Matronship – all have gone – died – and will never wake up to life again! and yet I long for love and pine for a home!

I am working on my new book[1] and have written three chapters of it. The *Saturday* sent me down by post Mrs Wood's last novel, *Elster's Folly* [1866] to review, and I could but cut it up. I have cut up every book I have had from them, save *A Life's Love* by a Scottish writer,* I opine. I cannot help it! If they send me trash, and abuse the writers for putting forth such rubbish. Mrs Wood is to me a very, very shallow writer, a shallow observer of society and a puerile and vulgar one, and I have said so. But still

* Mrs Linton is doubtlessly referring to Anna C. Ogle's *A Lost Love*, written under the nom de plume Ashford Owen.

67

*Eliza Lynn Linton*

this does not give *me* a good review, which would be more to the purpose! I wish I had had a good review, then – there has been some reason why I have not.²

Linton and Eliza were never officially separated or divorced. Incompatibility was the one and true reason she gave for the parting. From time to time she helped Linton financially, though he was for many years to make more money in America than he had ever achieved in England. She was once reprimanded by one of her relatives who was aware of her gifts and told her, 'What a little goose you are! Do you intend to be a little pigeon all your life for Skimpoles to pluck?' She was forlorn and sad for a while, but time softened the parting and Linton always wrote to her with great affection.

During her marriage, Eliza had been out of touch with publishers. She needed to catch up with lost time, for she badly required money. One publisher she had approached was Blackwood, who was George Eliot's publisher as well as the owner of *Blackwood's Magazine*. Her correspondence was not fruitful. Her first letter dated 8 April 1862 asked '£100 for the edition or £150 for the copyright' of a book of essays on women. These essays, which were eventually titled *Ourselves: Essays on Women*, did not appear until 1869, and then were published by Routledge, and subsequently reprinted by Chatto and Windus in 1884.

Having had no success with Blackwood over the essays, she wrote to them again the following year, trying them with her first modern novel since *Witch Stories* in 1861. The only previous contemporary novel had been *Realities* (1851). This novel was at first called *Lady Aylott of the Chase* but was eventually titled *Grasp Your Nettle* (1865) and was published by Smith Elder. Blackwood appears to have left her letters unanswered and she was rightly angry at the discourtesy; thirty years elapsed before she approached them again.

Save for the charming *The Lake Country*, which as already mentioned was a joint effort with her husband, fourteen years had passed since she had published the ill-fated *Realities*. In 1865 she came to an agreement with Smith Elder to publish *Grasp Your Nettle*, which was the first of a steady yearly output until her death. During her marriage Dickens was the only editor she had kept in touch with and she had been a regular contributor to *Household Words*. This magazine, however, had folded after Dickens had had a dispute with his publisher, Bradbury and Evans. Meanwhile, Bradbury and Evans had launched a new magazine called *Once A Week*, and Dickens had founded, in 1859, *All The Year Round*. Bradbury and Evans had written to Eliza requesting contributions to their paper, but she felt she could not accept without first referring to Dickens, with whom she had always been on the most friendly terms. Dickens's reply was that he considered her as one of his own valued contributors and that he would take it amiss if she were to write for a rival paper. She refused Bradbury and Evans's offer.

Feeling that as she was no longer living with her husband she would be ostracised by society, her sympathies doubtless turned towards George Eliot and George Lewes, who themselves were ostracised. They had been living together at 16 Blandford Square, but in May 1863 they moved to The Priory at 21 North Bank, by Regent's Canal, which much attracted them; in due course they purchased the lease for £2,000. In 1866 Eliza wrote to them suggesting she might visit them, and received a reply from her:

> It was very good of you to write me. We had thought it particularly unfortunate for us that just the Sunday when you were able to come we should have happened contrary to rule, to be away. But I hope we shall be able to see you before we take our longer flight, for Mr Lewes has some work which he cannot bear to leave unfinished, and his wretched health hinders him so much that we are not likely to get away till far on in January. You know how prompt and quick a worker he is when he is well, but he is often compelled to sit through the whole morning.
>
> I assure you we both feel a strong interest in everything of moment that befalls you, and we hope you will not keep from us either joys or griefs in which you care for sympathy.
>
> Pray come to us the first Sunday you can.

The meeting never took place.

Eliza, however, was never to attain the status of a major

*Eliza Lynn Linton*

novelist; indeed, she has found her place among a number of minor Victorian novelists, even though her work is far more deserving of serious critical recognition. She was an observant chronicler of her age and she was a writer of courage. The fact that society has so radically changed since her day does not invalidate her acute deliberations. But she was first and foremost a journalist rather than a novelist; she used her novels to propagate her then unorthodox, violent and prejudiced views. She never found it easy to establish a plot, but in all her novels she sought to assess the social life of her times. Even today her narrative powers carry one along with an assurance that makes it hard to stop reading. Like most fiction writers of her day she was obliged to conform to three-volume fashion which resulted in a great deal of padding.

All her novels are used for discussing the social problems she was concerned with, and if she clothed her fiction in melodramatic terms this was quite normal at the time. In both *Grasp Your Nettle* and *Lizzie Lorton* she aired her caustic views of village and parochial life, becoming increasingly obsessed with the position and emancipation of women. *Grasp Your Nettle* gives an amusing account of small-town gossip, fed by the owner of the 'manor house', a Rochester-like character. Melodrama is plentifully provided when he claims the sensible daughter of the rector, Aura Escott. The cleric is a charming but completely ineffectual old man married to an incredibly stupid and interfering woman, whose ignorance is matched only by her silliness.

*Lizzie Lorton* ranks high among Eliza's novels. As in nearly all of them, one can see in her heroines aspects of Eliza herself, though the physical description of the heroine – 'a tall low-browed foreign-looking girl, with almond-shaped eyes '– hardly resembles Eliza, while her rival, the fair and not so beautiful Margaret Elcombe, reflects only some characteristics. Between the two women, however, we see the conflicting revelations that Eliza was experiencing as her own marriage was failing. The action of this novel is set in the dales of Cumberland, where she herself was born: she was able to draw upon her own experiences with authority, for she retained all her life a great love for the beauties of Cumberland. The village where she sets the novel is in the region of Wastwater, Buttermere

## Life without Linton

and Grasmere, including Scaw Fell Pikes, which she 'paints' both in storm and sunshine. Her dalesmen talk in their local dialect, and Jobby Dowsthwaite, the chief dalesman, is a shrewdly and beautifully drawn character. Within the parochial scene we can see the gradual social changes that were beginning to intrude with the new university-educated vicar, whose prying questions into the local ways are resented.

Lizzie, who has never experienced any true home life, having been brought up by a stepmother, dreams of a romantic life and imagines herself as a sort of Hester Stanhope. She falls in love with the new overseer of the local mine, as also does a more placid heiress. Lizzie, who is the loser in this contest, drowns herself in the lake where she has spent such happy hours with the man she loves.

The book received particularly high praise from the *Spectator*, whose reviewer considered it 'infinitely superior to the mass of those we are so often condemned to read'.[3] The *Saturday Review* disliked the character of Ainslie, with whom Lizzie fell in love, a point difficult to understand. *The Times*, however, in a three-column review, apologised for the delay in reviewing the book:

> Books of a grave and solid character, if worth anything at all, usually retain their popularity for a considerable period after publication, – in fact, they need time to get a proper hold of the public mind, but novelty is the very life-blood of novels. With a few notable exceptions they are the mayflies of the bookseller's shop, and, unless they are of singular excellence, the wrinkles of age visit them with terrible rapidity. Thus it comes to pass that the commonplace novel of the present season is preferred to the good novel of the past season, or before they are twelvemonth old they are relegated to class B of Mr Mudie's monthly circular, just as ballet-dancers whose charms are on the wane are placed in the back-rows by the inexorable stage-manager.[4]

*The Times* concluded that *Lizzie Lorton* was a notable exception.

# 8
# The *Saturday Review*

In 1855 was founded one of the most influential journals of its time, the *Saturday Review*. Its redoubtable editor was none other than John Douglas Cook, for whom Eliza had worked on the *Morning Chronicle*. Cook was to make a tremendous success of the *Saturday Review*; he assembled some of the most outstanding writers of the day. The paper was the joint property of Beresford Hope and Cook, the former providing most of the capital. The first issue appeared on 3 November, as the *Saturday Review of Politics, Literature, Science and Art*, to give it its full title, and it was registered under the Newspaper Act as a weekly newspaper to sell at 5d unstamped, 6d stamped for transmission through the mails.[1] It was an immediate *succès d'estime*, although it was some time before it became financially successful. It cost £25,000 to establish.[2] In *The Times* of 9 September 1858 the circulation of the *Review* was given as 12,000 for the first quarter, 11,000 for the second, 15,000 for the third, and 21,000 for the fourth.[3] Lord Bryce was to comment, '. . . there surely never was a journal which enlisted so much and so varied literary talent as the *Saturday Review* did between 1855 and 1863.'[4]

Eliza began her regular contributions to the 'Saturday' in 1866, although she had before this written some fiercely critical book reviews. Her commissioned articles contributed greatly to the paper's success, for she lashed out in a sensational manner. Her attitudes had completely altered from those of the young and fiery republican and advanced thinker. The fact of her failed marriage had caused her much anguish and thought; any further thought of ever marrying again vanished, while her love of children was to cause her more suffering when Linton's offspring decided to follow their father to America. Now her pent-up emotions were to find outlets in her journalism.

> I wrote what struck and made its mark on the things of the time. But my connection with this paper brought me more obliquy [*sic*] than praise. I had something to say, and I said it with what literary force and moral vigour I possessed, indifferent to personal consequences, as I have always been, and as I must ever be to the end. And those at whom I struck were naturally indignant, and gave me back blow for blow, sometimes hitting below the belt, with even a few odd scratchings thrown in.
>
> At this time my portion was a strange mixture of literary kudos and personal enmity. I was publicly cut by irate partisans, and no one seemed to think it possible that I had a conscience and was not merely an *advocatus diaboli*, opposing that which I knew to be good and bolstering up that which I knew to be evil. But I lived through it, for I do not think anything enlarges the sympathies or humanises the mind more than undue condemnation. By what we suffer experimentally we can measure the pain of others; and the injustice which we have to accept we are careful not to pass on.

The *Saturday Review*, she wrote, was

> ... frankly utilitarian, empirical, and relativistic in its morality, insisting that rules and patterns of conduct are valuable only so far as they are the accumulated wisdom of experience, conceding that morals as well as manners are largely conventional, but nevertheless attaching great importance to the conventions as guides to living in a civilised society. It paid occasional deference to the religious sanctions and gave great weight to tradition, but the chief test for innovations in morality was the question: What, in the present state of historical development, will best conduce to the general good of the national society?[5]

Eliza's first contribution was a review of *Hester's Sacrifice*

*Eliza Lynn Linton*

(21 April 1866). A further twenty-one articles were published that year. In the following year she contributed only ten articles, but in 1868 as many as thirty-three appeared, which included the famous *Girl of the Period* essay in the issue of 14 March. The tremendous furore that the 'Girl of the Period' article caused resulted in her continuing in the same vein, and she attacked her sex pretty regularly throughout that year.

Her final summing up on the question of the emancipation of women appeared in 1885, when she wrote that

> . . . women should have an education as good in its own way as, but not identical with, that of men; that they ought to hold their own property free from their husbands' control without the need of trustees, but subject to the joint expenditure of the family; that motherhood should be made legally equal with paternity, so that no such miserable scandal of broken promises and religious rancour as this later Agar-Ellis* case should be possible. But these are only the alphabet of the movement; the main theme goes far beyond.[6]

Her observations on the time when the Talfourd Bill was passed were cogent:

> . . . giving the custody of young children to the mother had been passed after a stout resistance from the Law Lords on the Obstructive side. One of these said that, should this Bill become law, the avenues to the Court of Chancery would be choked with applicants for legal separation, as nothing but the fear of being parted from her children kept many a wife with her husband. The prophecy was disregarded; the Bill passed; and married life in England has gone on much the same as before.[7]

She continued to be incensed that a husband could make a will leaving all his property to others than his wife and children. 'The argument of trust in the natural softness of the parental instinct is about as solid as a drum. It makes a fine sound when nicely struck; but it is a rickety kind of foundation to build on.'

\* George James Wellbore Agar Ellis, Lord Dover, 1797–1833.

*The 'Saturday Review'*

Continuing with her theme, she writes in *The Autobiography of Christopher Kirkland:*

> Though the core of this question of woman's rights is just and reasonable, some of its supporters were even then too extreme for my ideas of what was fitting. I could not accept the doctrine that no such thing as natural limitation of sphere is included in the fact of sex, and that individual women may, if they have the will and the power, do all those things which have hitherto been exclusively assigned to men. Nor can I deny the value of inherent modesty; nor despise domestic duties; nor look on maternity as a curse and degradation – 'making woman no better than a cow', as one of those ladies, herself a mother, once said to me indignantly; nor do I join in the hostility to men which comes in as the correlative of all that has gone before.[8]

The article which was to cause the most sensation was the one of 14 March 1868, the famous 'Girl of the Period'. It was an attack on the frivolity of the advanced woman, who was antagonistic to her ideas of feminine charm.

> ... a fair young English girl, meant the ideal of womanhood, to us at least, of home birth and breeding. It meant a creature generous, capable, modest; something franker than a Frenchwoman, more to be trusted than an Italian, as brave as an American but more refined, as domesticated as a German and more graceful. It meant a girl that could be trusted alone if need be, because of the innate purity and dignity of her nature, but who was neither bold in bearing nor masculine in mind; a girl who when she married, would be her husband's friend and companion, but never his rival; one who would consider his interests as identical with her own, and not hold him as just as much fair game for spoil; who would make his house his true home and place of rest, not a mere passage-place for vanity and ostentation to pass through; a tender mother, an industrious housekeeper, a judicious mistress.[9]

No longer were such delectable young women to be found, instead

*Eliza Lynn Linton*

> 'The Girl of the Period' is a creature who dyes her hair and paints her face, as the first articles of her personal religion – a creature whose sole idea of life is fun; whose sole aim is unbounded luxury; and whose dress is the chief object of such thought and intellect as she possesses. Her main endeavour is to outvie her neighbours in the extravagance of fashion . . . the 'Girl of the Period' has done away with such moral muffishness as consideration for others, or regard for counsel and rebuke. It is all very well in old-fashioned times, when fathers and mothers had some authority and were treated with respect, to be tutored and made to obey, but she is far too fast and flourishing to be stopped in mid-career by these slow old morals; and she lives to please herself, she does not care if she displeases everyone else.[10]

She equally deplored skirts being short, and two things she could not abide were cheap jewellery and 'general lack of taste'.

After Eliza's death a leading lady of female emancipation declared that Eliza found it 'more profitable' to attack rather than defend her sex. That may be, but her acumen as a journalist was always foremost. 'When', she wrote, 'I was in my fighting age, it was either the crime of indifferentism or of time-serving, and I put it behind me as high-treason to truth! This is the penalty attached to earnestness – the harsh lining of enthusiasm.'[11]

She was a blunt woman and had little time for the dissembler. This was clear enough in *Grasp Your Nettle*. She felt that

> 'The Girl of the Period' had blunted the fine edges of feeling so much that she cannot understand why she should be condemned for an imitation of form which does not include imitation of fact. She cannot be made to see that modesty of appearance and virtue in deed ought to be inseparable; and that no good girl can afford to look bad, under pain of receiving the contempt awarded to the bad. This imitation of the *demi-monde* in dress leads to something in manner and feeling, not quite so pronounced perhaps, but far too like to be honourable to herself or satisfactory to her friends. It leads to slang, bold talk and general fastness; to the love of

pleasure and indifference to duty; to the desire of money before either love or happiness; to uselessness at home, dissatisfaction with the monotony of ordinary life, horror of all useful work; in a word, the worst forms of luxury and selfishness – to the most fatal effects arising from the want of high principle and absence of tender feeling.[12]

Eliza attacked the girls of her time because she averred they married for money and she considered their attitude to their children was that of a 'step-mother'. She believed men had become afraid of women.

If we must have only one kind of thing, let us have it genuine, and the queens of St John's Wood in their unblushing honesty rather than their imitators and make-beliefs in Bayswater and Belgravia. For, at whatever cost of shock, self-love or pained modesty it may be, it cannot be too plainly told to the modern English girl that the net result of her present manner of life is to assimilate her as nearly as possible to a class of women whom we must not call by their proper – or improper name.

When discoursing on woman's 'make-up' Eliza was doubtless pursuing an argument true to her tenets, for she had never indulged in anything but the plentiful use of soap and water. Her spartan upbringing allowed no thought of either powder or perfume; on the other hand, she had long prided herself on her tolerance: 'And we are willing to believe that she has still some modesty of soul left hidden under all this effrontery of fashion, and that, if she could be made to see herself as she appears to the eyes of men, she would mend her ways before too late.'[13]

As for the 'modern mother', she considered that 'Society has put maternity out of fashion, and the nursery is nine times out of ten a place of punishment, not of pleasure, to the modern mother'.[14] Her barbs were aimed at the woman who at all costs must employ a nurse or some poor slut to look after her children, notwithstanding how lacking they might be in a knowledge of how to bring up children.

A great deal of other evil, beside these sly beginnings of deceit, is taught in the nursery; a great deal of vulgar thought, of superstitious fear, of class coarseness. As, indeed, how must it not be when we think of the early habits and education of the women taken into the nursery to give the first strong indelible impressions to the young souls under their care? Many a man with a ruined constitution, and many a woman with shattered nerves, can trace back the beginning of their sorrow to those neglected childish days when nurse had it all her own way because mamma never looked below the surface, and was satisfied with what was said instead of seeing for herself what was done. It is an odd state of society which tolerates this transfer of a mother's holiest and most important duty into the hands of a mere stranger, hired by the month, and never thoroughly known. . . .[15] As the children grow older, the women by whom they are moulded come higher in the social and intellectual scale, but they are no more than before subordinated to the mother's personal supervision. She, for her part, cares only that her girls shall be taught the correct shiboleth of their station; and for the rest, if she thinks at all, she cradles herself in a generous trust in the goodness of human nature, or the incorruptibility of her brood beyond that of any other woman's brood. When they come under her own immediate hand, 'finished' and ready to be introduced, she knows about as much of them as she knows of her neighbours' girls in the next square; and in nine cases out of ten the sole duties towards them which are undertaken by her are shirked when possible, as a *corvée* which she is too wise to bear unnecessarily.[16]

She had little regard for the average woman and her abilities in the upbringing of her family. 'The benevolence which gives out of its own impulse, with no hope of reward save in the well-being of the recipient, has no place in the drawing room code of morals!' She certainly always deplored pretentiousness:

. . . women pay their shot – when they pay it individually, and not through the vicarious merits of their masculine relations – by dressing well and looking nice, some by being pretty; some by being fashionable; a few by brilliant talk; while all ought to add to their private speciality the generic virtue of pleasant manners. If they are not pretty, pleasant, well-dressed nor well-connected, and if they have no masculine pegs of power by which they can be hooked on to the higher lines, they are let to drop through the social meshes without an effort made to retain them, as little fishes swim away unopposed through the loops which hold bigger ones. These things are their social duties – the final cause of their drawing-room existence; and if they fail in them they fail in the purpose for which they were created socially, and may die out as soon as convenient. They have other duties, of course, and doubtless of far higher moment and greater worth; but the question now is only of their drawing-room duties – of the qualities which secure their recognition in society – of the special coinage in which they must pay their shot if they would assist at the great banquet of social life. A dowdy, humdrum, well-principled woman, whose toilette looks as if it had been made with the traditionary pitchfork, and whose powers of conversation do not go beyond the strength of *Cobwebs to Catch Flies* or *Magnall's Questions* may be an admirable wife, the mother of future honest citizens, invaluable by a sick-bed, beyond price in the nursery, a pattern of all household economies, a woman absolutely faultless in her sphere – and that sphere a very sweet and lovely one.[17]

Strangely, she castigated artistic men and those who had achieved something in their lives yet who were so often married to dowdy women, an assertion which seems unfair when she herself damned 'The Girl of the Period' for trying to improve herself. Equally, she never ceased to chastise the stupid woman. But in those days a housewife had little chance of educating herself; even later generations were slow to take advantage of opportunities. In an article, 'What is Woman's Work?', Eliza wrote:

> It is strange to see into what unreasonable disrepute active housekeeping – woman's first social duty – has fallen in England. Take a family with four or five hundred a year –

and we know how small a sum that is for 'genteel humanity' in these days – the wife who is an active housekeeper, even with such an income, is an exception to the rule; and the daughters who are anything more than drawing-room dolls waiting for husbands to transfer them to a home of their own, where they may be as useless as they are now, are rarer still. For things are getting worse, not better, and our young women are less useful even than were their mothers; while these last do not, as a rule, come near the housekeeping ladies of olden times, who knew every secret of domestic economy and made a wise and pleasant 'distribution of bread' their grand point of honour.[18]

However, she appreciated the difficulties with which 'the little woman' had to contend:

When the lymphatic giantess falls into a faint or goes off into hysterics, she storms, or bustles about or holds on like a game terrier, according to the work on hand. She will fly at any man who annoys her, and she bears herself as equal to the biggest and strongest fellow of her acquaintance. In general she does it all by sheer pluck, and is not notorious for subtlety or craft. Had Delilah been a little woman she would never have taken the trouble to shear Samson's locks. She would have stood up against him with all his strength untouched on his head, and she would have overcome him too. Judith and Jael were both probably large women. The work they went about demanded a certain strength of muscle and toughness of sinew; but who can say that Jezebel was not small; freckled, auburn-haired Lady Audley of her time, full of concentrated fire, the electric force, the passionate recklessness of her type? Regan and Goneril might have been beautiful demons of the same pattern; we have the example of the Marchioness de Brinvilliers as to what amount of spiritual devilry can exist with the face and manner of an angel direct from heaven; and perhaps Cordelia was a tall dark-haired girl, with a pair of brown eyes, and a long nose sloping downwards.[19]

Women's taste, she considered, was deteriorating. 'Pinchbeck' was 'deeply ingrained' in the modern woman. She was buying imitations of the real thing whenever she could. But if she could not afford the real thing, why should not imitation serve her purpose? To what harm had she come because she wore 'ornaments made of painted wood, of glass, of vulcanite'?[20] Was she so degraded when 'she must break out into spangles and beads and chains and *benoîtons*, which are cheap luxuries and effective decorations'?[21]

Eliza could not countenance vulgarity: the new fashions that were just appearing, when women could bedeck themselves with imitation jewellery and wear clothes that were not bespoke, were heralding a preference for cheap finery over solid structure.

> The *simplex munditiis*, which used to be held as a canon of feminine good taste, is now abandoned altogether, and the more she can bedizen herself according to the pattern of a Sandwich islander the more beautiful she thinks herself – the more certain the fascination of the men and the greater the jealousy of the women. This is the cause of all the tags and streamers, the bits of ribbon here and flying ends of laces there, the puffed-out chignons, and the trailing curls cut off some dead girl's head, wherewith the modern Englishwoman delights to make herself hideous. It is pinchbeck throughout.[22]

Eliza had no patience for feminine affectations. The woman

> ... who wears a double-breasted coat with big buttons, of which she flings back the lapels with an air, understanding the suggestiveness of a wide chest and the need of unchecked breathing; who wears unmistakeable shirt-fronts, linen collars, vests and plain ties, like a man; who folds her arms or sets them akimbo, like a man; who even nurses her feet and cradles her knees, in spite of her petticoats, and makes belief that the attitude is comfortable because it is manlike. If the excessively womanly woman is affected in her sickly sweetness, the mannish woman is affected in her breadth and roughness. She adores dogs and horses, which she places far above children of all ages. She boasts of how good a marks-

man she is – she does not call herself a markswoman – and how she can hit right and left and bring down both birds flying. When she drinks wine she holds the stem of the glass between her first two fingers, hollows her underlip, and throwing her head well-back, tosses off the whole at a draught – she would disdain the lady-like sip or the closer gesture of ordinary woman. She is great in cheese and bitter-beer, in claret-cup and still champagne, but she despises the puerilities of sweets or of effervescing wines. She rounds her elbows and turns her wrist outward as men round their elbows and turn their wrists outward.[23]

There was no feminine trick which Eliza did not hold up as absurdity. The affectation of a girl knowing herself to be pretty and pretending she is not, but expecting adulation; the flirt who takes her flirtations as far as she thinks she can go and then retracts; innocence of design and over-familiarity with men to show off. As to the pretty penitent, lifting her eyes furtively to see who has noticed her self-abasement – she is only one of the many whose affectations are derided.

> . . . that affectation pure and simple which is the mere affectation of manner, such as is shown in the drawling voice, the mincing gait, the extreme gracefulness of attitude which by consciousness ceases to be grace, and the thousand little *minauderies* and coquetries of the sex well-known to us all. And there is the affectation which people of a higher social sphere show when they condescend to those of low estate, and talk and look as if they are not quite certain of their company, and scarcely know if they are Christian or heathen, savage or civilised. And there is the affectation of the maternal passion with women who are never by any chance seen with their children, but who speak of them as if they were never out of their sight; the affectation of wifely adoration with women who are to be met about the world with every man of their acquaintance rather than with their lawful husbands; the affectation of asceticism in women who lead a self-enjoying life from end to end; and affectation of political fervour in those who would not give up a ball or a new dress to save Europe from universal revolution.[24]

The woman of fashion is not to be let off lightly. Eliza considered the age one

> ... of extraordinary wealth and of corresponding extraordinary luxury; of unparalleled restlessness that disdains all quiet and repose, as unendurable stagnation. Hence the fashionable woman of the day is one of extremes in her own line also; and the idleness, the heartlessness, the self-indulgence, the want of high morality, and the insolent luxury at all times characteristic of her were never displayed with more cynical effrontery than at present, and never called for more severe condemnation.
>
> The fashionable women of Greece and Rome, of Italy and France, have left behind them names which the world has made typical of the vices naturally engendered by idleness and luxury. But do we wish that our women should become subjects for an English Juvenal? that fashion should create a race of Laïses and Messalinas, of Lucrezia Borgias and Madame du Barrys, out of the stock which once gave us Lucy Hutchinson and Elizabeth Fry?[25]

Eliza appeared to have no doubts that the lady of fashion frittered her day away in endless frivolities and stupidities.

Victorian standards were poised on a knife-edge. If you were not all you pretended to be and there was any hint that you had something to hide concerning your background, some stately matron would make it her business to inquire into the matter and reveal the truth. Time and again Eliza returned to this theme in her novels. Many of her matronly characters resembled bloodhounds straining at the leash to pounce on any irregularity or odd demeanour. In *The Atonement of Leam Dundas* (1875), when a newcomer, a French lady who calls herself Madame de Montfort, arrives at a small county town, she is accepted by the male population because of her attractiveness and charm. But when she pays her official calls, the ladies are wary. After leaving the widowed lady at the Hall, the youngest daughter is delightfully 'taken with her'. 'Now, Mama, is she not charming?' she asks. And the cold reply is:

> My dear girl, what Madame de Montfort really is I do not

*Eliza Lynn Linton*

know, nor who Monsieur Montfort was; but of this I feel sure, there is something that I do not like at all. I say nothing against her character because I know nothing; but if I had had my way we should have had a detective down from London and have learnt all about her before we accept her.

From that moment we are quite sure that poor Madame de Montfort's position will be under scrutiny until she is proved to be a satisfactory person to receive. The 'skeleton in the cupboard' was something Eliza wrote about continually, but she was not by any means without compassion, but she cannot overlook the inherent weaknesses of her sex, who at that time had plenty of leisure to absorb themselves in examining the minutiae of their society. In her essay 'Sleeping Dogs' she says:

> If there has been absolutely no sinfulness to speak of, nothing but a little imprudence and a big glossary of scandalous explanation, a little precipitancy and a great deal of ill-nature, by all means wake up the sleeping dog and set him howling through the streets. He may do good, seeing the truth would be your friend. But if there be a core of ugly fact, even if it be not quite so ugly as the envelope which rumour has wrapped round it, then fall back on the dignity of 'living it down' and let the dog lie sleeping and muzzled.[26]

Of the physical aspects of her sex she was very fully conscious. She herself was by no means beautiful, but had striking looks; she was tall with a fine complexion and a commanding presence, and had a soft and beautiful voice. She considered that

> A lovely woman fulfils only half her mission when she is unpersonable instead of beautiful . . . When we are young, the beauty of women has a supreme attraction beyond all other possessions or qualities; and there are self-evident reasons why it should be so. It is only as we grow older we know the value of brains, and while still admiring beauty – as indeed who does not? – admiring it as one passing by on the other side – as a grace to look at, but not to hold, unless accompanied by something more lasting.[27]

She warned of the foolishness that made men hastily contract a marriage with a pretty little fool, only to regret it bitterly later: divorce was no easy matter in those days.

> The successful men of small beginnings are greatly liable to this curse of wifely hindrance. A barrister, once briefless and now in silk; an artist once obscure and now famous – who in days of impecuniosity and Bohemianism married the landlady's pretty daughter and towards the meridian of life find themselves in the front ranks of *la haute volée* with a wife who drops her h's and multiplies her s's, know the full bitterness of the bread baked from that hasty brewing.[28]

Misalliances have now lost their terrors, and it matters not whether you marry a barmaid or a girl from the 'county', or whether she be white or black. But then it was a very different matter if a man

> ... had married for beauty and nought else; thus the case of a rising politician whose dolly faced wife leads to imperilling his position, because she is too simple to comprehend what is going on in his life ... Each woman may have been beautiful in her youth, and each man may have loved his own very passionately; but if she has no brains to fall back on, by which she can be educated up to her husband's present social position as the wife of his successful maturity – she is a mistake.
>
> Dickens was quite right to kill off pretty childish Dora in *David Copperfield*. If she had lived she would have died like Flora in *Bleak House*, who indeed was Dora grown old but not matured; with all the grace and beauty of her youth gone, and nothing else to take their place.[29]

Yet Eliza can sometimes be contradictory:

> Men do not care for brains in excess in woman. They like a sympathetic intellect which can follow and seize their thoughts as quickly as they are uttered; but they do not care for any clear or specific knowledge of facts. . . . To most men, indeed the feminine strong-mindedness that can dis-

*Eliza Lynn Linton*

cuss immoral problems without blushing is a quality as unwomanly as well-developed biceps or a 'shoulder-of-mutton' fist.[30]

Her concept of the kind of woman a man desired to marry was one who could show ample common sense, good judgement, patient courage, and could surmount the daily difficulties of married life with 'dignity and good temper'. In the choice of a marriage partner, Eliza commends, if diffidently, the French way, which she says is more sensible, of the parents arranging the marriage without consulting the girl. She contends the unfledged virgin has not much knowledge on these matters, save a passing passion:

> The young people of the two lonely lighthouse islands, who made love to each other through telescopes, are good examples of the way in which instinct stimulates the impulse which calls itself love when there are two or three instead of one to look at. For we may be quite sure that had the lighthouse island youth been James instead of John, fair instead of dark, garrulous instead of reticent, short and fat instead of tall and slender, the lighthouse island girl would have loved him all the same, and would have quite believed that this man was the only man she could have ever loved, and that her instinctive gravitation was her free choice.

As there was little free love, if any, in Eliza's class, no sampling, no jumping in or out of bed, no guide books detailing the excitements or variations upon the theme of sex, her own blueprint was not exactly amiss:

> A man and woman of mature age who know what they want may make a *mésalliance*, but it is made with a full understanding and deliberate choice; and, if the thing turns out badly, they can blame themselves less for precipitancy than for wrong calculation. The man of fifty who marries his cook knows what he most values in women.[31]

She was fully aware that more often than not the woman has the worst of marriage, that it was her life that was so often destroyed. Novelists and poets, especially, were at fault in their unrealistic sentimental predictions of happy endings to difficulties in marital life. Not for her 'the Romantic novelists'.

It is all very well to talk of fighting the battle of life together and welding together by time. Many a man has been ruined by these metaphors. The theory, partly true and partly pretty, is good enough in its degree; and, indeed, so far as the welding goes, we weld together in almost all things by time. We wear our shoe till we wear it into shape and it ceases to pinch us; but, in the process, we go through a vast deal of pain, and are liable to make corns which last long after the shoe itself fits easily.

The 'Girl of the Period' essays became a catchword, and a famous caricature by Matthew Morgan produced not only fashions in clothing but a spate of publications named after this essay. The first of these was the *G. P. Almanack*, followed by the monthly *G. P. Miscellany*, and another *G. P. Almanack*. The *G. P. Almanack* was edited by Henry Vizetelly, who was an engraver before he became a publisher, and it was financed by Ashley-Terry. Among the contributors were Mortimer Collins, poet and novelist; Augustus Mayhew, one of five literary brothers; Savile Clarke and Edward Draper.

Because Eliza's articles in the *Saturday Review* were anonymous, speculation was rife as to the identity of the author. *Punch* vouchsafed that 'If the "Girl of the Period" is as she is represented, the sooner a *stop* is put to her the better.' It was mostly thought that the author was a man. Thomas Hardy, who read her articles, adhered to that opinion. Sixteen years later, Bentley published the articles in two volumes and Eliza wrote the following Preface:

> So many false reports followed the appearance of these essays, that I am grateful to the authorities of the *Saturday Review* for their present permission to republish them under my own name, even though the best of the day has a little gone by, and other forms of folly have been flying about since these were shot at. The essays hit sharply enough at

the time and caused some ill-blood. *The Girl of the Period* was especially obnoxious to many to whom women were the Sacred Sex above criticism and beyond rebuke; and I had to pay pretty smartly in private life, by those who knew, for what they termed a libel and untruth. With these passionate repudiators on the one hand, on the other were some who, trading on the enforced anonymity of the paper, took spurious credit to themselves for the authorship. I was twice introduced to the 'Writer of the *Girl of the Period*'. The first time he was a clergyman who had boldly told my friends that he had written the paper; the second, she was a lady of rank well known in London society, and to this hour believed by her own circle to have written this and other of the articles included in the present collection. I confess that, whether for praise or blame, I am glad to be able to at last assume the full responsibility of my own work.[32]

Naturally, many of those who attacked her were women and she records some of the incidents that happened to her. Thus, when going on one occasion to a meeting at St James's Hall, a fellow authoress refused to shake her hand. She received numbers of abusive and critical letters: 'Surely you must feel for your own sex!' But she did receive some tributes. One admirer wrote regarding her '... as a female Quixote ready to set your lance'.

Although she told Layard (who was to publish a life of Eliza in 1901) that 'the milk-and-water male was no more to her taste than the brandy-and-water female', it was always the dominant female type which drew her attention. One of her most outspoken letters was received by the editor of the *Daily Graphic* after she had seen an illustration of 'lady footballers at play'.

> Sir. The Illustration you gave on March 2nd of the lady footballers at play, is one to make all but the most advanced of the sexless men and unsexed women who head this disastrous movement pause in dismay at the lengths to which it has gone. Has, indeed, all sense of fitness, of feminine delicacy – not to speak of decency – left these misguided girls and women, whose sole endeavour seems to be to make

themselves bad copies of men, while throwing off every attribute that constitutes the charm of women? Say that modesty is conditional to the age and country; still, the sentiment is intrinsic if the manifestations vary. The woman who violates the canons of modesty of her own times is as reprehensible as if those canons were as essential as the elementary crimes and obligations of organised society. The Spartan girls ran their races naked and were not ashamed. What was accepted then as blameless would be a police offence now. We go about with unveiled faces and are not disgraced, but the lady of the harem who should discard her veil would be a good-for-nought in heart and rightly repudiated by her sisters. These boy-girls – these worse than hoydenish football players – sin against the laws of modesty in force at the present day, and we look in perplexed disgust at the exhibition they make of themselves. . . .

In 1868 Eliza moved from Russell Place to Fitzroy Street, remaining there for a year, after which she took up residence at 28 Gower Street. In addition to her steady contributions to the *Saturday Review* and other journals, she finished another novel, *Sowing the Wind* (1871). By now the momentum of female emancipation was gaining ground. One of the most important pieces of legislation had been the passing of the Marriage and Divorce Act in 1857, which, twenty years before, Caroline Norton, granddaughter of Richard Brinsley Sheridan, had fought to bring about to help all those who like herself were innocent partners of divorce actions but unable to have access to their children. This was followed by the Women's Property Bill in 1870. *The What-not or Ladies' Handy Book* drew attention to the fact that 'It is probably not generally known that when once a woman has accepted an offer of marriage all she has or expects to have becomes virtually the property of the man she has accepted as her husband and no gift or deed executed by her is held to be valid; for were she permitted to give away or otherwise settle her property between the period of acceptance and the marriage he might be disappointed in the wealth he looked to in making an offer.'

In England of the 1860s 'The Rights of Women movement began to assume the form of an organised campaign',[33] and

*Eliza Lynn Linton*

among the active feminists whom Eliza met at that time was Dr Mary Walker. Dr Walker was an American reformer who had obtained her MD in 1855. She was appointed a surgeon to the United States Army. She was also a lecturer on temperance and equal rights for women. She instituted a 'Garden of Eve without Adam', where Colonists lived in one large house, the supervision of which was directly carried out by herself. All applicants for membership had to be pledged to celibacy and 'bloomers' were compulsory. Only candidates over fifteen years of age and under twenty-five were deemed eligible. The principle of the scheme was the regeneration of humanity and the resurgence of a new race of women who, in the fullness of time, would spread the doctrine all over the land. Apart from the lectures she gave while in Britain, she drew considerable attention by her eccentricity and form of dress. She would appear clothed in a long frock coat and black trousers. Eliza commented:

> I may as well say here that the 'bloomer costume' which she wore, with that huge red rose in her hair as a sign of sex, did much to retard the Woman Question all round. The world is frivolous, no doubt, but here as in France, ridicule kills, and you can force convictions sooner than tastes. When that handsome barmaid in the Tottenham Court Road put on trousers as a greater attraction to gin-drinkers, not only Bloomerism received its death-blow, but the cause got a 'shog 'maist ruined' a'.[34]

She also met Dr Elizabeth Blackwell, the first woman doctor in the United States, and her sister Emily. Elizabeth and Emily had been born in Bristol but emigrated with their family to New York in 1832, Elizabeth then being eleven years old. In 1838 they moved to Cincinnati, where their father suddenly died, leaving a widow and nine children destitute. Elizabeth with her two elder sisters opened a school and ran it successfully for several years. Elizabeth then decided to study medicine and, after fruitless applications for admission to various medical schools, was finally accepted at Geneva in New York State. A friend suggested she should change her name to a masculine one and assume male attire, but this she refused to do. She

*The 'Saturday Review'*

graduated in 1849, and in 1859 she and her sister Emily revisited England. In London she delivered an important series of lectures on the necessity of medical education for women. She concerned herself with the National Health Society and the Society for the Repealing of the Contagious Diseases Acts. It was due to the efforts of women like Elizabeth Blackwell, Elizabeth Garrett (who qualified at the Apothecaries' Hall in London in 1865 and obtained her MD in Paris in 1870 and was also the first woman mayor in England) whom Eliza also met, and Sophia Jex-Blake (who fought a lifelong battle for the admission of women to medicine, and opened the London School of Medicine for Women in 1874 and founded a medical school in Edinburgh in 1894 from which women were finally allowed to graduate) that the profession became open to women.

Another friendship Eliza formed was with the celebrated orientalist, John Crawfurd, whom she held in great affection and respect. Crawfurd (1783–1868) was a particularly remarkable product of his age. He lived in Penang for a number of years, acquiring an extensive knowledge of the people and their language, went on an expedition to Java shortly after Britain had wrested it from the Dutch, and found himself responsible for its administration. When the Dutch had again taken over the country he returned to England, but soon set off for India and was subsequently appointed envoy to Siam and Cochin-China by the Marquis of Hastings. In 1823 he succeeded Sir Stamford Raffles as administrator of Singapore. His role in establishing peace between Pegu and Burma, as well as his work at the Court of Ava, one-time capital of Burma, are among his many achievements. He came back to England a greatly esteemed person. Eliza wrote of him:

> No truer soul ever lived than he; no kinder, juster, nor more faithful friend and father. His tall and powerfully built figure, just touched by the hand of time, and slightly, very slightly bent – his handsome face, with the eyes still bright, vivacious, penetrating, where the lightning-lines of latent passion flashed across the sweeter and more placid tracts – his noble white-haired head, and that look of a man who has won all along the line, and who enjoys and who does

*Eliza Lynn Linton*

not regret – all made him one of the most striking features of the learned societies where no one was commonplace.[35]

She also enjoyed the friendship of William Spottiswoode (1825–83), the president of the British Association, whom she described as 'a character as free from base alloy as gold that has been tried in the fire . . . to the furtherance of pure science and to the good of his fellow men', and who in 1847 had gained a mathematical scholarship, and followed his father as a member of the great printing house that bore his name and were printers to the Queen. In 1856 he went to eastern Russia and four years later to Croatia and Hungary. In the meantime he had published his first important mathematical work, *Meditationes Analyticas*, and then immersed himself in the study of 'curves and surfaces', his theories being outlined in *Philosophical Transactions*. In 1865 he was appointed President of the mathematics section of the British Association. Following this he devoted himself to the study of the polarisation of light. His lectures at the Royal Institution were acclaimed by large audiences on account of his clear and fine voice as well as his erudition as a speaker. He died of typhoid fever and was buried in Westminster Abbey.

The English scholar, James Spedding (1800–81) was also counted among Eliza's friends. The Speddings had been neighbours of the Lynns; James was born in Cumberland. He was a close friend of Tennyson, who said of him: 'He was the Pope among us younger men – the wisest man I know.' Spedding had lived in Cambridge until 1835, when he entered the Colonial Office; but, receiving only £150 a year, he resigned. He devoted himself to editing the works of Bacon, which proved to be a monument of scholarship and industry, while his edition of Fitzgerald's *Life and Letters* drew from Carlyle the comment that it was 'The highest and faithfulest bit of literary work I have ever met with in this generation . . .'. All who met him were enchanted with his personality and charm, not least Eliza, who wrote of him:

> He was one who touched the crown of the ideal student, whose justice of judgement was on a par with his sweetness of nature, whose intellectual force was matched by his

*The 'Saturday Review'*

serenity, his patience, his self-mastery, his purity. In the midst of the violent clashings caused by the arbitrary and contradictory dogmatisms which afflict and bewilder us, his quiet breadth, his godlike serenity and all-embracing liberalism, were as refreshing as silence after uproar, as shade in the noon-day heat.[36]

Among other friends were Edward Flower, W. K. Clifford, the mathematician, and Arthur Balfour. Also Sir George Lewis, the criminal lawyer, Ford Madox Brown, Henry Morley, writer and editor of English classics, Edmund Yates, novelist, William Hepworth Dixon, writer and editor of the *Athenaeum*, and many leading Jewish families, for besides having a liking for Jews she was inquisitive about their religion. Indeed, all religions interested her:

> By the law under which I live and suffer, I have to work out my difficulties for myself; and no personal admiration for the moral results in an individual can carry me over to the faith from which these results have sprung. I am like one standing in a barren centre whence radiate countless pathways – each professing to lead to the Unseen Home.[37]

Her own strong feelings on religion were to be reflected in the novel she wrote after *Sowing the Wind*, *The True History of Joshua Davidson* (1872). One of her main themes of contention was that so many of the clerics of the Church of England were out of touch with the working classes and were themselves class-conscious. From the days when she first gave any serious thought to theology, her mind had been full of doubts, and with the passing of the years she had not resolved any of her distrust. In most ways she was liberal-minded about religion in general, but she saw it without exclusiveness of favour, and deplored 'our poor discredited prophets, the Communists, with their altruistic dreams of a universal Utopia, where there shall be no lack and no injustice'.[38] She continued:

> The parable of Lazarus and Dives synthesises the whole matter. Leaning on Abraham's bosom – safe in the arms of the Saviour – I and my beloved are happy, no matter who

else is in torment. I have made my own calling and election sure; and for the rest, it is not my affair whom God in His infinite mercy and justice may think fit to torture for all eternity. The great gulf fixed between us cannot be passed, and Dives must call out for water in vain.[39]

Asked 'Why should we be virtuous when we get nothing from it?' and 'Why should we forego the present, which is our own, for a future by which we shall not profit and where we shall not be found?' Eliza replied:

Because of the law of moral evolution, which is just as irresistible as that of the physical ... It is the Law of Progress – the law under which all creation lives until it changes into that dispersion of forces we call death and disintegration, to be followed by a nobler reconstruction. We have no explanation to give. Agnosticism has no pillar of cloud by day nor flame at night, marking the way and illuminating each step as we go. It has only the guidance of experience and scientific truth as its waylines. But the Wherefore and the Whither are as obscure as the Whence and How – as the future destinies of the race or the undetected relations of the spheres.[40]

When Coventry Patmore published his *magnum opus*, *The Angel in the House*, which celebrated his courtship and marriage, Eliza admired it so much that she was urged to write to him, and received this reply:

I am much gratified to hear that my verses have found so warm a welcome from you. You can do, and you prove, what I have striven and failed to do in my verse – which seems to be, like the bat's voice, admire your self-control even more than your indignation. If I were to try and write my thoughts in prose, it would be a shriek and not an articulate protest like yours. I live here, like Ben Jonson at Hawthornden (was it not?), 'hating all mankind', and conscious that the only use that I can make of such faculties as I have is to show by utter silence that I hold them, in the present state of things, to be of no use.

Hoping some day to have the pleasure of making your acquaintance ...

# 9
# *Sowing the Wind* (1867)

As with all her novels, the male characters of *Sowing the Wind* (1867) are drawn as types, but the two contrasting females are well drawn. Isola the constricted wife and Jane the journalist are contrasted persons. The one is married to a jealous recluse who expects complete obedience from her, while the other, Jane, is obviously a self-portrait, and the editor in the story is John Douglas Cook. Isola is rewarded in the end for her womanly patience by marrying the man she truly loved, after her husband goes insane and dies, but Jane pursues her lonely and difficult path even as Eliza herself had been obliged to do.

This novel is yet another example of Eliza's habit of using a good plot to illustrate an argument. She was all for sound sense, she was intolerant of the subjugation of women and of turning them into mere cyphers; she was contemptuous of the idle '*domestica symphonica*' of the mundane, well contented, class-conscious middle class. At the end of this novel she writes:

> The most desolate creature in the world is a married woman whose husband has ceased to be her support. Women cannot help her and men must not. As lonely as a widow and without a widow's liberty – as unprotected as an orphan and without an orphan's future – she is like one with bound hands turned adrift into danger, unable to help herself and not suffered to be defended. Any one may help an unmarried woman, but a wife must bear her own cross without a friend to share it, if her husband fails.

The *Athenaeum* thought this book better than her previous novel, *Lizzie Lorton*. The *Saturday Review* asked: 'What can have been the writer's secret impulse, if not her avowed motive, unless that of showing what pitiful, feckless and ill-governed creatures men are, and how much wiser, steadier and more full of capacity are their wives.'[1] But only in real life does Eliza find men of quality; she rarely depicts them in her novels as behaving well to their womenfolk. It was religion that came under attack in her next novel. The educated Victorian was invariably concerned with religion and morality, and Eliza was no exception, and throughout her life expressed herself frankly and forcibly upon theological questions. Most of her novels revolve around the Church, especially the clergy, in *Under Which Lord* and *The True History of Joshua Davidson* and there is a particularly virulent portrait of a biased and arrogant cleric in the former novel. She would not have denied that many curates were ill paid and possibly deserved a better reward, but she was highly censorious of what she alleged were their narrow minds, ill equipped for serving their congregations. She attached great importance to the need for broad minds and a good education in the clergy. She must have been aware of the expanding Unitarian and Evangelical movements of her time and of the followers of Bentham, but the dictum that 'Christ died for our sins' was something she could not subscribe to, and she was no believer in personal salvation. She deplored the Oxford Movement and Puseyism, and in *Joshua Davidson* exposed the progress of the Anglo-Catholic and High Church:

> Men suffer individually from the moral grip of the Low Church ministers; yet, as this grip is more congregational than organic, it can be shaken off when desired, and is by no means so dangerous as that other. The 'Sin of Erastianism'* which the Tractarians denounce, is the only safeguard of national religious freedom; and while the Church remains national, and holds in its hands any kind of directing power over the lives of its citizens, it ought to be essentially, not

---

\* The complete subservience of the Church to temporal powers. 'They [Newman and his friends] asserted that the essence of the Church was prior to any connection with the State. They turned the quiet Erastianism of the old High Church on its head, and said the State ought to obey the Church.'[2]

nominally, Catholic; that is, it ought to include in its bounding line as much diversity as may be without self-stultification.[3]

According to Lord Robert Montague, the 'Church' at that time contained 16·5 per cent Baptists, Congregationalists, Jews and Mormons, etc; 16·5 per cent mixed Wesleyan; 16·5 per cent Catholics; 42 per cent Church of England, and then, of course, the irreligious, the down and outs. The *Saturday Review* expressed nothing but contempt for 'the Ultra-protestant fanatics, in Church and Chapel, who were afraid of the Pope'. It gave the fitting name of Prurient Protestantism to a meeting in St James's Hall at which speakers regaled their audience with innuendos about 'goings on' in convents; it demanded the prosecution, under the Obscenity Statutes, of the Protestant Electoral Union for publishing *The Confessional Unmasked*, and castigated the Bishops of Durham and Carlisle for stirring up hatred of Roman Catholics by circulating a twopenny anti-Romanist pamphlet.[4]

Eliza's attack on Christian morality and the position of the Church of England was published in 1872. *The True History of Joshua Davidson* was couched in the form of a novel, and became one of the most successful of her books.

The Christ returned to earth was Joshua Davidson, the son of a Cornish village carpenter. As a boy he was considered an embarrassment to the established Church. He grew to believe, as Eliza herself believed, in a rational and scientific church and to dismiss completely a superstitious church. Joshua himself worked for the republican cause. He defended the cause of prostitution and participated in the Paris Commune of 1871. His life was ended when he was finally kicked to death by those who thought him a dangerous communist.

Only a few leading journals reviewed the book. The *Athenaeum* wrote: ' "An infidel", we felt inclined to call this little work after reading its first fifty or sixty pages; but we soon find as we read on that the earlier canting tone, however much it may mar the earlier portion of the book, is not the author's.'[5] But the journal sniffed at it. More favourable by far was the *Graphic*, which rightly surmised it would set people thinking. It did.

*Eliza Lynn Linton*

Charles Bradlaugh, the social reformer, bought a thousand copies to distribute, and the philosopher and lawyer Frederic Harrison commented: 'It afforded me new and singular matter for reflection.' Even such a radical statesman as John Bright records in his *Memorials and Impressions* how he gave a short résumé of *Joshua Davidson* 'with so much fervour and pathos as to reveal the secret of his influence over large audiences'.

Of the many people who wrote to Eliza about this book, one in particular was the Reverend Charles Voysey. She had sent him a copy, pseudonymously calling herself 'John'.

Charles Voysey was a direct descendant of Susannah Wesley, a sister of John Wesley, and the son of Annesley Voysey who was a well-known church architect of Jamaica. Charles was born in London in 1828 and was educated at Stockwell Grammar School and St Edmund Hall, Oxford. When he had been ordained he was appointed curate at Hessle near Hull, where, he asserts, he spent seven years without a stipend. He then had various livings and quite obviously was a thorn in the flesh of the ecclesiastical authorities on account of his views and sermons against the doctrine of perpetual punishment. When he was preparing his sermons for publication, the Archbishop of York (Thompson) wrote to him several times to dissuade him, and was heard to have said '. . . at present I never hear the name of Healaugh [Voysey's parish] without a sharp pang.' In December 1869 Voysey was arraigned before the Chancery Court of York on charges of heresy and was deprived of his living, which was confirmed by Privy Council court on 11 February 1871. He then removed himself to London and began holding services at St George's Hall, Langham Place, where he founded the 'Theistic Church'.

Eliza's first letter to Voysey was of 26 February 1873:

> I will not tell you who I am yet, because you may not like me or my book when you know me. I have never been more touched by anything than by your frank and affectionate letter. It will always be to me a ray of the purest sunshine, a dear and exquisite note of music. Some day I hope to know you. I have seen and been hurriedly introduced to you, but you will not remember me. I question if you would even know my name again.

## 'Sowing the Wind' (1867)

The preface to the third edition is not yet out. I have not had the proofs, but I have said a few words I hope boldly and yet reverently. Neither do I think Joshua or Christ wholly right. But if Christ is not right as a guide, an example, why maintain his divinity? Why make us confess what we cannot believe, and hold only the good of the doctrine, not to the mythology grafted on to it? The book means simply a plea for sincerity . . .

I shall go and hear you next Sunday, and see my unknown 'friend and brother'. . . .[6]

Voysey replied:

> I little thought of the pleasure that I was giving you by most sincere words of thanks and sympathy. I am glad that you have written, and I am deeply obliged to you for telling me the design of your work. I will abstain from public reference to *Joshua* till I read your new preface. I go heart and soul with you in your hatred of *shams*. Of all the shams in the world the most shameless is that of *professing Christians* in their 'Great Example', as he is called. . . . I shall trust you to disclose yourself to me some day. If even you are a Bradlaugh or an Odger. The man who wrote that history of 'Jesus the Son of David', A.D. 1872, must be my friend and brother . . .[7]

Eliza went again to hear him preach at St George's Hall, and was impressed by his services. She wrote to him again whilst staying in South Wales:[8]

> I could not find even that little moment of time before I left London in which I could write to you with your books. I hope you have received them. I left them to my maid to put up and send. Thank you for them very much. I need hardly say how much I admire them and how I sympathise with your courage; your faith is more robust than mine. In abandoning the dogma of the Revelation, it seems to me that we are necessarily plunged into a sea of absolute Doubt. The immortality of the soul, the prescience of God, the destinies of the human race, and the part we play in the great

whole – all seems to me a mere chaos. And this is where I think we looked for you to go further and to make confession of Doubt brightened only by Hope. Conviction means nothing. Conviction is the product of a man's present state, and is no proof at all. But it is a comfortless state, to feel floating in darkness, unanchored, unrooted, only hoping in due time the Light will come here or hereafter! or if it does not, then *this* burning heart and yearning thought will be stilled, and it does not much signify to the dead in their graves what truth is!

I write, you see, now in my own name. So many people know that I am the author of *J.D.* that it would be affectation to keep up the disguise to you only. Thank you very very heartily for your kind words . . . .[9]

*The True History of Joshua Davidson* was the only one of Eliza's books that continued to sell in large quantities, and was reprinted as late as 1916.

Her next novel, *The Atonement of Leam Dundas*, she regarded as her best, and yet it was one of the least successful. The reason was not hard to find. Her heroine, for whom she had obvious sympathy, was a murderess, and it is unlikely that Victorian matrons would approve. Once again the tale is set in a country village, a perfect background for dissecting the social scene and examining its daily life, the class distinctions and parochial gossip, the life-blood of the community. This was the sort of exercise she enjoyed.

Among those who lived in this village was a Mr Dundas, who had married a Spanish lady. His wife was bored and disliked the English society in which she lived. They had a daughter, Leam, who adored her mother. Dundas was no longer in love with his wife and when a mysterious French lady arrives at the village he is enchanted by her. Conveniently his Spanish wife dies and Dundas asks the French lady to marry him. Leam is so incensed at the French woman living in her mother's house that she poisons her. The crime is undetected. Leam falls in love with a man who is so stainless that when she discloses the past he rejects her. Leam goes to Cumberland where she dies of heartbreak on the fells.

Eliza felt sympathy for her heroine and this created in the

## 'Sowing the Wind' (1867)

fiction of the time a new standpoint which horrified the press. Though she had great difficulty in constructing the plots and she obviously gave much thought to this novel, she unfolded the tale with a good deal of verve and skill which gave the book considerable readability even if we find her social and moral tenets no longer hold – then they were considered 'evil society'. The figure of the narrow and strict British matron who is the lady of the manor, a widow with three marriageable daughters, and a priest well educated but condescending, are well drawn.

The novel received a very harsh press. The *Examiner* considered it '. . . vulgar and false to nature' and even called it 'revolting', while the *Quarterly Review* condemned it as '. . . abnormal, defiant and execrable'. The *Athenaeum* was kinder, saying that '*Leam* was far above the average novel',[10] while the *Graphic* wrote, '. . . this novel impressed us as decidedly superior to anything we have as yet had even from a writer of whom we had already such good reason to think highly of as Mrs Lynn Linton.'[11]

10

# Beatrice Sichel and A. W. Benn

From 1875 to 1879 Eliza travelled extensively. These years were, she recalled later, among the happiest of her life. In 1876 her valued maid, Sadler, married, and Eliza took herself off to Florence. She wrote to her favourite sister Lucy:

> I am trying to get as much of my book done as I can, and I give myself little time for play . . . so many people have called on me – half the English in Florence – that I have spent and lost all my time in visiting. The very thing that I thought to escape in leaving England! . . . Among the people who called were Ouida and the Landors . . . Both live about three miles out of Florence in different directions. Ouida has the most splendid villa, magnificently furnished and standing in large English-like grounds, with a view that would make you happy for life. She has a huge dog, or rather three immense creatures, horses, ponies, and small dogs by the dozen, and she dresses magnificently. She makes an *immense* fortune by her books. . . .
> The Landors' visit was of a sad interest. Old Mrs Landor is really not unlike the dear old man himself. Her hair is white now, not golden, and she speaks something in the same way as he did. She is dressed in a half-dressing gown of grey, and an old-fashioned cap, but very, very kind to me. So was the daughter Julia. . . . Miss Landor bought the house, and lives there with the old mother. . . . It is full of pictures – a beautiful place, and there were the terraces and walks and myrtles, etc., that the dear old man used to speak of. . . .

I am working hard at my book,* which is going to be *pretty*. I have done only five numbers yet – that is, I am two months only ahead. We stay here till the 8th of January, I think, then go to Rome for six weeks, and then to Naples for about three weeks. . . . The weather to-day is heaven, but we have had the most uncertain and abominable weather you can imagine. For the last week it has been damper than England – wet and damp, as well as honest rain – a peculiar kind of thing that goes through every part of you and the house; 'sirocco', it is called – one can scarcely breathe in it. . . . Then we have the tramontana or north, to which our worst east is a baby. No, the winter climate of Florence is not good, and very, very trying. . . . As for flowers, they do not exist. London is out and out the best-supplied city that I have ever seen. You have to pay for things, certainly, but you can get them. Here neither love nor money can give them to you. In the spring I believe it is a paradise for flowers, but not now. The market is a narrow, dirty, filthy little street, where you buy fried fish and everything else. The side-walks scarcely hold two abreast in the broadest and finest street, and for the most part we have to walk *in* the streets with the carts and carriages at our heads and heels. I expect every day to be run over; but they drive very carefully, and one never sees a horse down nor hears of an accident. But the grand old buildings and quaint narrow streets, and the lines against the sky of roof and tower, etc., compensate for everything. All the streets are paved in large slabs, and when they are covered with mud they are like glass. How the horses keep their feet I do not know.

Eliza's particular reason for enjoying her life on the continent so much was her overwhelming love for a young girl called Beatrice Sichel. She had first met her at Dinard when staying with a Mr and Mrs Julius Sichel, the girl's parents. Shortly after this Beatrice's parents both died and she was sent to school at Brighton. When her schooling days were completed, Eliza asked her to spend a holiday with her at Hennequeville. They got on so well together that it was decided they would move on to Italy. Beatrice was then eighteen

* *The World Well Lost.*

years of age, shy and nervous, but Eliza's warmth and kindness to her broke down her reserve and they established a great regard for each other. Beatrice was later to describe Eliza as 'very handsome, with a beautiful figure, always well-dressed by an expensive dressmaker in Germany'. She considered her 'becoming more beautiful as the years went on'. She was never intimidated by Eliza; indeed, she was the only person ever to call her by a nickname, – 'Bones', for the reason that she wore 'a large lace bow at her neck, like a Christy minstrel'. The nickname stuck, though nobody else ever dared to call her by it. Together they went to Florence, Sienna, Rome and Naples, where they met Ouida, Sabrini, and the actresses Adelaide Ristori and Fanny Kemble, among a host of other celebrities. They were invited to the apartments of Thomas Adolphus Trollope (where they had to climb eighty-nine stairs) and where, on Sunday evenings, large gatherings were held.

Regularly Eliza would work from nine to three; they would then sally forth sightseeing, and spend the evenings visiting friends. Beatrice records that Eliza would get up at six o'clock in the mornings to clean her room, having a poor opinion of the manner in which Italian servants worked, and, with her intense dislike of slovenliness of any kind, would even darn the hotel towels.

They returned to England in 1879, when Beatrice married and the idyll was over. But Beatrice continued to see Eliza and found for her a flat in Queen Anne's Mansions, which became a famous literary salon. Every Saturday, when she was in residence, Eliza would hold an 'at home'. Beatrice was constantly 'in attendance' for shortly after her marriage her husband had died.

Apart from Beatrice, Eliza became very friendly with Alfred William Benn, a prominent and distinguished philosopher and a well-known member of the Society for the Promotion of Hellenic Studies. After graduating, Benn, younger son of the Reverend William Benn, and who had been born in County Westmeath in 1843, went abroad and remained there for most of his life, living in Italy and Switzerland. His first important work, published in 1898, was *The Philosophy of Greece*, followed eight years later by *A History of English Rationalism in the Nineteenth Century*.

Eliza met him in Rome in 1877 and they were naturally drawn to each other, he being an agnostic and a disciple of Nietzsche. He said of her:

> Years before this I had formed a very favourable idea of her personality from the courage and eloquence with which she gave expression to advanced or unpopular opinions; and this impression was deepened by her conversation. I must confess, indeed, that in appearance Mrs Linton did not at all agree with the fancy picture that I had formed of the author of *Joshua Davidson*. I looked for something concentrated, austere, unworldly; and found, to my surprise, that this free-thinking Communist had apparently taken for her model the most comfortable and complacent type of British matron. One of her first observations was that she set her face against slang, but that sometimes one could not express one's meaning without using a slang word. I shall therefore make no apology for saying that the lady struck me as being decidedly 'jolly'. But nobody of any intelligence could talk to Mrs Linton for half an hour without discovering that the enthusiasm which forms so dominant a characteristic in her writings was no less an essential element of her individuality, where, however, it co-existed with a sense of humour somewhat wanting in her literary compositions. Another conspicuous trait, especially piquant in one who first won celebrity as the most caustic of Saturday Reviewers, was a vein of childlike innocence, of which she herself was perfectly conscious, and, indeed, rather proud. . . .
>
> Like many self-taught persons, she exaggerated the importance of systematic training, and considered that she might have done much better if she had had the advantage of a more regular education. It might have made her more discriminating in the choice of those on whom her admiration and confidence were lavished: but as a conversationalist I think she would have lost rather than gained by passing through such a discipline as that to which the promising girls are now subjected. Mrs Linton was a charming talker, ranging without effort over an immense variety of topics, as well as, what all good talkers are not, a good listener, always ready to receive information from others where her

own was incomplete, and to hear what could be said for opinions that she did not share. Her voice, which seems to be carefully cultivated, was rich, sweet and well-modulated; and she listened with an air of rapt attention, probably cultivated also, but at any rate very flattering to the speaker on whom it was bestowed. . . .

She evidently thought that what was good enough for her was good enough for her sisters; and the necessity of keeping them within the limits of their sex, and of drawing those limits somewhat closely, had become a fixed idea, a fanaticism to whose service all the resources of her picturesque and passionate rhetoric were devoted. In truth, the relations of the sexes interested her above all other phenomena of life, and she feared that the romantic complications to which they give rise would disappear if the characters of men and women were assimilated, or if they were arrayed against one another in two hostile camps. . . .

At the same time it must be mentioned that in her private conversation at least Mrs Linton supported some important items in the programme of feminine emancipation. She thought that the rights of mothers to the guardianship of their own children ought to be considerably extended, and she advocated a greatly increased facility of divorce expressly in the interest of married women, her argument being that in the United States applications for divorce come much more frequently from the wife than from the husband. I believe she would have made marriage dissoluble at the pleasure of either party; and at the very least she would have granted a divorce in every instance where a judicial separation can now be obtained. . . .

When I first knew Mrs Linton she was a professed Communist; nor am I aware that she had ceased to be such when I saw her for the last time in 1886. . . .

Benn spent several holidays with Eliza, and at Mentone he saw her every day for three weeks. He also spent nearly two weeks with her at Bex in Switzerland and in the Engadine. He thought she was a 'fairly' good walker, 'doing ten mile stretch at a time'. She was then fifty-seven. After her last meeting with Alfred Benn in June 1886 he recalled that 'her intellectual vitality, and what with many is more perishable, her interest in the affairs of her friends, seemed as vivid as when I first knew her; nor would it surprise me to hear they continued in equal freshness to the end'.[1]

From January to April 1877, Eliza, accompanied by Beatrice Sichel, was staying at the Hotel du Sud in Rome, their rooms being of an immense size. Eliza wrote to her nieces Lizzie and Ada Gedge:

> I have seen some of the old part of Rome today, and I cried as if I had been standing by the grave of someone I loved. It overcame me, dears, and I was quite low. If a young man whom we know had not been there I should have cried plentiful. As it was, I just loot [sic] down some tears and sniffed the rest up. But I was really overcome. It was the realisation of a life. Those grand old ruins where the heroes of old time walked and talked and suffered and died. The air was full of spectres; and when I realised Cicero and Caesar and the gladiators in the Coliseum there, and the poor Christians cast to the lions . . .

On 20 January she wrote to them again:

> I am waiting in all impatience for the springtime and the flowers. I want to see the Italian flora, and am quite looking forward to it. It is not always easy to get the flowers; they build such high walls round the vineyards, that one cannot see anything, still less find anything.[2]

Her love and knowledge of wild flowers is expressed in all her novels; throughout her life she continued to look for species and describe them, and few of her correspondents would receive letters without, at some time or other, reference to 'botanising'. She had written to her friend Alfred Benn in 1882, 'Do you know what the "lily of the valley" orchid is? I am worried nearly into the gaping doors of a lunatic asylum by people talking to me of the lily of the valley orchid found in abundance in the Riviera. I never heard that name for any orchid, and no one knows any other.[3] And later she wrote to him:

> I remember when I first noted the different shapes of certain

## Eliza Lynn Linton

buds of trees, *e.g.* the difference between those of the horse-chestnut and the lime; I can yet put back certain rose-bushes and honeysuckles found in the hedges; and if it still exists as a field, I could walk straight to that corner of the field where I once found what I suppose must have been an oxslip. But it is more than fifty years since I have seen the place.

I remember the smell of the laurestinus and the bay trees the first evening we arrived at my father's Kentish home;* and the kind of awe with which those two cedars in the shrubbery opposite inspired me.[4]

In April 1877 they left Rome for Naples, where they remained for ten days, before moving on to Vico Equense, lodging in an old palazzo. It was a ramshackle place, furnished 'appallingly', with a staff that consisted of a boy of eighteen who was their cook, a small girl and a child.

Luigi is a pretty boy and a good cook, but we ought to dine at half-past-six, and we dine at a quarter-past-seven, because Luigi has been taking a lesson on the guitar from an old ragged brigand up from the mountain, or playing at bowls in the public street. Hitherto it has been dead cold, and the cold of a comfortless old barrack like this is dreadful. To-day it is the loveliest summer day of June. The scents of orange blossom and acacia come up, and the view is the most divine thing you can imagine. From one window we look over the town on to the bay and to the islands of Ischia and Procida. Another, the north window of my room, we see Vesuvius and Naples. The little town of Vico Equense goes in steps, and is the most picturesque thing to look at possible. When you are in it, it is the dirtiest. The streets are just wide enough to let a carriage or cart pass without touching you if you squeeze flat up against the wall. In the piazza, where there are fountains, there is a stand of donkey-carriages, etc. and we are almost mobbed when we go through. The children follow up in troops begging. Every one begs – men, women, and children, all are filthy in person, and in rags.

* *Gadshill.*

They spent June in Capri and then returned to Vico Equense. Meanwhile, Eliza was turning out articles for the *New Quarterly*, the *Queen* and the *Saturday Review*, as well as working on a new novel. On returning to Naples she wrote to her sister from the Hotel Nobile on 10 November:

> I have been *very* ill for a week, but I am all right now – was as if poisoned by something. . . . Then my Bee and I went over to the island of Ischia, which is *mountaineous* [*sic*], and where we lived in the purest and loveliest air, and I got quite well and came back jolly. . . . But I am thin all over, with a small face and quite withered hands. I am going to be thin and I am getting quite grey, and my 'abundant' hair, Lucy, has fallen off till it is thin hair and no longer abundant, and all in all I am a wretch. . . . I am not *very* strong these later days, but never other than cheerful and perfectly resigned to all that comes. I see the realities of life as facts and not to be sorrowful for. These they are and we have to make the best of them! It is no use kicking against the pricks, and all the inevitable circumstances of life – as death and old age – we must accept cheerfully. The remediable misfortunes are another matter. These I would strive against to the utmost, but for the rest! they are painful, Heaven knows, but how can we help them? For sickness and incompetence, these are remediable with more knowledge, and the world is growing better, and will one day be, if not perfect, indefinitely improved.[5]

Her next letter to her sister shows her in another light:

> I have been up Vesuvius – walked the whole way, and nearly died! We went on a bad day, and got into the smoke. We were nearly suffocated, it was all sulphur, and I was sea-sick. The guide wiped my mouth and then my face with his filthy pocket-handkerchief, and I was so humiliated by suffering that I was grateful! I would not be carried, and so I suffered. And when we got to the top it was all smoke! We could not see into the crater one bit – no more than looking into a white plate, only the white moved! It was awful. The way is one mass of loose cinders or ashes, where you sink into

your calf (coming down) and over your ankles (going up). Every step up you slide half-way back. I had two men to pull me with ropes around them and through a stick that then I held, and a man to push. It is almost at times perpendicular. I had to stop 'ferma!' 'aspetta!' every six or seven steps at least, and fling myself on the ground face downward, and I almost died! But it is done, and was a sell all throughout![6]

Eliza had finished her new novel, *The World Well Lost*, which she herself considered greatly inferior to *The Atonement of Leam Dundas*, and before starting *Under Which Lord?* she and Bee returned to Rome, where they went to stay at the Hotel du Louvre. Writing to her sister on 12 January 1878 she says:

> ... as for the spiritualism, dearie, I do not believe in it as anything beyond whatever hysteria may mean. All the so-called manifestations of hands, etc. when seen by many, *are without exceptions frauds* – when seen by one only, are hallucinations. It is a thing that does not bear the light of day or reason. Look at it – if a force is so powerful as to move a heavy table and so material as to be able to make tangible hands – where do you stop? ...
>
> All the city is in mourning and consternation at the death of the poor King.* It has been a dreadful blow to everyone, and the state of every one on Wednesday was really pitiable. It struck me to the heart, and I was as cold and white as this paper for hours after. It is a dreadful thing for Italy at this moment. Things are not sufficiently consolidated to bear a shock of any kind, and this is a shock; and unless Humbert† is wise and moderate, on all sides there will be grave troubles!

After leaving Rome, Eliza went to Jenbach in the Austrian Tyrol, and from there to France, going to Hennequeville

---

\* Victor Emmanuel II (1820–78), King of Sardinia and first King of Italy, who devoted himself to his duties as a constitutional monarch with great conscientiousness. He died in Rome of a fever on 9 January 1878.

† Humbert I succeeded his father and was equally well liked and popular.

where she had spent the first holiday with Beatrice. But she was still restive and made her way to Munich, then back to Scholastica near Jenbach and on to Venice.

All this time, in addition to her articles, she was hard at work on *Under Which Lord?* (originally titled *Under Which King?*, its name when serialised in the *Gentleman's Magazine*). She wrote to her sister Lucy, '. . . it is going to make a noise, but *you* will not like it. No orthodox person will. I cannot help that! I must write according to my conscience, and I must take the blame and bear the brunt when it comes in consequence.[7] *Under Which Lord?* was her most virulent piece of work and she was attacked violently, though she also had her supporters.

This novel was an even more searing piece of religious propaganda than *The True History of Joshua Davidson*. If its characters (with the possible exception of the wife, Hermoine) had been drawn with more subtlety and humanity, Eliza might have established herself as a novelist of some stature. But it was a brave and wholly absorbing book revealing the highly disturbing influence that surged through English theological life of that time of the Anglo-Catholic Church and its beliefs, and the ominous results that its ritualism produced among those who were intimidated into its activities. The theme drew attention to the plight of Protestant parishes where vague priests of the Church of England were unable to influence their parishioners in the invidious manner of the higher church practices. Once again Eliza has drawn her characters with no half-measures. A free-thinking husband, with no love for the ritualistic Anglo-Catholic Church, is forced to witness his wife and her wealth being drawn into the clutches of the local priest, while his daughter is coveted in the same manner and is forcibly taken to a nunnery in Rome. Many Anglo-Catholic priests pressed on wealthy women warnings of eternal damnation unless they fully and unquestioningly embraced the aims of their all-powerful church. So many women had had no emotional outlet and were prey for such men as Lancelot Lascelles who unmercifully asserted their authority and denounced any individuality the women might have. These attitudes where the Roman Church is concerned are hardly exaggerated.[8]

This remarkable and forceful novel was naturally received with hostility by the press, which could not afford to offend

*Eliza Lynn Linton*

Catholic readers by praising Eliza's outspoken opposition to Anglo-Catholicism.

No sooner had Eliza returned to England than she longed to be abroad again. She had been staying at Hayter House, Marylebone Road, and, writing to her sister on 28 May 1879, said:

> I went over the largest hospital in England last night, with all the wards quiet, the lights turned down, many sleeping, many awake feverish and restless. There was one poor fellow, a butcher, who had nearly missed killing himself unintentionally by a missed blow of an axe, which did not chop the meat, and did cut his own stomach. He was getting on, but first they thought he would not live. A baby three months old had a broken thigh. One man, with awful abscesses on his legs, had hundreds of small bits of healthy flesh taken from the rest of his body to engraft in the sore places. It was all very interesting. I went with Mrs Priestley,* and we were received and carried round by the governor and one of the young doctors. I am to write a magazine article about it. We did not get home till twelve.

She left London to stay with the Priestleys in Scotland, and then went to the home of her sister Lucy at Ludborough Rectory, Lincolnshire. When she returned to London she wrote to her nephew, Ernest Gedge:

> There is one thing you must hold fast by – Duty. That includes self-respect and ambition. Do what is right and don't do what is wrong, for the sake of the good for which we ought all to live, and for that self-respect which we ought never to outrage.
> And remember that what you have got to do in this life is to succeed – not only to enjoy yourself, but to work well and bravely and manfully to the end . . . If you want a safe and understanding friend, and whom to take counsel, come to me. Your loving aunt and true friend, Eliza Lynn Linton.[9]

Eliza could not forget her affection for Bee Sichel and she

\* Later Lady Priestley.

now felt a lonely and saddened woman. She recorded her feelings in *The Autobiography of Christopher Kirkland*:

> I tried hard to be grateful for what had been, and not sour the past by lamentations in the present; to be cheerful, and to take an active interest in things and people as I had done when my heart was at rest and I was happy in my home. But human nature was too strong for me; and I had again the old conflict to go through – again to fight with my wild beasts of sorrow and disappointment and loss, till I had conquered them – unless I would be conquered by them.
>
> The time was very, very sad. I thought that all love had died out for the rest of the years that I had to live. I promised myself that I would have no more enthusiasms, make no more close friendships, open my inner heart to no ideal for the future; – never again – never again! Love had ever brought me pain in excess of joy; and henceforward I would live on the broad common-land of friendships that were kindly, refreshing, sustaining, but not exclusive to me; friendships where I was one among others, and where I made numbers stand in stead of specialities. I would have no more private gardens cultivated with my heart's blood, to see them laid waste by disappointment, separation, death.
>
> What supreme folly it was to put one's happiness into the powers of others – to hang one's peace like a jewel round another's neck! The wise man keeps his own possessions sure. It is only lunatics who scatter their treasures far and wide among those who, by the law of their own life, cannot guard them. And what was I but a lunatic, with this insatiable need of loving – this inexhaustible power of giving? Why had I ever let this dear child creep so far into my heart, so that when the appointed end of a girl such as she came, as come it must, I should suffer as I did? For indeed her loss was quite as severe a trial to me as the break-up of my married life had been, when I had to begin again the struggle proper to youth, without the hope, the energy, the unworn nerves of youth, and further handicapped by the sense of disappointment and illusion. Truly I was an unlucky investor of affection! – but the strange law of loss – the strange ruling of fate – that I should not root – had never pressed so

hardly on me as now. For long months I was physically sick, so that sometimes I despaired of my own recovery.[10]

Bee had married a Mr Hartley and soon after the wedding had written to Eliza, who replied:

My Beloved Bee – I cannot tell you what supreme joy your letter has given me. Peace and rest – those two words darling are worth a volume. That is *the* feeling to have! You are at peace now, you have rest. You have your friend, your protector, your lover, your caretaker, your home in your dear husband's arms for life. And all that you have is to be your own sweet, best truest self, to love him, to study him, to give him all that he gives to you – and that is no task, no difficulty! It is all done with; your home is secured, your happiness, and no one now has the right to bring a moment's sorrow to your dear dear heart. Oh, Bee, how glad I am that it has turned out so well! For that engagement time was trying, and if you had both got fretful and irritable even with each other, I should not have been surprised. However it is all over. Every care and sorrow lies behind you, and we have only joy and love, rest and peace, in the present and the future. . . . It makes me happy to think of you – and if I have not let my rooms by then how glad I shall be to see you – return! I think I shall go to the station to meet you if I knew when you would come. You are so like my own child, Bee! I have never taken to a girl such as you. No one of your own age ever came so near to me. I never loved like *my own* child any girl as I love you. . . .[11]

Eliza published in 1880 one of her most attractive books, *The Rebel of the Family*. It contains much autobiographical material and discusses with considerable clarity and verve the conventions of her time, class-consciousness and female emancipation. Mrs Winstanley, daughter of a bishop, is left a widow with a small income and three daughters. The eldest daughter, Thomasina, is an upright, highly controlled girl; the youngest, Eva, a little flirt, ingenious but under the influence of her mother. It is Perdita, the middle child, who is not blinded by the conventions of her age and who is a forerunner of the emancipated girl who insists on earning her own living and is not to be tied to mother's apron strings. She is therefore treated as 'a rebel of the family', ridiculed by her sisters and held in constant horror by her conventional mother. Perdita longs to be a male so that she could leave the constricted female household in which she is forced to live. But at last she wins her way and to the horror of the family takes a daily job. She meets a lesbian lady, Bell Blount, who invites Perdita to live with her. But she is such a monstrous woman who already has 'a wife', and Perdita has met the local chemist's son to whom she has become attracted, and cannot subscribe to Bell Blount's outpourings against men. Finally, it is the savings of the chemist's son, so abhorred by the Winstanleys, which rescues the family from ruin.

Eliza's attitude, however, was still inconsistent, because she herself still thought that a woman's life was best secured in looking after and helping her husband. But she equally derided the false position women found themselves in, in a world dominated by men. This is expounded by Bell Blount:

> Men have made us what we are. For their own abominable purposes they have demoralised us, denied us freedom and education that they might govern us more easily through our follies and weaknesses. They are responsible for all our vices. When we have shaken off masculine influence and dominion, we shall then improve, indefinitely. When we can develop according to the best law of our being, we shall cast off this slough of vanity and indirectness which now afflicts you and every honest soul among us. It is only the consequence of our dependence. Men make us deck ourselves like slaves to please the master; and we are driven into deceit because they are tyrannous and strong and we are enslaved and weak.

*The Rebel of the Family* is one of the best of Eliza's works. The characters take possession of the reader and are drawn with knowledge and understanding, and the arguments for women's emancipation admirably presented. If Charlotte Yonge could define the close family relationships of the middle-classes of the time, Eliza on a more candid canvas revealed

*Eliza Lynn Linton*

the trials and tribulations of a wider social segment. Contemporary reviewers were lukewarm, rather by reason of Eliza's ambivalence on the woman question than for reasons of literary merit.

## 11

# Mrs Tweedie and Henry James

In 1880 Eliza met Mrs Campbell Praed, one of the first Australian novelists to achieve fame in Britain. Born in Queensland in 1851, Rosa Caroline Murray was educated at Brisbane and before her marriage saw a great deal of social and political life in Queensland. On 29 August 1872 she married Arthur Campbell Bulkley Praed, the son of a Fleet Street banker and nephew of the poet Winthrop Mackworth Praed. For a while they lived on their station on Curtis Island, Queensland, before coming to London in 1876. Four years later she began her literary career with a successful novel entitled *An Australian Heroine*. From then on she poured out a stream of novels, later collaborating with Justin McCarthy, the Irish novelist and politician, of whom she became a close friend and correspondent.[1]

Mrs Praed and Eliza first met at a dinner party given by Frederick Chapman, the publisher. Mrs Praed told Layard: [2]

> The contradictions in her nature always puzzled me. She had the reputation – founded on her *Saturday Review* articles, I imagine – of being very hard on women. So she was – on the women whom she thought unwomanly, or in any way false to themselves and to her ideal of womanhood. I have heard her speak of such in the bitterest terms; yet, in actual intercourse, the only side of her I ever saw was that in which womanly sympathy with other women seemed the most prominent characteristic. I have never known a woman more intensely sympathetic with all the little cares and troubles of domestic life and womanly weaknesses and emotional frailties. Her tenderness with such was extraordinary.

*Eliza Lynn Linton*

She was such a curious mixture too, of the man and the woman. She liked things gracious and well-ordered. I have seen her at the rooms where she was staying darning the tablecloths herself because she could not bear to see them unmended. She liked pretty clothes – was always the first to admire and commend a becoming gown – yet when talking on intellectual and social problems would horrify some women by her 'masculine' views.

Her materialism was another puzzle. She would listen indulgently to me when I talked of my own hopes and beliefs; would attribute them to weak health; would to a certain point be sympathetic with them, and would even tell me of half-mystical experiences of her own – then would demolish all by some unanswerable materialistic assertion. I wasn't clever enough to argue with her, yet the subject had a fascination and was often brought up between us.

I used to be continually struck with Mrs Lynn Linton's ever-springing youthfulness and pleasure in the mere fact of existence. It was either her seventieth birthday or just afterwards, and she was sitting with me one evening and telling me of the fact, and how she had a sort of animal delight in nature and in the joy of life, so that when she rose in the morning – and the expression struck me as coming quaintly from one of her age – 'it is my dear,' she said, 'as though I were going forth to meet my love'; and in one of her letters comes this, 'I am at the present moment ridiculously well. I believe I completed my five-and-twentieth year last week or so – at Arundel, where I have been for a fortnight, and where I found somehow an atmospheric Castalia that made a new woman of me.'

The year before her death in 1898, Eliza wrote to Mrs Praed:

I am not strong! I am all to pieces. I can neither rest nor work. Do you know that terrible unrest of weakness – the enforced idleness which you feel you must in all duty break into activity – and, when you try, you sink back and pant and faint? I am in that state, and to an active person like myself, whose desires travel fast and whose powers slink behind, it is painful beyond measure. Well, I shall get well in time, and I shall some day see you again. . . .[3]

In conversation with Mrs Praed, she recorded:

> I will not barter my sense of self respect, for anyone or anything in the wide world, I am too old now to be very supple in the knee or back. Only when I believe and respect do I bend my knee and bow my head. Where I do not, I cannot and will not for any advantage to be gained by subservience or loss by stiffness . . .[4]

She carried her hatred of deceit and shams into everything. Her greatest commendation for a woman was that she was 'loyal' – that was the quality on which she prided herself. Those who knew her mostly loved her gracious and charming manner. Those who did not, and there were many, were venomous about her.

When she was seventy-two she was interviewed by a Mrs Alec Tweedie for an article in *Temple Bar*. The interview took place in Eliza's famous flat in Queen Anne's Mansions. Seated within the large working-room, Mrs Tweedie observed numbers of bulky manuscripts lying about and questioned her about them.

> Not one is my own. Bundles of manuscripts like these have haunted my later life. I receive large packets from men and women I have never seen and know nothing whatever about. One asks for my advice; another, if I can find a publisher; a third inquires if the material is worth spinning out into a three-volume novel; a fourth lives abroad and places the manuscript in my hands to do with it exactly as I think fit, etc.*

In answer to Mrs Tweedie's question what on earth she did with all these manuscripts, Eliza told her:

> One I once returned unread, for the writing was so bad I could not decipher it, but once only; the rest I have always conscientiously read through, and corrected page by page,

* What famous author is not similarly pestered?

if I thought there was anything to be made of them. But to many of my unknown correspondents I have had to reply sadly that the work had not sufficient merit for publication, and as gently as I could, suggest their leaving literature alone and trying something else.

When one thinks of the labour of having to read handwritten manuscripts, this was no easy assignment for an elderly and busy writer. Yet she would not fail them. To one she wrote:

> You had better begin by writing quite short stories. You have not power or experience yet for a novel of any length and there is no use in beginning anything before you have a clear idea of what you want and mean to write about. A title is all very well, but the title is only a finger-post, remember, it is not the temple itself. Get your mind clear before you begin the actual work, and do not be afraid of your own ideas, for you will never do anything in life, or in literature, if you begin on no foundation, and then get sick of this bit of froth only to begin another in the same way.
> Try your hand at quite a short story, of not more than three actors and of a very simple plot; write it with a method; know first of all what you want to write about, and have the characters quite clear in your mind. If it **is** to be a love story, devise the sorrow or obstruction, and plan the action and the persons, before you write a word. Then jot down the skeleton idea as you have thought it out, and then clothe it in words, enlarge and elaborate. But always remember to have your *skeleton* idea clear in your own mind before you set down a word. As for handsome young men and silly girls, I don't think you know enough of life, my dear, to do without them. You are but a girl, and only its truth to your own nature and experience would make it valuable.[5]

On the other hand, her sense of values was not easily shaken. Asked why she did not use a typewriter, she replied:

> I hate them, they lack individuality. All the hours I have written, I am thankful to say, I have never used it. I use a

broad holder and a fine pen, and that squat glass inkstand has been my constant companion for fifty years. It has travelled everywhere with me, full of ink, and tied round with an old glove. I am very particular about wiping my pens, and every morning I have the mouth of my inkstand washed, so that it is quite clean when I begin work. I do not like anything dirty or untidy; in that I am an old lady spoilt.

I always work in the morning, from four to five hours a day contents me as a rule; formerly I often wrote eight and even ten and eleven; but that is no longer necessary, and I could not endure the strain. . . .[6]

Despite her dislike of the typewriter, there was an occasion when she went to the expense of having a manuscript typed, in order to see whether it would read better, for it was a work which she thought was worthy of it.

In an undated letter to Rider Haggard she wrote:

I scarcely know the feeling of jealousy – professional jealousy not at all. I have plenty of indignation, scorn, whatever you like against humbugs, touters, *made* reputations – people like X———, who sends me a form of subscription for her yet unpublished novel, and a request for a review of it, etc, etc,; men like that puny traitor who requested an 'interview' for the *Pall Mall*, and, kindly received and treated, made his dirty guinea by a slashing attack on me, accusing me of selfishness and ill-will towards the younger professionals – for all and such of these, yes, blows and lashes straight and strong – but for the good workers, if they have leapt to fame as you and Rudyard Kipling, and, soon will, Barrie, I have not the faintest feeling of chagrin but only one of hearty pleasure.[7]

It was in June 1880 that Eliza decided she had had quite enough of London and she gave up living at Hayter House and returned to the continent. She went first to Paris, from where she wrote to her sister:

I have made my grand move and broken with London for

*Eliza Lynn Linton*

> the present. When I return I am in a dozen minds to break with it altogether, and settle in some pretty country place where I can have a little garden, a man and his wife and the sunsets.
> I am growing too old for the racket and noise and turmoil of London life. I like a little of it, but it is impossible to regulate these things, and when you are in a rush you must keep in it.

From Paris she went to Bex, Switzerland, where she began work on her next novel, *My Love*, then moved on to Pontresina. Again she wrote to her sister:

> I calculate that you will get this and my little parcel on the dear old 19th with its flavour of cherry tart and the shilling's worth of goodies we used to have. How long ago those days seem to be, Loo! but the childish love, with all its quarrelling to keep it company. My new book goes apace, *My Love*. I will send you a copy of *The Rebel of the Family* when she comes out in three volumes.

She then heard that her close friend, W. H. Wills, was dying, and he was anxious that she and she alone should be with him at the end. She immediately set forth for England, but on the way was taken ill herself and was delayed. When she arrived in England it was too late, for Wills was already dead. She did not remain in England long, but set out for Como. It was there that a tremendous discussion took place about Henry James's *Daisy Miller*. *Daisy Miller* had appeared in the *Cornhill Magazine*, and was published in book form in 1878. It made Henry James's name and was discussed everywhere. 'We are still moved by *Daisy Miller*,' wrote Leon Edel, 'despite the fact that the world of manners has so utterly changed.'[8] The book has a spare economy, a quick painting of background and a chasteness of narrative, in its summary sketching of American ignorance confronted by American rigidity abroad. It remains also the prototype of the 'international' story. Henry James was to write many more important and more brilliant tales, but *Daisy Miller*, like its name, is a fresh and early flower still blooming among his works. Edel said that '. . . the achieved pathos of this predicament softens Daisy's hardness of surface, and makes her a victim not only of parental and national ignorance, but of her own innocence. Winterbourne, at the end, can only wonder whether he hasn't lingered too long in Europe, whether a civilisation – or absence of it – was developing in his native land which he did not know or understand.[9]

Eliza certainly must have felt a great sympathy for Daisy, for she herself had produced a most sympathetic and remarkable character, and of greater substance, in Perdita Winstanley,[10] but without James's economy of style. Eliza had had to follow current fashion in popular fiction and spin out her novel into the usual three volumes required for subscription library circulation. However, the later novels of James were not famed for their brevity! Eliza wrote to James:

> As a very warm dispute about your intention in *Daisy Miller* was one among other causes why I have lost the most valuable intellectual friend I ever had, I do not think you will grudge me half a dozen words to tell me what you did really wish your readers to understand, so that I may set myself right or give my opponent reason. I will not tell you which side I took, as I want to be completely fair to him. Did you mean us to understand that Daisy went on in her mad way with Giovanelli just in defiance of public opinion, urged thereto by the opposition made and the talk she excited? or because she was simply too innocent, too heedless, and too little conscious of appearance to understand what people made such a fuss about; or indeed the whole bearing of the fuss altogether? Was she obstinate and defying, or superficial and careless?
>
> In this difference of view lies the cause of a quarrel so serious, that, after dinner, an American, who sided with my opponent and against me, came to me in the drawing-room and said how sorry he was that any gentleman should have spoken to any lady with the 'unbridled insolence' with which this gentleman had spoken to me. So I leave you to judge of the bitterness of the dispute, when an almost perfect stranger, who had taken a view opposite to my own, could say this to me! . . .

*Eliza Lynn Linton*

> I hope that you are well and happy. I have read your *Confidence* and *The Madonna of the Future*, etc., since I saw you. My admiration of your work increases if that were possible.

In due course the reply came:

> I will answer you as concisely as possible – and with great pleasure – premising that I feel very guilty at having excited such ire in celestial minds, and painfully responsible at the present moment.
> Poor little Daisy Miller was, as I understand her, above all things *innocent*. It was not to make a scandal, or because she took pleasure in a scandal, that she 'went on' with Giovanelli. She never took the measure really of the scandal she produced, and had no means of doing so; she was too ignorant, too irreflective, too little versed in the proportions of things. She intended infinitely less with G. than she appeared to intend – and he himself was quite at sea as to how far she was going. She was a flirt, a perfectly superficial and unmalicious one, and she was very fond, as she announced at the outset, of 'gentlemen's society'. In Giovanelli she got a gentleman – who, to her uncultivated perception, was a very brilliant one – all to herself, and she enjoyed his society in the largest possible measure. When she found that this measure was thought too large by other people – especially by Winterbourne – she was wounded; she became conscious that she was accused of something of which her very comprehension was vague. This consciousness she endeavoured to throw off; she tried not to think of what people meant, and easily succeeded in doing so; but to my perception she never really tried to take her revenge upon public opinion – to outrage it and irritate it. In this sense I fear I must declare that she was not *defiant*, in the sense you mean. If I recollect rightly, the word 'defiant' is used in the tale – but it is not intended in that large sense; it is descriptive of the state of her poor little heart, which felt that a fuss was being made about her and didn't wish to hear anything more about it. She only wished to be left alone – being herself quite unaggressive. The keynote of her *character* is her innocence – that of her *conduct* is, of course, that she has a

little sentiment about Winterbourne, that she believes to be quite unreciprocated – conscious as she was only of his protesting attitude. But, even here, I did not mean to suggest that she was playing off Giovanelli against Winterbourne – for she was too innocent for that. She didn't try to provoke and stimulate W. by flirting overtly with G. – she never believed that Winterbourne was provokable – she would have liked him to think well of her – but has an idea from the first that he cared only for higher game, so she smothered this feeling to the best of her ability (though at the end a glimpse of it is given), and tried to help herself to do so by a good deal of lively movement with Giovanelli. The whole idea of the story is the little tragedy of a light, thin, natural, unsuspecting creature being sacrificed as it were to a social rumpus that went on quite over her head and to which she stood in no measurable relation. To deepen the effect, I have made it go over her mother's head as well. She never had a thought of scandalising anybody – the most she ever had was a regret for Winterbourne. . . .

It is not hard to see that *Daisy Miller* was a work that would attract Eliza. At that time she herself had written a long-short story, *Within a Silken Thread*. It does not compare well with Henry James's work, dealing as it does with one of her many aspects of class-consciousness. It concerns the daughter of a Cumberland guide who is 'not well up in the accidence of refined living'. A gentleman on holiday in Cumberland falls in love with the beautiful daughter and wishes to marry her, and therefore invites her to his home. The girl

> . . . could tat and crochet and embroider with creditable dexterity . . . she was a country girl of the modern school – rather delicate in health, with a tendency to hysterics and no digestion to speak of; who could play a little on the piano and sing prettily in the choir; who dressed by the fashion-papers; took in her weekly instalment of penny literature; wore an elaborate chignon and a great many beads (chiefly of wood and glass) and would have as soon have thought of swearing as of talking 'broad Cumberland' . . . In a word, she was the half-bred of the summer show place; neither

gentlewoman nor peasant . . . But she was a good girl in both mind and conduct; and if not thorough in polish, was at the least substantial in propriety.

However, her suitor's mother perceives that the girl is unsuitable and determines that her son shall not marry her. So she arranges a dinner party with the local gentry as guests in order to discomfort her. She is clearly made to see that she is far from welcome and returns swiftly home, glad to be amongst her own people once again. Eventually she marries a Cumberland farmer within her own class.

Eliza's story has none of the subtlety that Henry James brought to bear on Daisy Miller. Eliza's girl is sympathetically drawn, as most of her heroines are, even if she is not Henry James's Daisy. The two girls are both confronted with the same world of class-consciousness. Its barriers were impregnable and any attempt to breach them was fraught with danger. In all Eliza's fiction she draws heavily on experience. She never forgot her early upbringing in Cumberland, nor did she forget the Cumberland dialect or her love of the scenery. Her accounts of local gentry leave a strong impression.

*Mildred's Lovers* is another story which appeared in her collected edition. It is mostly autobiographical, a jaunty account of her early years in London, when she worked at the British Museum and lived at a boarding establishment. It is a tale which shows Eliza at her best; the character of Mildred Smith admirably portrays the author herself. Many of the other stories in this collection show a considerable inventiveness. They range from small domestic issues to melodrama pure and simple, but they were tailored for the popular magazines of the time.

Of her excursions into melodrama, one of her most successful stories in this style was *The Last Tenants of Hangman's House*. This is an episode of a shipwreck on the Cornish coast and tells how a single survivor, a Spaniard, is rescued by a forger, how this forger seeks to 'use' the Spaniard for his own ends and how the Spaniard murders the forger. It is a tale well told and could well have come from the pen of Wilkie Collins. This time Eliza had no axe to grind and the tale is all the better for it.

Perhaps the most moving story in the three-volume collection entitled *Within a Silken Thread* is *Dear Davie*, a tale of much charm concerning two maiden ladies who are awaiting the arrival of the widow of their youngest brother. She is the sole heir to the estate. The old ladies are faced with a new, unfamiliar head of the family. Their worst forebodings are realised. The dictatorial, unpleasant young widow from India, together with her own retinue of servants, sweeps all before her. How the old ladies suffer under this woman is presented without sentimentality.

Not unnaturally, there is a story about a governess. *The Family at Fenhouse* is not a sentimental portrait, but a grim one involving murder, reminiscent of Le Fanu, with an ending that is not conventional.

As a contrast there is a story in the same collection of a rich and beautiful heiress determined not to become the slave of any man, despite the fact that she has so many local admirers, though she is eventually captured by a gallant captain after a hunting accident.

In *Galloping Dick* there is a study of a more cunning female. Two old sisters living in an isolated cottage employ a distant cousin to look after them, since no one cares to work for them because of their meanness and the fact that a ghostly horseman is purported to ride by their cottage at night. The miser sisters are known to have hoarded wealth. The cousin puts up for a while with the appalling discomforts and the sisters' tantrums, until one stormy night the 'horseman' gallops past the cottage. Shortly afterwards a man calls and begs to be admitted; the sisters refuse, but the cousin takes charge of the situation and forces the two old women to admit the stranger, who 'is exhausted from the wild night, and tells of the horseman'. The sisters are soon bound and gagged, their cottage ransacked and their so-called drudge and her lover have decamped. It is an exciting story and the atmosphere well held. Equally enthralling is the story *The Fate of Madame Cabanel*. Jules Cabanel lives in a hamlet in Brittany and marries an attractive Englishwoman. Sickness comes to the village, which in reality is due to the primitive drainage, but suspicion falls on the Englishwoman, who is suspected of being a vampire. The tale is a perceptive study of village superstition and ignorance.

*Eliza Lynn Linton*

By today's standards, with the advances in technique of short-story writing, these tales may be considered naïve; nevertheless they show an economy of writing that was very difficult, sometimes impossible, to achieve within the convention of the three-volume novel of the time.

12

# Return to Italy

In the early part of October 1880 Eliza decided to go to Florence. She has left us a record of that journey:

> At 9 I started for the train, picked up my luggage, took my ticket, fee'd my doctor, and got into a carriage full of Italians. They were all innocent of soap and water and of clean linen, and smelt! They would not have a window open, and if they did open one at any station where we stopped, a man was sure to lean his whole body out and effectually stop the fresh air. It was the Black Hole of Calcutta and worse, but their good tempers and amiability to each other and to me! When they left – which thank goodness they did at Bologna at two in the morning! – the fat, frowsy, handsome, dirty lady by me shook hands and thanked me for the grace of my company! Their sweet smiles! Their graciousness! I do not wonder at people loving them – but their dirt, their lies, and their dishonesty!!![1]

When she arrived in Florence she became seriously ill with 'brain fever', which the doctors thought would affect her already bad sight. But she had courage and great strength of will and recovered. On 3 December she wrote to her sister, Mrs Gedge:

> ... Don't be anxious about me; my health is now quite good ... My eyes are still untrustworthy and bad. I am not quite sure of my sight; but if I am to be blind, I shall find philosophy and strength enough to support that trouble and to organise my life in comfort, usefulness, work, and dignity.

> So long as I can keep the clearness of my intellect and sense of vigour and enjoyment and health and sympathy with all forms of beauty and life, of joy and of suffering such as I have now, I shall be happy.
>
> I may not lose my sight of course; the doctor says I am in less danger than I was, and he gives me every hope of preserving it so I do not worry myself or fret in any way. I do my work, and go out and do my social duties and my sight-seeing as blithely as ever. When I have to be bled and go to bed in the dark for twenty-four hours, I go and don't fret a single moment. All my old strength of will and of patience has come back to me, and I am not more than thirty years old![2]

Another letter which is thought to have been written about the same time, but which lacks both date and destination, shows her old verve:

> All publishers are tradesmen; not all are swindlers, but they drive a hard bargain when and where they can, and care no more for their author's *rights* than a sharp merchant cares for the loss to a bankrupt of goods bought below cost price and sold at 200 per cent advance. It is a war, but war may be civilised – that is, strictly honest – or barbarous – that is dishonest. X——'s are honest; they will take the skin off you, if you let them, but they will not rifle your valise.[3]

Despite an attack of pleurisy, Eliza, accompanied by a trained nurse, a Miss Johnson, who looked after her like 'a daughter', moved on to Rome, where she went to the Hotel du Louvre. On 6 February 1881 she wrote to her niece Amy Murray, who was the daughter of her elder sister, Rose Cecilia,[*] who had married the Reverend James Murray:

> Dearest Amy, – I have to thank you, darling, for two sweet letters, the first of which I have been intending to answer for a long time, but I was prevented by my illness, and this last which came as the accusing spirit in a very sweet and

---

[*] Born 1814.

*Return to Italy*

gentle and loving form, an appeal to my own conscience rather than a rebuke! Well, darling, I have been very ill and almost blind, but now I am all right. I had, and have still, congestion of the retina, and then I had gastric fever and pleurisy; but a kind, dear lady in the hotel nursed me night and day, and I had a good doctor; so I am all right again, save for a certain little adhesion of the rib to the pleura or the pleura to the rib, whichever you like to call it, which will go away in time. Meanwhile I am all my old cheerful and energetic self, if not quite so strong as I was. But I do not make troubles in life – 'borrow troubles' as the Americans say – and I try to live down and live through all that oppresses and worries me, and to look up into the sunlight and not back into the darkness. It is the best way, but difficult to get at. In early youth all troubles are so gigantic, all sorrow so insurmountable, so eternal. By and by, as time goes on, we feel that eternity has come to an end, and we are quite ready to enjoy as we used, to love as we did. Then we begin to feel that it is as well to distrust our own passionate despair, and to try to control our anguish. It is hard, hard! Perhaps we only come to it when age has helped us and we have less passion to conquer and weaker emotions all through.[4]

From Rome she wandered about Sicily for four months, returning to Castellamare and then back to Rome. Like Henry James, she could not resist Rome, and there she remained until March 1882. In April she was in Florence once more and finally arrived back in London in May. For the next few months she visited a number of friends in England and afterwards returned to Rome, where she said she was more at home than in London. 'The atmosphere of London is so terrible, and the wealth oppresses and *impoverishes* me. I feel such a pauper there!'

In 1883 her famous essays from the *Saturday Review* were published in a collection under the title *The Girl of the Period and Other Social Essays*. Nearly twenty years had elapsed since she had written the essay from which the book's title derived, which, with 'Modern Mothers', so shocked those who thought that Eliza was the champion of the emancipated woman. In the Preface, she wrote that her views were unchanged. Furthermore:

> One of the modern phases of womanhood – hard, unloving, mercenary, ambitious, without domestic faculty and devoid of healthy natural instincts – is still to me a pitiable mistake and a grave national disaster. And I think now, as I thought when I wrote these papers, that a public and professional life for women is incompatible with the discharge of their highest duties or the cultivation of their noblest qualities. I think now, as I thought then, that the sphere of human action is determined by the fact of sex, and that there does exist both natural limitation and natural direction.[5]

It was the publication of these two volumes of reprinted essays that gave lasting fame to her name. Eliza originally suggested to her publisher, Bentley, that they should be called 'Saturday Morning', but quite obviously 'The Girl of the Period' essay which gave her so much notoriety in the end seemed proper. There was now no doubt about the identity of the author. The *Academy*, which had never liked her novels, was delighted to give a further bad notice to the latest book. 'It is curious', they wrote, 'to be reminded of the fuss and indignation which were excited by the setting up and demolishing of that monster of fiction, "The Girl of the Period", and to note how far, and to what good purpose the world has travelled since then.'

How things had changed was indeed indicated by the fact that Bentley sold only 657 copies of the book and lost £173.[6] Eliza had herself to blame to a certain extent for this, because she had published *Ourselves: Essays on Women* in 1869 and the market for her attacks on her sex had obviously diminished. She was now engaged in writing her own strange autobiography – in which she transposes her sex and calls herself Christopher Kirkland. This work is a basis for any evaluation of her life and work.

Her relationship with publishers, incidentally, was by no means good. Blackwood, as we have seen, refused to publish her, and Chapman and Hall, whose reader was George

Meredith, also rejected her work on account of her attitude towards women.

The bond between Eliza and Swinburne was undoubtedly Landor. Swinburne's respect for Landor was as great as Eliza's adoration. In March 1864 Swinburne had journeyed to Florence with an introduction to Landor from Monckton-Milnes (later Lord Houghton). Landor was then eighty-nine years of age and in the last year of his life, for he died in Florence that September. He was by then more than tired of life; he had written to his brother:

> I do not expect to live many days beyond my birthday, so that what I am now writing to you is probably for the last time. It will be a great comfort to me to hear that you suffer less than I do. Sciatica cramps me sadly. It is late and with difficulty that I creep out of bed. Many friends, English and strangers come to visit me, but I can receive few. My earing [*sic*] and sight are almost gone.[7]

It is therefore not surprising that Landor no longer welcomed strangers, and he had a horror that someone might approach him to suggest writing his biography. When Swinburne did call, his mannerisms confused the old man. Swinburne recorded that he '... found him, owing I suspect to the violent weather, too much weakened and confused to realise the fact of the introduction without distress ... he seemed so feeble and incompatible that I came away in a grievous state of disappointment and depression'. When Swinburne returned to his hotel he wrote 'a line of apology and explanation ... expressing (as far as was expressible) my immense admiration and reverence in the plainest and sincerest way I could manage'.[8] As a result, Landor sent him a message to come to see him again. This time the old man had recovered and received Swinburne most graciously.

Swinburne's admiration for Landor was real and lasting. All his life it remained with him, and the fact that Eliza had been so close to Landor too obviously drew Swinburne to her. They first met in the 1870s, and in 1874 Swinburne asked her if she would accompany him to a private view of Whistler's works.

*Eliza Lynn Linton*

In 1877 Swinburne paid Eliza a very handsome compliment when he published his *Note on Charlotte Brontë*. He wrote:

> I can trace it in no living English authoress one-half so strongly or so clearly marked as in the work of the illustrious and honoured lady – honoured scarcely more by admiration from some quarters than by obloquy from others – to whom we owe the over-true story of *Joshua Davidson* and the worthiest tribute ever yet paid to the memory of Walter Savage Landor.

How much they continued to see of each other is not recorded, but we find Swinburne writing to her in 1880:

> It seems to me you are always leaving England just when I begin to hope that an occasion is about to offer itself for our meeting again: a fact which would – if anything possibly could – shake the very foundations of my sure and certain faith in the Beneficent Omnipotence of the Personal Governor of an Universe which reflects such infinite credit as does ours on the All-Wise Design of its All-Merciful Creator. I did hope at least that you, like our friend Mrs Burton,* would have once – if but once – honoured and gratified us with a visit before flying off to foreign parts where – even if not beyond 'the sound of church-going bell'[9] – I have reason to fear that you may not find the Gospel preached in all Its purity.... I want you too to see my books and pictures 'and cetrer' (as Miss Squeers has it)[10] now that they are in something like order. Your approbation of my sonnet[11] against 'the soft Dean'[12] – more shamefully soft than any of Pope's time – is even more delightful to me than the delightful and most flattering abuse of his fellow sycophants.
>
> And now I come to a little matter in itself which is great to the little mortal now addressing you. I am by no means unmindful of dear old Mr Landor's oft-repeated reflection, to the effect that he never could bring himself to understand how any man living could be so incomparably the basest of all living creatures as to ask another to accept the dedication of a book, nor how the other could be so infinitely more base

---

* Wife of Richard (later Sir Richard) Burton, the explorer.

than this one as to do so. I need not say, therefore, that I am not about to descend to the lowest imaginable depth of infamy by asking you to descend to a depth immeasurably lower than my own. But I take leave so far to count upon your fellow-feeling in the matter, that I have addressed to you some verses in dedication of a yet unfinished memorial poem – begun five years after date – on the centenary of our dear and glorious old friend. . . . Hoping that your kindness will accept it for his sake as cordially as his own kindness did after all receive the dedicatory tribute of my first adult poem.

At this time Eliza was working on a novel entitled *Ione*, which was eventually dedicated to Swinburne. A later letter from Swinburne contains the following:

If you derived as much pleasure and satisfaction – or half as much – from the inscription of my poem as your letter has given me, I have had as complete and grateful a success as the most exacting vanity could desire or dream of. But I am perplexed and vexed at the too evident fact that you did not receive the copy which I desired our common – if not unclean[13] – publishers to send you in my name before the day of publication. . . .

There is hardly anything, I think, better in life than fellowship in love and reverence. And when the partner is one with whom one has such cordial sympathy in faith and hope, love and also hatred of the same things (the last I always hold a very precious bond), as I have with the author of your noble books, the most heroic in temper since the Brontës', and of so much wider intelligence than theirs – the community of worship becomes doubly precious and delightful. And I do not know the Englishman born between Milton and Landor so wholly worthy of loyal and whole-hearted worship as were and are they. Do you? I should like to know what you think of (the new) James Thomson's poetry.[14] He is surely a man of genius – 'and yet I feel I fear' there is a vein of what can only be called vulgarity (in the genuine rather than the conventional sense) underlying or running through his democratic and free-thinking effervescence which would have displeased Mr Landor as much as

*Eliza Lynn Linton*

the man's honest outspoken daring and sometimes very noble inspiration would have been sure to engage his ever too generous sympathy.

Eliza, who was in Sicily, where she remained for four months, next heard from Swinburne on 24 March 1881:

... I hope it will please you to hear that I am now writing (as the Church Catechism says – 'with all my heart, with all my mind, with all my soul, and with all my strength') a biographical and critical article on Mr Landor for the *Encyclopaedia Britannica*. I feel the greatness of the undertaking and the sense of my own unworthiness as keenly and deeply as any one can: but I must – and shall – do my best, and if I fail it will not be for lack of love and loving labour, as you (and possibly he – who knows after all?) will know. I have just got to the year 1812 and *Count Julian*. What a glorious poem is that! Its splendour of spirit and moral anguish puts all younger English verse to shame.

I have also just 'done' Keats and am just going to do Marlowe for the *Encyclopaedia Britannica* – so you see I am like to end as a minor English Diderot (the typical encyclopaedist). . . .

For myself and the book of which you speak so kindly, I can only say in the words of Imogen – 'Poor I am stale, a garment out of fashion.'[15] All the reviews but one (the Athenaeum) have agreed either to revile or to ignore it. The sonnets\* on the yacht of a certain unhappy wretch who since they were written has been sentenced and executed have, I am told, hopelessly ruined the chances of the book. So be it – I must say what I think and what I feel that I have to say, now and henceforward and before. I am more disappointed by the seemingly utter failure of a small attempt in comic verse, and by the detection of its anonymous authorship: on the keeping of which secret I had (to confess the truth) counted for a little quiet amusement in case of the little venture proving other than the hopeless fiasco I am told it is. But why should I trouble you with my failures, when I have to congratulate you on such a book as 'The Rebel of

\* 'The Launch of the Livadia.'

*Return to Italy*

the Family',* which I have just finished reading? Thomasina strikes me as an especially perfect and admirable success. Your studies of grave realistic humour are in my poor mind as thorough as your triumphs in tragic passion and circumstance.

In May 1882 Eliza was back in England, staying with friends, as already related, and there was further correspondence with Swinburne, including one letter of great length from Guernsey, where he was staying with Watts, containing amongst other things thanks for her praise for *Tristan of Lyonesse*. The next two letters were an effort to arrange a meeting before she left England to return to Rome:

> I am cruelly disappointed to hear that I am in danger of missing a sight of you during your stay in London. It is a moderate eternity since we met, and you know how much I should have valued the opportunity of seeing you again. I am here with Watts for the first night of *Le Roi s'amuse* – an engagement made some time since, which of course could not be deferred. . . .

Eliza set out for Rome in January 1883 and remained there for four months. The weather in Rome was very bad and she wrote:

> I think the seasons must have changed immensely since history began. How the Romans could have gone naked, I cannot understand. *We* find sealskins and furs barely enough to keep us warm. Yesterday and today we have a sun like a great vault of hard metal, with a wind that is positively wolfish . . . There is to be a large evening party at the Embassy to-night, and I am going. Oh, how I hate these large evening parties! I am always so tired and sleepy, and I want to go to bed instead of dress and flourish out.[16]

She journeyed on to Florence and then decided to go to Palermo, where she planned to pay a visit to Lord Bridport's place, Maniace on Etna. She imagined she would be in time

* Published 1880.

for the wine harvest and would at least find people she liked, but she wrote:

> ... it is about eight miles from the dirtiest hole of a town Bronte, which gave the title to Lord Nelson when the King of Naples created him Duke of Brontë. ... It is thirty miles to drive, all uphill, through the wildest, bleakest-looking mountainous region you can imagine. A guard came for me from Maniace, armed to the teeth. We live in a state of preparation, not of fear. At sundown the gates are shut, and no one is allowed to go out or come in without special permission and a grand parley.

She endured the bleak slopes of Etna for about two months, when she returned to Palermo. Later that year (13 November), Swinburne wrote to her telling her he had not yet received a copy of *Ione*, and he wrote again on 8 December 1883, about his essay on the Cenci:

> ... am sincerely glad to know that you like my essay on the Cenci – I wonder how you will like a longer one, on Wordsworth and Byron,[17] on which I am now expending my best industry. Our dear old master would (I know) cordially have agreed with at least two-thirds of it – though I think he would in some of his later moods have demurred to what I say of Wordsworth's greatness – on the occasions, *bien entendu*, when he *was* great, and not small.
>
> I should think it impossible for the spitefullest stupidity to dream that it could detect in the book to which you have so highly honoured my name by prefixing it 'any falling off' whatsoever 'in vigour and freshness'. That the catastrophe would be 'painful' and 'shocking' to the *too* gentle reader you must of course have anticipated. I did not forsee quite such a crashing *finale* myself – but I suppose it was unavoidable, and it is unquestionably just and logical no less than powerful and impressive. All the characters, great and small, seem to me drawn with quite equal power and skill of touch – a proof (if any were wanting) that this story cannot, will not, and must not, by any manner of means 'be among your last.'

*Return to Italy*

Eliza was attracted by Tunis, where she had gone from Palermo, and described it as 'the Arabian Nights in person'. She very much wanted to go still further east, but was, nevertheless, back in London by May 1884, and stayed with her friend Mrs Wills. In June she wrote to her sister, Mrs Gedge:

> The doctor said that if I remain in England I shall have to be shut up for three months, in which case, Lucy, you may go to the joiner's to order a coffin, and when you come back the poor dog will *not* be laughing. . . . Then I have all my interests here, pecuniary, literary, intellectual, emotional . . . I feel I am being punished for my sybaritism in going abroad so much. Now I cannot live in the old cold, damp climate though I wish to do so.[18]

Nevertheless, she remained in England, staying with friends, and then found a flat that suited her well, and where she held her weekly 'salons'. It was on the eighth floor of Queen Anne's Mansions. She wrote to Lucy, 'I look over St James's Park and all London and on to Highgate and the Infinite. If you come to London, as I hope you will next Spring, I shall expect to see you come into my stationary balloon.' And in another letter to her sister she wrote: 'I infinitely prefer a flat to a house. You are well out of the way of burglars and sneaks; you are the proprietor of a splendid view; you enjoy a maximum of luxury at a minimum of cost; and, as my democracy is practical and not theoretical, the servants are my friends.'[19]

Eliza stayed in London for the rest of the year and began work on a new novel, *Paston Carew, Millionaire and Miser*. In the meantime, she heard from Swinburne again on 25 May 1885:

> If I could be very glad of anything just now, it would be to hear from you and to know that you are again so near us. I am trying to work off the first sense of stupid bewilderment by writing a short account of my dear Father's and Master's work, touching especially on points unfamiliar to the run of foreign readers. (If you think it is conceited or affected of me to call Victor Hugo 'my dear father' I must excuse myself

by saying that almost his first words to me when we met were 'mon fils'.)

I am still so stupid – there is no other word for it – that I can hardly write a decent letter. I hope you will not think me no more of a man than Armine St Claire (in *my* book,[20] which I treasure in sign of your kindness and regard); but I have lost the gift which your dear 'father' and mine retained – and if ever there were manly men and heroes, were not they such! – the gift of tears,[21] which women and children and Homeric heroes, and such men as Landor and Hugo do not lose. (If I could but 'cry like a child' – or a hero – I should be better again afterwards – like them.) Only I cannot quite understand yet how the sun manages to go on rising. Please don't show this to any one, but burn it. It is really rather an effort to write anything – even stuff such as this – even to so kind a friend as you. I know all about his immortality, and the survival of his essential part – but I am selfish and childish, and I do so want the man – the hand that pressed mine, the mouth that smiled on me, the glorious eyes that deigned to rest on mine with such unspeakable kindness.

But of course after all it is much better for me than if – as I used to fear – he had died before ever I set eyes on him. Though I might not have felt all that I now feel, I should always have had a regret at heart with something of a remorse in it (that I had never gone to see him)....

Eliza subsequently paid a visit to Swinburne.

*Ione*, the novel Eliza dedicated to Swinburne, was written while she was depressed and living alone in hotels in Italy. It, like its predecessor, is concerned with class-consciousness and revolves around an impoverished doctor, practising in Eliza's usual county town. He falls in love with Monica, daughter of a well-to-do woman who has called him in professionally. But the mother will not allow him to marry her daughter, considering him not an adequate match. The girl is completely submissive to her mother's wishes, and as a result the doctor, ill and distraught, takes himself off to Sicily where he becomes involved with Ione, the fiery adopted daughter of an English captain. Not until the pair are married does Ione discover that her husband is still in love with Monica, whereupon she murders him; their child is eventually adopted by the wretched Monica.

The novel is readable enough and quite skilfully written, but Eliza was not deeply concerned as to its fate for she was negotiating with Bentley about her *Saturday Review* articles.

# 13

# *The Autobiography of Christopher Kirkland*

Not unnaturally, Eliza considered *The Autobiography of Christopher Kirkland* 'the book of my whole career . . . the best I have ever done'.[1] She chose to write her autobiography in the shape of a three-volume novel, and as already mentioned, to transpose the sexes. Her reasons were, of course, that for so frank a credo she would be unable to identify the partners of her 'love affairs' or of many of those close to her, though she freely gives the true identity of her many friends and acquaintances.

There were considerable delays in publication, for Bentley was not very happy with parts of her manuscript and made several suggestions for revision, especially regarding her religious beliefs. These delays brought from her a *cri de cœur*:

> If you could realize my sufferings, I am sure you would end them. My book is being ruined by delay, and I cannot understand why there should be this hitch. I have softened as much as *possible* all the parts to which you objected, but as a really truthful exposition of thought and mental development I am obliged to keep the main lines as they were. I cannot make the mental part of the work in any sense fictitious . . . think of the long, long months I have waited patiently for your decision . . . Do you think this throbbing fiery heart is *quite* dead! . . . I have put my very Soul, my Life into these pages and I feel as if I am being slowly killed through them.[2]

*The Autobiography of Christopher Kirkland* has naturally been used throughout this study as a basis for the assessment of much of her character. A great deal in the three-volume work is devoted to the 'Woman Question', her opinions remaining unchanged through the years. She still maintained that women should not have equal rights with men; she obviously never deviated from asserting that 'women were a gentler sex, who should be protected, guided and comforted by men', though she thought they could well assume the role of *éminence grise*, and guide the men, but not 'melt the two into one so that you scarcely know which is which'.

*Christopher Kirkland* was not successful. To her Victorian public it must have seemed a strange and confusing novel; the author's heartfelt outpourings fell upon many deaf ears. She received a bad press; much of the criticism was not surprising. The *Spectator*'s objections were historically unjustified, as she was censored for the realistic picture she revealed of her early life in Cumberland. She was accused of being 'dismal'; Wordsworth's picture of the region, it was said, was far more to the point: 'We would sooner trust Wordsworth than the anachronistic Mr Kirkland.'[3] We now know that this is untrue, and that her own record of her upbringing and of the life then led in remote villages in the early nineteenth century had changed little socially from that of a hundred years earlier.

She was equally called to account for her unhesitating agnosticism:*

> We hear of the 'great truth of moral evolution, whence springs the doctrine of Duty' (though surely Duty was known before that most dubious and dangerous doctrine of moral evolution was ever heard of); of 'the vitalising faith in indefinite expansion which makes all things possible'; of 'the practice of Altruistic Duty as the absolute law of moral life', and so forth.[4]

Her attacks on the clergy were reiterated:

> ... those ecclesiastics whose very personality sends one's blood the wrong way. Manners, look, voice, enunciation,

---

* Originally Bentley suggested to her that the book would be better named *Confessions of an Agnostic*.

gestures, all are studied and artificial with these men, who talk of glory and knowledge, saving grace, the blood of Jesus, and the new birth, as others talk of the crops and the weather. Everything is subdued, nothing is spontaneous about them, and there is the ever-present consciousness of superior holiness, like a visible varnish, over them. The thin lips, tightly closed, seem unable or unwilling to take a deep draught of vitalising air. Who knows what sobbing breaths of sinful passion may not have profaned it? – what rude impulses of vigorous life may not have stirred it? – unlawful for those whose castigated pulses may never throb beyond the chill regulation beat. The smooth, clean-shaven face is as impassive as if cast out of wood. No generous flash of quick emotion brightens the cheek nor softens the eye, dilates the pinched nostril nor dimples the sterile mouth. You detect the clerical impress on that impassive face the first instant that you see it, for the episcopal laying-on of hands has left the thumb-mark for ever.[5]

She accused the clergy of pronouncing that the devil 'was a personage as real as that next-door neighbour the Socinian, and hell is actually a place like Paris or Rome.'[6] 'Logical and literal, they admit no refining away of words nor enlargement of sense by the doctrine of development.'[7]

For any woman to utter such sentiments was considered intolerable. 'Women, because of their sex could merely do good in a small way. This attitude was especially marked in "Church families" when the women had been bred in an atmosphere of reverent submission to the opinions of their men-folk.'[8] Her contemporary, Harriet Martineau, of similar outlook, published an article on Practical Divinity and was praised by her brother Thomas, but few had the temerity to chide Miss Martineau. One of Eliza's sisters was to discard her, for she

> ... had become a believer in the theory of the Ten Tribes – in universal Jesuitism, so that a Free-thinker, a Socinian, an Evangelical, a Tractarian, have each and all been supposed by her to be so many emissaries of the Jesuits – in secret poisonings as matters of weekly occurrence – in the

'*The Autobiography of Christopher Kirkland*'

Apocalypse, and the Seas now being opened (witness thereof the potato disease and the phylloxera) – and in ghosts, apparitions, presentiments and warnings as among the ordinary phenomena of this solid earth.[9]

She investigated original sin, and quite clearly stated that it did not exist:

Cut away the base of anything – even of murder – and you cut away a necessary and integral part of human nature. Exaggerate this absolutely necessary base, and you come to disproportion and selfishness – that is to sin; as in the instinct of self-preservation, of which anger or revenge, culminating in murder, is the excess, the exaggeration, the disproportion, the crime.[10]

An influence on Eliza was her meeting with Robert Owen, the Welsh social reformer. He was no longer young, but to his advanced principles she was ardently converted: 'I felt sure that these principles of co-operation would ultimately prevail . . . I should have liked to have seen the question fairly tried, and to have proved for myself what was the moral hitch to prevent smooth-running.'[11] She was not, however, easily swayed into accepting Robert Owen's anticlerical views, for she had studied widely over the years, especially the ideas propagated by Comte, the French philosopher and sociologist, and was continually in search of the answer to the question 'What is Truth?' – but unsuccessfully.

Later she records, after experiencing life in Paris:

One gets to see too, that although to obey existing laws is the duty of every citizen, to change them is the right of the community and to criticise them that of the individual. Without doubt there is a better and a worse, a higher and a lower, but nothing is absolutely final; and that 'fourth dimension' may be applied to society as well as to Space, and to morals and even matrimony as to other things. I saw that in Roman Catholic countries the Sublime theory of the sacramental quality of marriage is wholly in operation in practice, and that this is none the more sacred because it is indissoluble. On the contrary, the unyielding nature of

*Eliza Lynn Linton*

the tie forces consideration for human weakness, and adultery is condoned because divorce is impossible.[12]

Eliza also gave good account of the changes that she had witnessed during her own lifetime, while her blueprint for the future state of this country would hardly be amiss if she had announced it yesterday:

> The miserable conditions of the poor; the injustice of existing arrangements, both in the tenure of the land and in the relations between capital and labour; the need of 'levelling-up' – of inculcating greater self-respect among the masses by improved education – by better material conditions in food and dwelling – these were the subjects which now sat nearest to my heart. They made the more mature phase into which had passed that crude academic ideal of Liberty with sword and banner, wild hair and floating plumes, crying, 'Death to the Tyrants' on the ramparts, and shouting the 'Song of the Greeks' to the winds, which had been my dream in the boyish days of romance. This kind of thing had gone for ever; and I had come to the knowledge that reforms, to be lasting, must be legal, and that true liberty comes by the slower process of growth and gradual fitness, rather than by the sudden leap into supreme power of men unused to responsibilities and incapable of self-government. To be sure, armed revolution has been, and still is, necessary where supreme power is backed by the army, where abuses are maintained by the law and peaceable reforms are impossible. Then there is nothing for it but a hand-to-hand fight for the freedom of the many against the tyranny of the few; and the sacred right of insurrection cannot be proclaimed too loudly nor too loyally upheld. But under a constitutional government, where liberty of speech, association and remonstrance is already won, armed rebellion is unnecessary; and bit by bit reform, so loftily despised by heady youth, manhood learns to respect as the only revolutionising method fit for rational people. '*Ohne Hast, ohne Rast*' is the best motto for the political reformer. But there must be that '*ohne Rast*'; and the nuisance to be carted away must not be left to obstruct the highroad.

## 'The Autobiography of Christopher Kirkland'

It was, however, in the sphere of Women's Emancipation and the Cause for Women that Eliza's name was held in such controversy. She had voiced her own beliefs over a long period of time, and she had declared that '. . . women should have an education as good in its own way as, but not identical with that of men; that they ought to hold their own property free from their husband's [sic] control without the need of trustees, but subject to the joint expenditure of the family . . .'.[13] She battled against the fact that a husband could make a will and exclude her property from his wife and children. She could not accept 'the doctrine that no such thing as natural limitation of sphere is included in the fact of sex, and that women may, if they have the will and the power, do all these things which have hitherto been exclusively assigned to men'.[14]

A woman once said to her that 'women are no better than cows' since all that was expected of them was to bear their husbands' children. This matter was ever uppermost in her mind, though she was equally suspicious of many of the 'bluestockings' and advanced theories of some of her eminent contemporaries.

She approved of the establishment of Girton and Newnham Colleges, of certain office occupations for women, and for women to enter the medical profession, though in this last respect she stated: 'Unless the demand for female doctors was strong enough to support female schools and hospitals, I maintained, and maintain, the inexpediency of providing a few lady-doctors by means of mixed medical education – just as I dislike mixed drawing-classes from the nude.'[15] And, of course, of all things that enraged her, worst, as we have seen in *The Girl of the Period*, were 'bloomers' and other new fashions.

Only one reviewer of *Christopher Kirkland* did Eliza justice – Julia Wedgwood in the *Contemporary Review*, who wrote that 'She translates a woman's into a man's experience, and does it less clumsily than we should have expected . . . the only sign that we are reading the story of a female life is the fact that Christopher Kirkland grew up without any education.'[16]

The 'autobiography' was never reissued, which greatly saddened her.

It is from *Kirkland* that we learn so much of her life, friendships and interests. She tells of her discussions with John

*Eliza Lynn Linton*

Crawfurd upon ethnological matters; of how indebted palaeontologists should be to Sir Roderick Murchison, the famous geologist, president of both the British Association and the Royal Geographical Society.[17] When Robert Chambers, a founder of the well-known publishing house, wrote *Vestiges of Creation*, which was published anonymously, Eliza recorded: '... he saw the true shape of things, if he did not fill in all the details with perfect accuracy; ... his *Vestiges of Creation* – which we may now take for granted was his – will take rank forever as one of the advance guard in the forces of knowledge as they stand arrayed against those of ignorance.'[18]

Commenting on John Stuart Mill, she wrote:

... the definition of liberty was not the household word it is now. The doctrine that exact laws could be applied to that inconstant quantity man; laws of average as precise as mathematics; laws of economic results as certain as chemical combinations; laws governing human conduct and forming the science of sociology as unalterable as those which govern the course of the planets and form the science of astronomy; – this was a new page in the great Book of Life, which many found hard to read; – and Herbert Spencer's laurel-crown was still growing on the bushes.[19]

Another famous geologist, also a President of the British Association (and repeatedly President of the Geological Society), Charles Lyell (later Sir Charles), also received her studied attention. 'He was not one of those who "builded better than he knew", for he looked his own conclusions fairly in the face, and accepted in its integrity every word of the writing on the living scroll which unrolled itself before his eyes.'[20]

In her early days, she tells us, she found great help in Max Muller's writings on philology and orientalism, and derived much benefit from the study of Grote's *History of Greece*. Years later a great 'joy' was Kinglake's *Eōthen*. George Eliot was 'a goddess behind a cloud', and she thought George Sand ran her close in genius; she had an even greater regard for Elizabeth Browning.

Her own views on matters intellectual and scientific were not without merit. At one point in *Kirkland* she wrote:

'*The Autobiography of Christopher Kirkland*'

The emancipation of the human intellect from superstition in the substitution of the scientific method for the theological, was the great event of the time and made itself felt everywhere. Brute absolutism and unreasoning authority were set aside in matters intellectual as they had already been in things social, legal and governmental. That which bestrode the reason was flung off into the dust; and even the Church followed with the rest. *Essays and Reviews* had brought on its authors the honour of ecclesiastical condemnation; and Colenso's book,[21] which is now a mere letter in the alphabet of distinctive criticism, had been stamped in gold by Convocation as 'full of errors of the gravest and most dangerous kind.' And yet how short it falls of both De Wette and Norton.*[22]

Another aspect of her life which she aired in *Kirkland* was her relationship with the Jews. She knew many. One of the first she had met was a Mrs Ben Israel, who collected for 'charities'. She would borrow from young married people, say, £300, on the faith of a will to be made out in their favour, also promising to leave them expensive shawls, rare lace, etc. With the secured money she herself manufactured the gifts of

> . . . embroidery very beautifully done, handkerchiefs, shirt-fronts, waistcoats, blotting-books and the like, which she said she herself worked in the solitude of her own room on those off-days when she did not receive. Our then greatest living novelist came in for a fine flowered waistcoat, which she presented to him as her own work and a tribute of admiration. She had paid for it at a shop; and I saw the entry in her book which she showed me. . . . As her husband objected to this crazy application of their income, and would not give her an allowance to cover this quite unnecessary margin, she raised the necessary funds in the way I have said. And only when she died did her several victims find out the practical joke that had been played on them, and learned the true value of the legacy which was to have been rich enough to go twice around the original loan.[23]

* Wilhelm De Wette (1780–1849), German biblical critic, and Andrews Norton (1786–1853), American Unitarian theologian.

*Eliza Lynn Linton*

When Eliza visited Jewish homes she would inevitably be offered cold fried fish cooked in the Jewish fashion, or kosher meat, of which she wrote 'This "cosher" [*sic*] meat, by the way, beyond its undoubted merit of superior wholesomeness, still remains as a sign and symbol of true godliness among the Nation. Or perhaps it were better to say, as a fact, which in itself is godliness.'[24] She considered that the Jewish people had many admirable qualities; she found them clever, brilliant and high-minded. 'In admitting me to their homes religious Jews did me signal honour.'

The closest and most important of her Jewish friends was Dr Asher. Born in Glasgow on 16 February 1837, he was educated at the high school there and at the university. He was the first Jew in Scotland to enter the medical profession. In 1862 he went to London and became medical officer to the Jewish Board of Guardians, and in 1866 was appointed Secretary of the Great Synagogue. In March 1871 he became the first secretary of the United Synagogue, which owed its success to his efforts, and he retained this office until his death. Asher was also medical adviser to the Rothschilds, as well as being a personal friend, and his advice on many communal matters was accepted by them. Of all the people of the Jewish faith with whom Eliza discussed the Jewish religion, he was obviously one of the most able. She, on her part, recorded:

> I have always done my best to put myself on the outside of things and to judge of my own standpoint as it would appear to others. If this weakens tenacity it strengthens liberality; and the thinking world knows the latter is better than the former in all matters of unprovable speculation, inasmuch as it is the result of that wider knowledge of men and things which makes the whole difference between cosmopolitism and parochialism.[25]

Asher told her, 'We are in truth a living miracle – preserved by God as perpetual protest against your idolatry.'[26] The word 'idolatry' struck her hard, even though she had no belief in the divinity of Christ. Asher, in continuing his argument, said to her:

What else can you call the religion of you Christians, which makes a human being of that Incommunicable God – that Supreme Deity – the Great Spirit of the universe, Jehovah our Lord, whom we Jews worship in spirit and truth. You pray to a man who, you say, was God Incarnate. You worship one who lived and died a man like yourselves, and who is still a man to you now in Heaven – specially moved to listen to human prayers because of His own human experiences on earth. But we hold that no one has seen God at any time, and that He to whom we pray is beyond all sense. God has been incarnate in man no more than in the Egyptian bull; and your worship of Jesus of Nazareth, the son of Joseph and Mary, is as pure idolatry – that is, the worship of a created and finite being – as was ever the faith which made Apis a divine Incarnation and Dagon a God in whom were light and life and power.[27]

Eliza commented:

It is always useful to see ourselves as others see us, and that Christians never realise the anthropomorphism of their religion, nor remember that the universal Saviour was but a man, subject to all the limitations of humanity, and that even now He is but the Divine Man deified. Nor do they ever reason out their belief in the Trinity – in those Three Persons and One God; nor ask, 'Was it always so? – was that part of the Godhead which afterwards became Christ, always the Divine Man He is now? – or was the essence split and made tripartite when Mary conceived?'[28]

Asher told her that he predicted the persecution against his people which had not then begun, but of which he saw the certainty as God's way of rebuking the pride, ostentation, laxity and luxury, which had crept in among them. These vices had to be scourged out of them, if they were still to be the chosen people.[29]

Eliza recollected that when the German Juden-Hetze began, followed as it has been by the still more shameful barbarities of Russia and the late disgraceful trial in Hungary, she remembered what Asher had said:

*Eliza Lynn Linton*

But I was none the more convinced of the Presidential Authority of God in these matters than in some others. Natural causes, arising from racial, ceremonial and religious separation – from anti-national tribalism, so that a man is first an Israelite and then a German or an Englishman – from those classes of business which gather in and do not produce, taking from the hoards of others but not adding to the general store – from a specialised financial faculty, so that they get the better of the slower European intellect – these natural causes are sufficient to account for all that has been of late, without calling in the aid of the Divine Hand. For their earlier persecutions we want only the reasons that (1) The Jews amassed portable wealth by the same methods as those by which they amass it now, namely, that specialised financial faculty already spoken of, which takes advantage of the duller brains and profits by the more wasteful habits of Christians. (2) They had no country, with ambassadors to represent them and an army to retaliate when they were evilly entreated. They were orphans of the world and that brutal, blustering, ferocious world treated them as undefended orphans have ever been treated.

Eliza was honoured by being invited to take Friday night supper with the Ashers, where Dr Cohen said prayers before 'bread and wine'. Decorum in the Asher household Eliza thought superior to that of the average Christian household. 'The whole tone struck me as – unhappily – archaic, with a little dash of Quaker quietism to intensify the disciplinary spirit. I liked it.'[30] She was well aware of the closeness then, and not merely then, of the Jewish community, but equally she comments upon the magnificence of their charities and their regard for the poor, their zealous attention to a liberal education, and their religious instruction. 'We also know how learned are their learned men – how to the forefront everywhere is the Jew. In art, science, philosophy, literature, finance – of itself a science – we have to acknowledge the value of the bright Semitic intellect.'[31]

With these thoughts in her mind, she was incensed at the emergence of such societies as 'Missions to the Jews', the 'Society for the Conversion of Jews', and the like.

'*The Autobiography of Christopher Kirkland*'

The Jews live in the midst of Christian communities, and have ample means of judging the working results of Christian doctrines in the morality, the philanthropy, the self-respect and education of all classes. If they saw that the Universal Brotherhood, which Christ taught as the foundation of all faithful human action, gave more satisfactory working results than their own trial solidarity – well and good. If they saw that we were more sober, more chaste, more humane, more generous than they, more liberal and more intellectual, they might then think that we had got hold of a higher law than any we know. . . .

Before she sent her final revision of *Christopher Kirkland* to her publisher, she sent the draft of the section on Jewry to Dr Asher to read and approve.

Dr Asher died in 1889. After his death she wrote about him:

Tender as well as firm, he could discuss and dissect to the very heart and bone any subject whatever with those with whom he disagreed, without acrimony, heat, or partiality. He would let no false statement pass uncontradicted. He allowed no fallacy to slip in that he could refute. But he always argued with such high-bred courtesy of mind and directness of method – he was always so straight as well as humane in his polemics – that one loved and reverenced him even when there was no intellectual agreement. For myself, I can speak of this with a full heart. . . . He was one for whom I felt the most entire respect, and I longed, had it been possible, for him to give me his dying blessing – the blessing of a good, pure-hearted, pious man, emphatically one in whom there was no guile.[32]

Although Eliza usually paid little heed to or interest in reviews of her books and apparently did not subscribe to a press-cutting agency, she was bitterly disappointed that *Kirkland* was not an immediate success. It is perhaps hardly surprising that it was never reprinted. Her public, accustomed to her novels, would hardly have known what to make of the book. It had no 'plot', and at the time it was published no one was to know that 'Christopher Kirkland' was Eliza Linton.

## Eliza Lynn Linton

The views of the press were unanimously unfavourable. The *Academy* thought it 'disjointed'; the *Athenaeum* merely debated whether Kirkland might be the author herself. Not even the *Saturday Review* gave her a good notice, maintaining that it was too loosely put together and that it was 'neither exciting nor edifying'.[33]

Eliza received many letters about the book. One was from Rhoda Broughton, a leading novelist of the time. She was naturally surprised at what was clearly an autobiographical work and asked Eliza why she 'adopted the odious, conventional, trammelling, and in this case, eminently misleading form of the three-volume novel'. Eliza replied:

> ... Mrs Hulme is a study partly true, partly evolved; so is Althea Cartwright, so Adeline Dalrymple. All the rest (so far as I can remember at this speed) are real persons. The real names given are those who are dead – the Machonochies etc. etc. Esther is Mr Linton. I am very glad the book interested you enough to make you write to me. You are a dear girlie for that same.
>
> The three-volumed form was chosen by Mr Bentley, and I don't know the fate of the sale nor have I seen many reviews. I have always felt that the book has a certain vitality of its own, and that it will not have one day's life only.[34]

A year before Eliza's death in 1898, Layard, her biographer, tried to persuade her to write her reminiscences, but he records: 'Her eyes blazed at me through her spectacles as she raised her hands and beat her knees, with a characteristic gesture, and cried, "Oh lor'h! oh, lor'h! George, my dear, I dare not! I know too much, I dare not!" '[35]

# 14
# A letter from Herbert Spencer

Before the year 1885 had ended, Eliza had published a short novel, entirely different in content from her other works of fiction – a melodramatic tale entitled *Stabbed in the Dark*. She also contributed to *Temple Bar* an essay on George Eliot, and wrote innumerable other articles. Eliza was to temper her opinions on George Eliot in a serious study of her works, but in this essay she again attacked her relationship with George Lewes, which brought her an angry letter from Herbert Spencer.

Marian Evans (George Eliot) had been introduced to Herbert Spencer in August 1851 while she was in London with the Brays to see the Exhibition at the Crystal Palace. She saw a good deal of him, and Spencer took her to the theatre and to the opera at Covent Garden. At one time it was thought he might propose to her. He certainly was very devoted to her, and he kept a photograph of her in his bedroom till the day of his death. But Spencer was never really in love with her and his excuse for avoiding an actual proposal was lack of money. All the same, he would never hear a word against her.

That Eliza should hold up her hands in horror that George Eliot would live with Lewes without marriage is a strange contradiction of character. She, who went out of her way to get herself talked about because of her vehement views, who expected women to show their individuality, who left her husband because her life was unhappy with him – she of all people should have shown tolerance to her rival. But Eliza was, in fact, jealous of Marian, though in her last assessment of her work she was not so stupid that she would not praise

155

*Eliza Lynn Linton*

her genius. By then, of course, Eliza was an old lady, and she too had made her name, but in a very different manner.

In her reply to Spencer she said:

> I am *very* sorry to know you are not so well as you should be, for all that you have still got to do for the world. Such men as you ought to be made of cast-iron, never and never know a day's ill-health. I have just been reading your church book, and delighted in it, as I do in all you write. Thank you for the gentle tone of your remonstrance. How quiet and generous and gentle you are! It was ———, not ———,* who told me about Miss Evans, as she was then. It was this story – for to me ——— was more antipathetic than any man I have ever known, and his love-making more purely disgusting – that for years prejudiced me against Miss Evans as a girl of infinitely bad taste, to say nothing more. How she *could* have liked him was to me a marvel! When I saw her two or three days I did not like her. It was only after her union with Mr Lewes that her beauty (in my eyes) came to the front. I remember telling Mr Linton once, after I had met and talked to her and Mr Lewes in St John's Wood, how infinitely ennobled she had become. But as time went on, and the falsehood of their true position increased with the reverence of the world, while Thornton Hunt, who was so thorough, so true to himself, so utterly and entirely apart from all time-serving, all worldliness, went to the wall and was reviled by those who worshipped these others, my soul revolted, and I went back to my first position and despised with loathing the (as it seemed to me) humbug and *pastiche* of the whole matter. . . . Mr Lewes and Miss Evans were perfectly justified in their union – perfectly – but they were not justified in their assumption of special sacredness, nor was the world, in its attitude of special reverence, which was more than condonation. It is the sense of favouritism and consequent unfairness that has animated me in all I have said. . . . I only say that his union with Miss Evans was no other, no more, than any of the same kind, and that the holiness and solemnity ascribed to it came solely from her success. Had she been exactly the woman she was, and not

\* Blanks in Layard.

the authoress she was, she would have been left in the shade by all those who sought her in the sunlight.[1]

It is obvious that Eliza did not by any means want to offend Spencer. She knew when she was up against a great intellect. Equally, she was frank enough to propound her precipitousness, and her easily raised wrath. But, as she had in the past suggested that marriage by the established church was something of an anomaly, why did she think it was so outrageous for two people to live together?

Whether Herbert Spencer was assuaged we do not know, for he does not refer to the matter in his autobiography.

*Stabbed in the Dark* might well have served as a plot for Verdi. It was actually based on the picture she had seen by Rudolf Lehmann entitled *The Confessional*. The setting of the novel was Naples, which, of course, Eliza knew well. Shorter, and in an entirely different vein from most of her novels, it is a highly melodramatic account of the illicit love of an Italian princess for her husband's guest, which ends in the guest murdering the husband after a ball. The wife takes the blame and retreats into a nunnery until her death.

On 25 January 1886 Eliza wrote to her sister:

I have been struggling over a bit of work that would not get done as it should, and I have put aside everything until it was finished, as it is just this moment. It is my new story, *Paston Carew, Millionaire and Miser*, in *Temple Bar*, and I have got into a coil! I have written these three chapters five times and today have re-patched and re-pieced them – but at last they are finished and away.[2]

*Paston Carew* made its appearance at the end of the year. It provides an outlet for Eliza's views on 'Grundyism' in local society. Despite her strong opinions on morality and her defence of respectability, she equally strongly argues against the narrow English conventions. *Paston Carew* was ignored by the press. It seems to have been reviewed only by the *St James's Gazette*. They considered it 'a clever book' but not up to its predecessors. Yet this book was important. It is the story of how Paston Carew has to fight against 'the blot' of illegitimacy. Only one person in the community shows true kindness to him. He dotes on his only daughter and she refuses to marry the man her father has chosen for her, preferring, naturally, the man of her choice. Paston finally dies a bitterly disappointed man. The character of Paston is drawn with much finer perception than most of Eliza's male characters and if her plea for greater understanding was ignored Eliza was undaunted.

She was writing more than she had ever done, and throughout the eighties her articles appeared constantly in all the principal periodicals. Her output was enormous. Among those periodicals to which she contributed was *Chambers'*, and she was flattered to receive from C. E. S. Chambers a letter asking her whether she would contribute a new novel to this magazine. She discussed the project but in the end her next novel, *Through the Long Night*, went to a new publisher, Hurst and Blackett. In earlier days she had been published by Bentley, from whom she secured very satisfactory contracts. *The Autobiography of Christopher Kirkland*, which Bentley insisted on publishing as a three-decker novel, was the first book he published on a royalty basis: she received an advance of £250 and a royalty of five shillings on every copy after 1,000 had been sold. If a one-volume edition was required, she was to have sixpence for each copy.[3] Bentley spent £173 6s 3d on advertising and it was published at 31s 6d a set. Quite obviously it was a mistake to have published the book as fiction; on the other hand, Bentley's problem was an insoluble one, as 'Christopher Kirkland' existed merely as a mask for the real author. It sold 648 copies and made a loss of £86 2s 9d.[4] Of all her novels, the only one which sold effectively on publication was *The True History of Joshua Davidson*. Chatto and Windus probably did quite well, because a number of her titles were included in the successful series of popular cheap reprints called 'yellow-backs'.

In the meantime Eliza still kept hammering away at the 'woman question'. How deeply she actually believed in everything she wrote is open to question, when her correspondence is taken into consideration and her conversation with the many people she met, who mostly found a generous and kindly, if forceful, nature. But she had found a large market for her

*A letter from Herbert Spencer*

views. Editors saw her as one who could certainly stir up heated controversy in what she had to say in general about her sex. In the only critical work devoted solely to her writings on the 'woman question', Miss Nancy Bartlett Anderson deplores her views:

> Just as she sought to keep the sexes segregated into differing civic and occupational responsibilities, so she wanted to keep separate and different moral standards of the two sexes. She maintained that women, as the weak and inferior sex, should be severely restrained within the walls of strict morality. (Indeed, in the restricted boring lives of conforming women, their virtue probably was their own reward.) In contrast, Mrs Linton insisted that robust manly freedom must be preserved for the superior sex, a freedom which necessarily included overstepping the bounds of moral propriety.[5]

One of her foremost articles, 'The Higher Education For Women',[6] certainly laid stress on how women could preserve their charm and femininity while taxing their strength and brains at a job and at the same time marrying and bearing children and serving as responsible housewives. She emphasised the excess in numbers of women over men, 'making it impossible for all to be married'. Nor could they all become schoolmistresses or governesses, the two occupations mostly open to them. 'As authoresses or artists they may hold their own; the glamour of "fame" and "genius" gilding over the fact that they make their incomes and do not draw them, and have nothing capitalised – not even their own reputations.'[7]

Allowing that women led narrow lives at home and that Girton and Newnham Colleges were proper means of escape, she questioned how many could achieve even a modicum of true fame: '. . . such women are not many; voluntary devotion, irrespective of self-interest, to art, literature, science, philosophy, being one of the rarest accidents in the history of women – as, indeed, most needs be if they are to fulfil the natural functions of their sex.'[8]

Of course she argues against herself. We know that years earlier she herself had rebelled against her father and had been

159

determined to make a living for herself. Yet, in pursuing her argument she writes:

> Three important points come into this question of the Higher Education of women. These are (1) the wisdom or unwisdom for a father of limited means and uncapitalised income to send to college at great expense, girls who may marry, and so render the whole outlay of no avail; (2) the effect which this Higher Education has on the woman and the individual; (3) the physical results on her health and strength, especially in relation to her probable maternity.[9]

Eliza made clear that she did not understand why intelligent girls should seek higher education. On the other hand why, in *The Rebel of the Family*, did she show her heroine in such a pathetic light when Perdita so desperately wanted to escape from the deadening life her mother expected her to live? Had every girl to become a housewife? It is difficult for us to comprehend Eliza's attitude, but she obviously could not envisage a married woman having a career; it was sufficient that she ran her home with authority and was a guide and counsellor to her husband, but nothing more.

Eliza's pressure of work never let up. Writing to her sister she said:

> I am a kind of Mother of the world now. If you knew my life you would be amazed at all I have to do for others. . . . Every one comes to me for every kind of thing – references, plans, reading MSS – all sorts of things, and my time is just murdered among them all. . . . I grudge this rapid flow of years, they are all going too quickly, and my strength is going with them! I cannot do one quarter what I did ten years ago – not so much by half as two years ago. I have tumbled off my great strong perch on to a very slender little fellow. But there it is, and we cannot help it.[10]

On 28 August 1889 she again wrote to her sister: 'I am writing a new novel. It will, I think, be the last. I cannot write now as I did. I get so terribly exhausted. I have been a *hard* writer now for forty-two years exactly, and if I fail a little – a great deal of strength – I have done my darrack manfully while it lasted!'[11]

In May she had decided that she would like to return to Cumberland to revisit her childhood home. She left London in September, staying at the Keswick Hotel. On the 23rd she wrote to her sister:

> ... I went through the Limepots to the vicarage; asked the servant to go into the garden, and made her take me through the hall into the kitchen; saw the old chimney-piece in the dining-room, and found out our old faces; went into the study and touched the old book-shelves and cupboards; looked into the pantry and the larder place where we had the flour-bin; and then went over the garden. The gardener gave me a bunch of flowers, and I gave him a shilling. ... I feel half in a dream here. It is Keswick and yet not Keswick, as I am Eliza Lynn and yet not Eliza Lynn. I sat on the terrace wall while the man picked the flowers ... I heard the sounds come up from the road, the voices of children and wheels and dogs and cows just as we used. It was so strange I do not think a resurrection of the bodyguard would be a blessing, Loo![12]

The change of scene and revival of memories benefited her, and there was little abatement in the number of articles she contributed to the leading journals of the day. But as she became older so her views changed. She certainly continued her attacks on her own sex, but more politically now; she was no longer the strong republican; there were distinct shafts of less advanced liberalism in her new beliefs.

As the years passed many of her friends died. Age troubled her, as can be seen in her letters to her favourite sister. Writing to Fisher Crosthwaite, an old friend, she said:

> Oh, how I wish I was young and strong for just a year, and could go down to Keswick, climb all the mountains, go over all the passes, skate on the frozen lake (I would not despise Blea Tarn, where we used to go and slide), go along the Skiddaw Terrace Road, and row about the lake as we used. Whenever I am not quite well I dream of the lanes

and roads about that fairest temple of nature (to me), chiefly of walking in the Limepots or else on the road just opposite the vicarage. I remember it all so vividly *as it was*; it is an effort to remember the changes that are. Next year I hope to go over to Ireland, else I think I should take shelter under my friend Mrs Wilson's hospitable roof. In any case I hope to see the place again once more at least before I die, and shake hands with all my dear old friends, such as are left me.

Good-bye, dear Mr Crosthwaite. There comes a time in one's life when the old, long-tried love conquers all differences of creeds, and when we recognize the truth of truths, that sincerity to our belief, whatever it may be, and love for our fellow-creatures, make a creed and a practice in themselves where we can all meet.[13]

Shortly after this letter was written, her favourite brother, Arthur, died.

*Through the Long Night* was published by Hurst and Blackett, and was well received. The moral conflicts with which the main characters are involved have no longer the slightest relevance to the present-day problems. As in every novel of Eliza's, the centre character is a young girl. In this case it is Estelle Clanricarde, whose father is a financial failure and is scorned by his waspish, avaricious French wife. Clanricarde's precise occupation, like those of most of the male characters in Eliza's novels, is ill defined – 'trade' would put him in a lower class – and one can only assume he derived his income from investments which had obviously been a failure. In Mrs Clanricarde's opinion their only hope was her beautiful daughter. She was determined to find a rich suitor for her, come what may. Estelle, however, had fallen desperately in love with a poverty-stricken artist, Charlie Osbourne. What Eliza proves in this sorry tale is that ambitious parents may think they can marry off their children to their advantage, but of course it just does not work out that way. This is a sad tale of Victorian parental authority going sadly awry, for Charlie Osbourne eventually dies and Estelle poisons herself. Within the context of its time, this novel lives up to the review in the *Athenaeum* which praised its excellent narrative. Eliza had very purposely shown up the disasters of planned marriages and the overweening ambitions of small-town matrons for their daughters. As to the heroine, she is hardly a Hedda Gabler, her only purpose in life being her unswerving love for her man. She is not one of the great characters of fiction, but she is true to herself, and like all Eliza's heroines she draws our sympathy and illustrates the implications of the existing social scene – a pattern which Eliza has always woven with considerable ability.

Although she was much concerned with European events, expressing strong anti-Russian views, it was Ireland that was about to interest her far more deeply. She was now sixty-eight, very short-sighted, and prone to bronchitis. Nevertheless, she was determined to go to Ireland to see things for herself. She was a Liberal and thus had favoured Home Rule. At that time the English had

> no first-hand knowledge of racial strife, and very little historical knowledge or imagination; our people could not understand why the Irish tenant farmers were so unlike the British tenant farmers, who never shot landlords or houghed cattle, and why the Presbyterians of Ulster were so unlike the comfortable nonconformists of England.
>
> The only real hope would have lain in an alliance of British statesmen to settle Ireland, as an urgent Imperial problem, objectively considered apart from our home politics. But this proved impossible. Our two-party system showed off all the defects of its qualities, and artificially excited passions which the Irish question in its nature was only too well calculated to arouse.

It was in 1889 that Eliza was invited to Ireland. She had admired the novels of J. F. Fuller, a prominent architect and writer, and had written to him. Fuller lived in Kerry, near Kenmare. On receiving Fuller's invitation she wrote to him in June:

> . . . Tell the dear wife that slowest life is the best for me. I am not very strong, and I cannot do much. I cannot go long day-excursions without horrible fatigue, and I am such

*Eliza Lynn Linton*

a coward that I dare not go in dogcarts or rickety vehicles of any kind. As for an outside car, dear man! if you put me into one of those, you will have to bind me with ropes and straps and then blindfold me.

She spent a month with the Fullers. In Dublin Fuller met her and she saw 'the sights'; she was particularly anxious to see the spot in Phoenix Park where Lord Frederick Cavendish and Mr Burke were murdered in 1882. From Fuller's house she visited the Gap of Dunloe and also drove some thirty-odd Irish miles to Glasacree, stopping at Windy Gap to give the horses a feed, where she was overwhelmed by the beauty of the scene. She visited the houses of the peasants and spoke to all and sundry, though she naturally found their speech hard to understand, indeed, at times unintelligible. But she recorded her experiences by contributing two articles to the *Queen* called 'In the Wilds of Kerry' and 'A Touch of Kerry'.[14]

What she saw changed her opinions completely – only too naturally: staying with people whom she liked and who were in accord, she was bound to be influenced by their views. Fuller was a landowner and a Protestant, but he was no bigoted Orangeman and he deplored the agitators who murdered and demanded death for those who held allegiance to Popery. Fuller thought that the Act of Union was the greatest misfortune that had befallen his country.

When Eliza returned to England she set about writing two articles for the *New Review*. When finished, however, the articles were not published due to arguments with the editor, which, she comments, put her 'somewhat in the position of Balaam with Balak, when, called on to curse the Israelites, he was forced by superior power to bless them'.[15] When her first article did finally appear, she found that 'the backbone had been taken out of it' and all that was left were her arguments and extracts from the Land Acts. She now determined that her views should be adequately published, and signed an agreement with Methuen for this purpose. In the Introduction to this now rare book (*About Ireland* 1890), she said:

> All of us lay-folks are obliged to follow the leaders of those schools of politics, science or religion, to which our tem-

perament and mental idiosyncracies [*sic*] affiliate us. Life is not long enough for us to examine from the beginning upwards all the questions in which we are interested; and only by chance that we find ourselves set face to face with the first principles and elemental facts of a cause to which, perhaps as blind and believing followers of our leaders, we have committed ourselves with the ardour of conviction and the intemperance of ignorance. In this matter of Ireland I believed in the accusations of brutality, injustice, and general insolence of tyranny from modern landlords to existing tenants, so constantly made by the Home Rulers and their organs; and shocking though the undeniable crimes committed by the Campaigners were, they seemed to me the tragic results of that kind of despair which seizes on men goaded to madness by oppression, are reduced to masked murder as their sole means of defence – and as, after all, but a sadly natural retaliation.

Confessing that she knew nothing of Ashbourne's Act, that she considered that the Home Rule Act would set things straight, Eliza was now criticised for her changing opinions. She wrote to her erstwhile friend, the Reverend Charles Voysey, on 9 August explaining the change:

> ... I have been making a little tour of beautiful Kerry and now at Dublin on my way to London. Thank you very much indeed for all the handsome things you say of me; you have always been good to me. Now I am full of Ireland and of the folly that I and other Liberals have been indulging in. Home Rule and all that is bound up with it simply means ruin to the country, loss to ourselves, and the foul fiend to pay all round! I came a Home Ruler, I leave a strong Unionist, a strong believer in Balfour's wisdom, and in the need of a firm front opposed to popular clamour.
>
> I hope I have not chilled your friendly impulse toward me. Dear Mr Voysey, we Liberals are becoming riddled through and through with unworkable sentimentality. It is pitiable. Under this washy, treacly overflow we are losing all the fine old force that made us what we once were.[16]

*Eliza Lynn Linton*

Voysey agreed with her, writing back to say that he too no longer had any regard for Home Rule. She wrote to him again:

> Yes, I have come back a strong Unionist, having seen the utter fallacy of the Home Rule cry – its shallowness, its falsity. The peasants want the land without paying for it; the Catholics want to oppress the Protestants, and the agitators want to aggrandize themselves. We, the good, stupid, enthusiastic English, who are being ruined by our sentimentality, and whose politics are all riddled with fads, we are sincere, and we alone – no one else. . . . I am writing some papers about it. I hope I may do a little good, for, as far as things go, and have gone, it is the landlord who is being persecuted, *not* the peasant. So I am now on your side, boldly and wholly, with the proviso that Ireland ought to have a measure of local self-government such as we have in England; but Imperial Government must be one and indivisible.[17]

Eliza supported Balfour, whose firmness and directness was to win the applause of Parliament. After the Crimes Act troubles and the Parnell forgery letter in *The Times*, followed by the arrest and imprisonment of O'Brien, enraged by the indignity put upon O'Brien Eliza wrote an angry letter to one of the evening papers, whereupon she was chastened by her friend, A. F. Walter, editor of *The Times*. Eliza replied to him, 'My dear Mr Walter, I am very sorry if I have said anything to annoy you. . . '. She obviously did not want to cross swords with so eminent a person and wished to be convinced by him. What incensed her was that a man in O'Brien's position should have to submit to the indignity of prison dress.

In 1889 Eliza's husband paid his last visit to England. 'He had become frail and begun to limp. He allowed his immaculately white hair and scraggy beard to grow and he assumed the demeanour of a benign, full-lipped patriarch. His friends noticed that his skin remained smooth and unmottled. They found him uniformly sincere, gentle, and independent.'[18] He would see all his friends, and he had written to Eliza of his coming, but she refused to see him, which, in view of his last letter to her, seems rather sad:

*A letter from Herbert Spencer*

> Dear Old Love, we must not lose sight of each other again. Now that I am leaving, and satisfied that we have done wisely by not meeting, I may say that it has been hard for me too, I would have been glad to hold you to my heart again, my lips on yours – but the parting would have been too painful. Dearest, believe me, I would knit our lives together again if I thought it might be; but in some things we have been unsuited, and if in the first fervour of our love this difference could part us, might it not occur again? I could dare to face it but it would be rank unwisdom. God bless you, darling! It is a happiness that only good thoughts exist between us . . . .[19]

Back in America, Linton finally completed his memoirs. It was during the winter of 1896–7 that he contracted pneumonia and remained ill and listless for five months afterwards. In October 1897 he finally admitted himself too weak to operate his hand-press. Finally Margaret Mather and her husband removed him to their home in New Haven. He died there peacefully on 29 December 1897, a fortnight after his eighty-fifth birthday.

Eliza meanwhile continued her ceaseless struggle over the new movements towards the equality between the sexes. Thus she observed that, though women were now allowed to vote in municipal elections, they still could not become county councillors, nor were there any women mayors or jurors; she chafed at the absurd inconsistencies.

> It was indeed a most curious inconsistency, and one may think perhaps that the denial of the parliamentary vote to women was occasioned not by belief in women's ability or lack of ability or because of the upset to the electoral see-saw which it was presumed it would make, but more fundamentally because 'Votes for Women' had become symbolic of the whole contentious change in the status of women.[20]

Eliza was still adamant over any change in the *status quo*. She feared the 'masterful woman' just as she disapproved of the effeminate man. Yet she was such a mixture herself. Gentle with people, especially her many friends, her pen was

*Eliza Lynn Linton*

quite the reverse. She had constantly shown her approval of The Women's Property Act, but she was equally shocked by Josephine Butler's crusade. She considered that prostitution was necessary, but she never advocated the desirability of licensed brothels. Consideration of prostitution was a matter with which women should not concern themselves. Presumably, she did not regard prostitutes as 'women' in her meaning of the word.

# 15
# The *Fortnightly Review*

From January 1887 to March 1889 Eliza had been contributing articles to the *Fortnightly Review*. There were nine altogether, on a variety of subjects. Outstanding was 'Italian Women in the Middle Ages', which appeared in February 1888. She thought the women of this period were passionately courted and tyrannously possessed, and, despite any political motivations, more often than not it was a woman who sparked off the sort of violence that took place in Florence in 1215 and in Bologna fifty-eight years later. She instanced the Guelf and Ghibelline feud; the Imelda Lambertazzi tragedy; the Medici and Orsini intrigues; the murders at the Villa Zenzalino at Ferrara, etc. She discoursed on Castiglione's *The Courtier*, proclaiming the work's value as 'an exact description of a thorough gentleman – in no wise a hero, a saint or a reformer, but simply a man of taste and good breeding such as would make him the favourite of women and the delight of society'.[1] She also reminds us that our own Sir George Etherege, Restoration dramatist, had made similar observations. Of her feelings about that violent age, she declared that the women were no better than the men.

In June 1888 Eliza followed her essay on 'Italian Women in the Middle Ages' with a paper on 'French Political Women', in which she gives a summary account of the many remarkable political ladies of France, from Frédégonde – the prefiguration of *les dames de la Halle* – to the Empress Eugénie. She stated that in 'No country in Europe have women played so important a part in politics as in France' and 'Everywhere they have launched their frail skiffs on the troubled sea of political affairs, not to speak of their more legitimate action in the arts, literature, the conduct of society, and . . . manners.' She did not, however, confine herself to articles on women. In September 1888 she wrote about the Abbé Galiani,[2] who, in her opinion, '. . . was as little priestly as Liszt or Cardinal Antonelli himself – men for whom the phrase "*l'habit ne fait pas le moine*" is so curiously apt'[3] and that the Abbé's letter to Madame d'Epinay 'contained not a dull page' in the then recently published two volumes:[4]

> The loud and boisterous Homeric laughter of Rabelais had given place to the polished sarcasm of Voltaire; the philosophic depth and calmness of Montaigne was lost in the violence of partisanship, the passionate tirades, of the new race of noisy politicians; for the healthy psychology of Molière was substituted the sickly sentimentalism of Rousseau; and for such men as Sully, Crillon and Coligny, Robespierre, Couthon, Marat and Saint-Just were the young vipers lying coiled beneath the great serpent of vengeance.[5]

She classed her sleek little abbé as one of the past wits, and, indeed, compared him to Horace and thought him 'as amorous as Catullus, as sensual as Villon, and as gay and careless and passionate withal, as only a faun or a Neapolitan can be. He was facile and *débonnaire* all through; not impeded by conscientious scruples nor oppressed by an over-chilly morality.'[6]

The October 1888 issue of the *Fortnightly Review* included her essay on 'The Irresponsibilities of Genius'. She had, throughout her life, witnessed a considerable change in moral attitudes. The age of Landor, Coleridge and Southey had now long passed: 'Prosaic virtues, like foresight and self-restraint, were good for those earth-bound folk who could not deliver their souls; but that superior condition of brain which enabled a man to seize, define, and crystalize the evanescent ideas and shadowy sentiments common to humanity, tossed moral obligations to the winds . . .'

She had never met Coleridge, nor Southey, though she knew Southey's children; but as Coleridge had asked Southey in 1800 to look after his (Coleridge's) children, she had probably met them too. However, in the early days of her friendship with Landor, there was much discussion upon Southey and

Coleridge. It was Southey who recognised Landor's genius after he had published *Gebir*, which led to the lifelong friendship between them, while it was Coleridge who published the poem privately. Eliza always felt that Coleridge had behaved badly to Southey. 'Humanity', she averred, 'should be held more sacred than the individual; and if the law is too hard for some it should be relaxed for all who need. . . . For the musical majesty of *Kubla Khan* and the sweet embrace of *Geneviève*, the world willingly bartered all the little dry bricks of a commonplace morality, and thought itself the gainer by the exchange.'[7] She remembered that the views of Coleridge and Wordsworth were considered sufficiently subversive at the time to prompt a government spy to investigate their activities. Coleridge, she considered,

> . . . wrote nothing like *Queen Mab*, nor *Don Juan*, and he only abandoned what we may call the secular moralities. He did not deface the tables of the Decalogue; and he believed all that lay between the first words of St Matthew and the last of Revelations. Hence, he was easily pardoned for his sins against those secular moralities, by which, however, society lives and thrives; and his genius was held as a sacred, if eccentric, quality, which condoned his indolence, his self-indulgence, his comfortable trust in ravens, and his preference for lying prone, dreaming in the sun, weaving sweet fancies as he lay, to sitting straight-backed at a desk, working so many hours for bread. But Shelley was pursued with a rancour which has broken out with fresh violence even in our own day; and *Don Juan* was pilloried as an obscene thing not to be mentioned by the fathers of daughters who read Zola without winking and discuss his imitators without a blush.
>
> In this licence given to genius the man, *quâ* man, does not count. As man he may be penetrated through and through with the loftiest thoughts, the most exquisite sensibilities, the sweetest fancies; but if he does not throw these into some concrete form which the world can see or hear, he has no more grace allowed him than has Hodge tramping at the plough-tail – his sole care to drive a straight furrow, and the amount of bread and cheese set apart for his supper at once his main anxiety and his highest reward. It is neither the

man nor yet the music which makes the privileged genius – it is both together, *plus* success. And to attain success, as has been said, the divine lyre must be in unison with the jew's harp in vogue – giving, if you will, fuller chords, nobler themes, a grander swell, a more subtle melody; but always in unison – never striking a discord with the popular melodies of morality – and above all, never drowning the psalms and litanies intoned by the Church and believed in by the people. How true this is let the difference between the popularity of *In Memoriam* and *Queen Mab* attest.

It is the same in practice as in theory. A popular and therefore successful genius finds life a wreck, wanting the connubial presence of a beloved person denied by the Ten Commandments and already anchored in a prohibited mooring-ground. The Commandments are defied, the mooring-ground is invaded, and the wreck is averted. Whereupon, in consideration of that success, the world celebrates the union with an epithalamium of the orthodox pattern, and crowns the adulteress with a chaplet of myrtle and lilies. An unsuccessful genius, or one who is altogether mute and inglorious – whose lyre has never been strung, or is out of tune with the key-note of the time – but a man whose passionate sensations and eager fancies match for intensity those of that other, does precisely the same thing.[8]

She insisted that humanity should be held more sacred than the individual. 'If the overwhelming emotions, the frenzied desires of the poet, are to be urged as extenuating circumstances when he breaks the law and boldly poaches another man's preserves, the grocer with a poetic temperament and the like frenzied desires may plead the same.'[9]

There is little doubt that Eliza hated personal disorder: '... the shipwreck of a life's happiness is always a shipwreck.' Hence her approval of Southey for taking on the responsibility of looking after Coleridge's family when he was already handicapped.

In this same essay Eliza touched on Thomas Moore and expressed the opinion that only *Irish Melodies* and *Lalla Rookh* would survive, while already, during her lifetime, Thomas Colley Grattan (1796–1864), novelist, dramatist and poet, had fallen into oblivion.

She recalled meeting the debonair Harrison Ainsworth, 'Who like a youthful Jove, pronounced his love for all the good things of life' but realised his fame was already decreasing. She thought Douglas Jerrold had a staccato style and an effervescent cynicism, while Bulwer-Lytton's affectations of style could no longer be endured – it was 'too gaudy and glittering for perfect taste'. She had met him at Knebworth,

> when he had drunk the cup of life to the dregs, and of all that clear and sparkling wine only the thick and turbid lees were left. Alone, deaf, in ill-health, his power of work diminished and his enjoyment with his work, he was waiting on the inevitable end. But he was always kind and dignified: always the courtly and considerate gentleman of his best days; and the fate he could not avert he knew how to accept like a man of courage and a philosopher.[10]

It was earlier, in 1886, that the essay 'The Higher Education of Women' had appeared.[11] To support her objections to the education of women, she quoted what a woman doctor, Dr Withers-Moore, had written about the effects on women's health of undertaking men's work, and she went on to record that one of the wisest and best trained women she knew had said:

> How much of all the grand force and nervous power, the steadiness and courage of Englishmen, may not be owing to the fact of the home life and protection of women; and how much shall we not lose when the mothers of the race are rendered nervous, irritable, and overstrained by the exciting stimulus of education carried to excess, and exhausting anxieties of professional competition![12]

Eliza, to illustrate her views, instanced that 'immortal' women such as Elizabeth Fry, Mary Carpenter, or Florence Nightingale were not particularly learned ladies, nor did she believe that men preferred blue-stockings as wives. Yet she mocked the incredible number of stupid women who figured in nearly every single novel she wrote. Most of the matrons that she depicts had not a single thought in their heads save the desire of marrying their daughters satisfactorily. Her article goes on to assert:

> We are in the midst of one of the great revolutions of the world. The old faiths are losing their hold and the new are not yet rooted. . . . In this revolution, naturally, one of the most prominent facts is the universal claim for individual freedom, outside the elemental laws which hold the foundations together, made by every one alike. We preach the doctrine of rights everywhere, that of duties straggles in where it can; and the one crying need of the world at this moment is for some wise and powerful organizer who shall recombine these scattered elements and reconstruct the shattered edifice. Women, who always outstrip their leaders, are more disorganized, because at this time they are even more individualized than are men. Scarcely one among them takes into account the general good. Even in those questions where they have made themselves the leaders, individual victories are of greater value than general policy, and they would always subordinate the practical welfare of the majority to the sentimental rights of the minority. An individual sorrow moves them where the massed results of a general law leave them cold. . . . Women ought to be individual, not for themselves but for others; and in that individualism there ought to be the injustice inseparable from devotion. An altruistic mother who would sacrifice her one child for the sake of her neighbour's two, does not exactly fulfil our ideas of maternal care; on the other hand, a mother who would rather her son was disgraced as a coward than that he should run the dangers of courage – or the partisan of her own sex who would sacrifice twenty men to save one woman inconvenience or displeasure, is as little fit to be the leader of large movements involving many and varied interests, as is that other to be a mother. In their own persons women carry out to a very remarkable degree this principle of individualism, the general good notwithstanding. Speak to an ordinary woman of the evil economic effects of her actions, and you speak a foreign language. She sees only the individual loss or gain of the transaction, and

a public or social duty to creatures unknown and unseen does not count. . . .

In another article, 'The Future Supremacy of Woman' in the *National Review*, she stated pretty forcibly that she was wholly against feminine emancipation. She had no two opinions about the abilities of the sexes: 'Men have been given, by nature and sex, heroic qualities and the larger crimes and vices; to women gentle virtues and smaller faults, and the restraining influence which comes by the very fact of their innocence, their goodness, their purity, their unselfishness.'

Paradoxically enough, Eliza's views and attitudes towards marriage were reasonable and sensible:

> The rudiments of orderly society lie in the voluntary restrictions of marriage as against promiscuity, just as the rudiments of political organization lie in the voluntary submission of a tribe to one chief as against individual independence. Whether the method of gaining the wife be by capture or purchase, whether she must be one of the same tribe or some dusky Sabina taken by force from afar, whether she never pronounces her husband's name or loses her own in his, nothing of this is integral to the question. Even polygamy or polyandry is only a fringe, an adjunct. The vital thing is that a man and woman marry with the consent and knowledge of their society, and that the children born of this authorised union belong emphatically to that society.[13]

She advanced strong views on a mother forcing a daughter into marriage against her will to a wealthy suitor, a theme she used for her novel *Through the Long Night*. On the other hand she admitted that a *mariage de convenance* worked well enough in France, whereas in England 'a match-making mother is a term of reproach. . . . It is part of our British pride not to stir a finger to help on a nascent love affair; part of our British prudery to ignore the discreet flirtations of our daughters, so long as they are discreet and not too violent to be overlooked.'[14] Whilst believing that a vigilant mother should allow her daughter freedom of choice, in her novels she frequently illustrated the restrictions to which girls are submitted. Equally, she warns against marriage on a shoestring when a girl has been brought up to enjoy the luxuries of life. Living when she did and observing how poverty can affect marriage, her viewpoint does not seem particularly out of focus. 'Romance does not reign quite so triumphantly in the present as it did in the past days of Lydia Languish, or even when the "Lady of Lyons" held the stage. Our roses and lilies have to be gilded, not perfumed; and for dewdrops we demand diamonds, and plenty of them.'[15]

Having disapproved of marriage on a shoestring, Eliza rather contrarily states that English society is far too concerned with money where marriage is concerned:

> Anyone with money can buy of the best in the open market; for money is power, and the old adage about knowledge is as rococo as that about love in a cottage and the dinner of herbs. Let that pass. We sell our energies, our brains, our time, our health and strength, for so much current coin of the realm. We sometimes sell our consciences and that thing, that 'sort of something' we call our soul. Why not our bodies as well? In the street it goes by an ugly name; but society and church call it marriage and society and church should know best.[16]

Eliza's own marriage had been a failure, and in her heart she considered marriage a very 'chancy' institution, ending in either a philandering husband or a boring relationship. 'If May elects to live with January, she must keep her lips dry and her eyes steady, else she will make pie of her marriage-lines before the year is out, when all that will be left her will be a broken law fearfully avenged by her everlasting disgrace.'[17]

One wonders whether she is speaking from experience when she says: 'The average man cannot bear vital obligation to a woman.' She thought it a mistake for a man to marry his paid mistress, and added: 'It is a psychological fact that many men are charming as proprietary lovers who are impossible as husbands, and many women make the most complacent and delightful mistresses who, as wives, would give points to Xanthippe.[18]

There was never any hesitation in Eliza's opinions, and her

pen moved as swiftly as her thoughts, which may account for her contradictariness: 'If he is a self-flatterer whose vanity goes to his morals, it is a daily pleasure to him to be able to peacock himself on his generosity, his voluntary fidelity, his greatness of soul all through.'[19] Women, on the other hand, she declares, apparently take on a different attitude with security:

> It is the old story of the coward and the bully – the villain by nature enriched of fortune and acting according to the law of her kind. Every student of humanity must have seen these two characters – the man who, a generous and kindly because voluntary proprietor, becomes hateful under obligations, and the woman who, a complaisant and delightful mistress, becomes just as hateful as soon as she has touched security.[20]

Another aspect of marriage which occupied Eliza's thoughts was the law which forbade marriage to a deceased wife's sister. Why should this be, she asked, when it affects no one else in society, and is a matter for the individual concerned? And she had little patience for the ritualists who refused to marry the divorced, and no time at all for the Roman Church which allowed no divorce. Why, therefore, did she not advocate easier divorce laws?

# 16
# Was He Wrong?

There could have been few weeks when Eliza was not the recipient of letters from angry ladies complaining bitterly about her writings and her opinions.

On 23 February 1889 the *Queen* began serialising a short novel of Eliza's called *Was He Wrong?*, the first chapter of which, appearing on its leading page, caused offence. It is the story of Fanny Fisher, a little gold-digger 'for whom men lose their wits and go down into fathomless depths of folly'. Fanny is such an admirable gold-digger that she is able to deceive her own son, but she is finally exposed. However, this tale was never published in book form.

In January 1890 Eliza heard from the editor of a periodical called *Men and Women of the Day*, who wished to include an article about her. When she had read the proofs, she wrote to him:

> Dear Sir, If you could, without over-running, put in that last little paragraph, I should be glad. I am so constantly spoken of as the enemy of my own sex. I was accused in the *Pall Mall Gazette* of that worst of all vices in my mind, *selfishness*, having now reached my own vantage ground, cruelly and coldly desirous of keeping back all others – that is if this one trait of my character could be brought forward, I should feel it an act of justice. I do not suppose anyone alive has done so much for others as I have. If I had to make an income by revising MSS., I should make a better one than I do now by writing them! I have a bevy of girls about me who look on me as a mother; who come to me for advice and sympathy, and who are no more afraid of me

than if I were one of themselves. I have been the mother and friend of more than one young man of letters, helping with all manner of help, and it does pain me to be set forth as a selfish villain who cares only for her *own* advantage. This is the one accusation that stings and rankles with me. No one *can* say that I have ever truckled or been a snob, or had that low kind of trivial ambition, desiring to be 'seen' at grand places – but the charge of hatred to my own sex, and because of my dislike to political rights of women, the charge of envious desires to keep them back, can be made with more plausibility, and hurts me terribly when made. . . .[1]

In October of that year she was invited to a dinner at the Mansion House given for 'the International Literary and Artistic Congress'. She went alone and her 'inside was all of a trimmle'. She was one of the principal guests and was taken to dinner by the Lord Mayor himself. She wore her best dress – a black striped silk and satin with a white front covered with jet and white facings. She ate modestly, 'some turtle soup, a small portion of filleted sole and only the vegetables belonging to the mutton that followed'. She refused the sweets, the fruit, and drank no wine. But she enjoyed the evening.

In 1890, in an article in the *Lady's Realm*, Eliza took up the cudgels against women riding bicycles, which brought back a fearsome rejoinder from Susan, Countess of Malmesbury. The bicycle had just come into its own and models had been devised for women. Touring clubs were instituted and enthusiasm for this new method of locomotion spread rapidly. The fact that women took to the bicycle gave Eliza an admirable opportunity to attack what she called an 'undignified' means of transport. The clothes women wore for the purpose were uncommonly ugly and it obviously made them hot.

> The prettiest woman in the world and the most graceful in riding, in walking, in dancing, in skating, in reclining, loses all her distinctive charm when 'biking'. The attitude is constrained, and pedal as she may, the action is ungainly, and the picture she makes is ungraceful. The skirts alternately flap and fill like the sails of a tacking boat; the eyes

are hard and anxious; the face is set; there is not left in her the faintest remnant of that sweet spirit of allurement which conscious or unconscious, is woman's supreme attraction.[2]

Eliza certainly hated any kind of trouser outfit – bloomers, knickerbockers, Norfolk suits, and the like – anything which in any way aped male costume. 'We cannot understand', she wrote, 'how pretty women of position and fortune, who look like so many Greek Amazons on horseback, should descend from their place of perfect beauty for anything so hideous as the bike, when there is no excuse to be made for the machine as a valuable and much-needed method of locomotion.'[3]

She relented a little when she admitted the utility of the 'cycle in the country', but deplored its use by women in London and other big cities. It was highly dangerous, she said, as accidents and other horrors came to her mind, not to mention the way women's complexions would suffer and how their noses would peel. Lady Malmesbury, on her part, wrote:

> Mrs Lynn Linton takes up in a belated way, a somewhat analogous position, having never asked herself the few simple questions which if honestly answered, would clear away the mists from her mind and allow her to view the wide, if rugged prospect now offering itself to our sex, bounded as it is by an horizon where fair promise is clouded by the storms inseparable from the life of both men and women in this strangely fascinating world.
>
> Women are, even more than men, from the greater delicacy of their constitution, liable to suffer from the effects of a luxurious and artificial existence – particularly the kind described by Mrs Lynn Linton in so affectionately alluring a way, and which would reduce the whole of an active, cultivated, well-developed class of Society to the condition of those fat and pampered lap-dogs which we sometimes see, sitting in open carriages, over-fed and snappish, by the side of a fond and elderly owner. Debarred as women have been – and as Mrs Lynn Linton would like them to remain – from healthy exercise and play, the love of which was implanted in them by their natures and only eradicated by many slaps and much repression, women cyclists would no doubt like

to apply the same light whip to their happy companions of the other sex sporting the turf, which Mrs Lynn Linton so kindly and gracefully suggests as the only way to reach their dull feminine understanderings.[4]

Lady Malmesbury considered that the widest gaps in society were between the middle classes and the upper classes, and that there was considerably more understanding between the artistocracy and the lower classes, who fully understood what a boon the 'cycle' was. 'It is we women of the upper class who have born the brunt of senseless ridicule and public insult, and have given the others a lead over the stiff fence of prejudice into a fairy playground of delight.'[5]

Whether working-class women were actually enjoying the new upsurge of sport is open to question. Certainly in 1889 the illustrations in *Punch* of ladies playing cricket, or golf, show the players in the highest fashion. The British Ladies' Football Club, which was founded in 1895, naturally horrified Eliza. When cricket clubs began proliferating Lady Milner advised girls '. . . to wear a white flannel skirt of walking length, a well-cut white shirt, a girthbelt, and a white sailor hat, tie and hat ribbon in the wearer's club colours'. In fact, Lady Milner went further than Lady Malmesbury in advising women upon their apparel:

> Let us not spoil our freedom of movement by encasing ourselves in steel armour, more commonly called 'the correct corset' . . . So much of our success depends on quickness of movement and suppleness of body that I may be pardoned for pointing out that if we are steel-bound and whale-lined throughout, the free use of our limbs which the game demands is rendered impossible.

In the same year Eliza was on a new crusade – freedom for writers in the matter of subject and length. One of the real problems that beset the Victorian novelist was the need to conform with Mudie's conventions. Charles Edward Mudie had established his famous lending library in 1842, and such was his eventual success that he was able to order very considerable numbers of most books, including, for example, 2,500 copies of volumes 3 and 4 of Macaulay's *History of England*.[6] His only serious competitor was W. H. Smith, who in 1858 began operations at railway bookstalls.

There is little doubt, however, that novelists were greatly constrained in the moral tone of their work if they were to be accepted by Mudie's library. Moreover, a novel had to be 'padded' to fit the convention of a three-volume work, as required by the subscription libraries. Shrewd and practised novelists like Anthony Trollope assessed that it was necessary to write 198,000 words to fill three volumes, and Mrs Henry Wood, for whose novels Eliza had little regard, had a tremendous success with *East Lynne*, which was 251,866 words long. Gissing, on the other hand, often found this tremendous length a great difficulty, and later George Moore rebelled against it, but in the main the popular novelists bowed to Mudie's dictates.

It was in January 1890 that the *New Review* published a symposium on *Candour in English Fiction* by three writers – Walter Besant, a successful novelist and founder of the Society of Authors, Thomas Hardy, and Eliza Lynn Linton. Besant took the view that 'he who works for pay must respect the prejudices of his customers'. If a novelist 'crosses certain boundaries' he will find that Mudie or Smith will not distribute his books. Eliza, far more sensibly, proposed a compromise. 'Such restraints', she wrote, 'cut off from fiction one of the largest and most important areas of that human life we pretend to portray. . . . If a novel is written for the inclusion of the Young Person among its readers, it does not go beyond the school girl standard.' She concluded that the novel could not exist if shorn of adult reading. 'A locked bookcase was necessary for readers who required volumes for more thoughtful and mature minds.' Hardy, for his part, attacked magazines (which serialised novels) and the circulating libraries as responsible for the 'indescribably unreal and meretricious' views found in fiction. When books are borrowed and not bought, Hardy pointed out, they are 'made to wear a common livery in style and subject, enforced by their supposed necessities in addressing indiscriminately a general audience'. To the circulating library he ascribed responsibility for the lack of sincerity, since fiction 'is conditioned by its surroundings like a river-stream'.

## 'Was He Wrong?'

Eliza's unerring flair for cultivating the acquaintance of talented persons could not be more happily recorded than when meeting with Thomas Hardy, then quite young, for whom she had the profoundest admiration. Of this meeting she wrote to her sister Lucy on 27 January 1891 from Queen Anne's Mansions:

> Yesterday a stranger called on me. The boy said *Harvey*. I was in a fume – could not make out who it was – went round and round the central point, till the stranger said he was going out of town to-day. 'Where?' says I. 'To Dorchester' says he. Then I ups with a shout and a clapping of my hands, and says I, 'Oh, now I know who you are! You are Thomas Hardy not Harvey. . . .

During March she heard again from Herbert Spencer who had read what was undoubtedly one of her best essays, 'Our Illusions', in the *Fortnightly Review* of April 1891. He wrote:

> . . . How I envy you your vigorous style, your telling metaphors, and your fertility of allusion! . . . Should you republish it, there are two additions which I would suggest. While you have given abundant illustrations of the truth that most things are not so good as they seem, you have not sufficiently emphasised the truth that in many cases things are better than they seem – acts are not unfrequently misinterpreted to the disadvantage of the actor. One may, for example, having paid a cabman more than the full fare, refuse to give him still more, and may be held by him and by bystanders to be restrained by parsimony; whereas the motive may be entirely the desire to check the growth of abuses – the feeling that resistance to extortion is needful for public welfare. Or, again, one may persist in putting down smoking in a non-smoking compartment of a railway carriage, not from personal aversion to the smoke, but from the desire to maintain wholesome law for the benefit of passengers in general, and one may be regarded for doing this as a selfish curmudgeon. You have referred to cases in which the fact, even when known, is illusively interpreted, but it is well to emphasise more fully the truth, that the real inter-

pretation may be more favourable than the interpretation which appears probable.

Another truth which I think you ought to point out is, that many of the illusions under which we labour are due to the non-adaptation of human nature to social conditions, and that when the adaptation approaches nearer to completion, the difference between fact and fancy will be by no means as great as now. . . .[7]

To which she replied:

You know what your kind letter is to me, one of the big honours of my life! You are quite right, as of course, and I might have made a point of the illusions of condemnation; perhaps, indeed, those are more frequent, and surely more disastrous, than the illusions of belief, respect, and of love! But I am always afraid of 'summering and wintering' a subject too much, and yet, try as I may, I cannot get to that most valuable of all literary qualities – reserve – the quality which no writer possessed to more perfection than my dear old 'father' Landor. He used to say that he always left a subject before he had sated his reader, and always left it suggested rather than explained. In fiction, Bret Harte has this quality of suggestiveness, of reserve, of indication rather than of exhaustive description, but I have the tendency to 'pour out' and 'slop over'. . . .

Her postscript to this letter read: 'From birth to death life is all phantasmagoria, illusive, conditional, and a dream; and when that death comes – what?'

The essay 'Our Illusions' concerns Eliza's 'search for truth' and the illusions of truth. Youth, she maintains, was amply rewarded by illusions of faith, hope and charity, while every succeeding generation demands the reformation of society, so human nature should be 'reconstructed to suit the spirit of the times'.[8] Poverty, war, inequalities of fortune must be swept away. There are some, of course, 'who hang their faith on the Apocalyptic millennium; others on that of the theosophical spiral; others again on the more scientific doctrine of evolution'.[9] But fundamentally a new code of morals, a new adjustment of principles, is to be applied:

> Religion which asserts itself as divinely given conviction, and is a clever calculation of bread and pence; political principle which means place, power and party, but has nothing to do with patriotism; philanthropy which is the profoundest egotism – vanity building its own monument during the lifetime – when it is not a means of living like any other trade; these and some other things are among the cold douches which experience pours over our burning faith – from the fervid fever of belief reducing us to the glacial coldness of scepticism.[10]

What of the truth that we believe is history, she continues:

> Were the men we have demi-deified in history no better than the men of the present day? Did the Gracchi despise the *plebs* for whom they fought and in whose cause they died? Was patriotism – was the old Law of Numa, a cleverly constructed stalking-horse behind which Brutus made his own ends when he consorted with Casca and planted his dagger in Caesar's breast? Was Marcus Aurelius an imperial Tartuffe given to his base love for a vile woman? and was Epictetus richer in phrases than fertile in action? Who knows now? Who can determine? The balance of truth is clogged with the dust of ages; and as the romance of history, the poetry of ethics, adjusted it so long ago, now must it forever hang.[11]

She examined her own personal illusions. Were our own past memories faithful, or are they not coloured by our own youthful inexperiences and our imaginations? 'Was it all an illusion, woven by the soft south wind?' As to love, we have little else there but delusion. 'What is it that makes us love that inferior A. and turn an unsympathetic shoulder to B., in all things superior?' For, she added, 'in this battle, it is by no means always to the strong, nor the race to the swift; and many of those who are most passionately beloved seem to outsiders the least worthy of regard'.[12] She illustrated her theme by citing cases:

> No one knows the root – the triliteral – of that many-sided word of Love. 'Instinct' touches one point only and falls

*Eliza Lynn Linton*

>short of all the rest; and 'spiritual fitness' leaves the cloud as beautiful and as bewildering as before. It is all maya – all delusion. Only when old age has couched our eyes of the blindness wrought by passion, and experience has cleared the tangle created by ignorance and belief, only then do we see the thing in its true shape. And yet no shape is real. Protean, illusory, evading the touch changing to the eyes, love is of the elemental mysteries of human life whereof no man has the key – one of those prepotent effects whereof the secret cause is sealed against the sharpest eyes.[13]

Are our memories of youth, seen in the light of experience and the disillusionment of time, only darkly glimpsed? 'Nothing was as it seemed to be, and its most sacred memories are self-evolved – due to our state rather than to the actual things themselves.' And what of our perfections? How do we deal with the confusions of thought that are constantly perplexing us? 'Even verbal truth itself would sometimes be more dishonouring than a lie. We know the paradigmatic instances which refute this absolutism and bring down truth itself to the relativity of the rank and file – as, the deception practised on the dangerously sick whose dead beloved are reported well or convalescent....'[14]

It would appear that Eliza did not often attend the theatre, but, writing to her sister Lucy in April 1891, she seems to have enjoyed Wormser's *l'Enfant Prodigue*.

>I went to see a play yesterday afternoon – for the first time for a year – almost a year. It was all in dumb show, *L'Enfant Prodigue*, and the male characters were dressed as *Pierrots* in white with chalked faces and scarlet clown lips. The first two acts were very good; the first amusing, the second interesting. The last was pathetic to such an extent that I *sobbed* – sobbed over the wonderful acting without words, of whitewashed faces and clown-painted mouths! It was marvellously done. The suitable expression given to these mask-like faces was simply marvellous.

In July she spent another holiday in Cumberland with the Gedges. Ruskin heard she was in the district and invited her to Brantwood, but she declined his invitation, feeling that she did not wish to reopen past memories.

It was in 1892 that Eliza first met her biographer, George Somes Layard. They were both taking the cure at the Raven Hotel, Droitwich Spa. Layard recognised her as soon as she entered the dining-room: 'As we filed out after dinner, I felt a touch upon my arm, and heard a never-to-be-forgotten voice saying – "Are you one of us? You must bring your wife to my room and have a talk" '. Thus began Layard's long series of many conversations with Eliza. In the same year a Mrs Gulie Moss published an anthology of excerpts from Eliza's novels, which highly delighted her.

In June she returned to Ireland, staying this time in the house of Sir James Henderson, Lord Mayor of Belfast, at Windsor Park. She immediately wrote a further book on the Ulster situation.

But more damaging to her reputation than anything else she had written was her next novel, *The One Too Many*, which was serialised in *Lady's Pictorial* in 1893 and published in book form the following year. This novel was inscribed 'To the Sweet Girls Still Left Among Us, who have no part in the New Revolt but are content to be Dutiful, Innocent and Sheltered'. *The One Too Many* is a virulent attack upon female emancipation and further education, and in particular upon the newly established Girton College, founded by Emily Davies at Hitchin in 1869 and moved to Cambridge in 1873. At Girton women were promised an education comparable to that of men, a promise that Eliza was unable to swallow. It is difficult to understand her inflexible attitude. A rather obvious reason comes to mind: she was jealous, perhaps, of the opportunities that were now being offered to young women, which had been denied to her, and like many people of an older generation she refused to accommodate herself in any way with the rapid advances that were being made towards the emancipation of women. The fact that a girl would answer her elders with presumption, that such an unpleasant habit as smoking among females was becoming prevalent, that they sought their own futures away from the parental home, that they had completely opposite views to those expressed by their parents, she could not tolerate. But the puppets she manipulated in *The*

*Eliza Lynn Linton*

*One Too Many* are jerked so violently that she heavily defeats her own case. Her male characters in this novel, especially the arrant coxcomb to whom the heroine is married, behave in such a manner that she seems to want to prove that marriage is an appalling risk for any girl to undertake. What was Eliza's purpose? What was the point of her dedication if her precepts were to praise the docile Victorian woman, 'content to be dutiful, innocent and sheltered'. Why commend the obedient, home-loving girl if, like Moira in the novel, she is doomed from the moment of marriage? Yet Eliza may have a dual purpose, of which there is a hint in the review of the *Athenaeum*: '. . . the plain person can hardly fail to rise from a perusal of the story without an impression that in the view of the writer, it is wiser to revolt than submit.'[15]

George Saintsbury in the *Academy* considered 'the characters were exaggerated, but the story amusing'. Today the characters appear utterly grotesque, but they served Eliza's purposes, hammering in her point, which she blunted, however, by lack of subtlety and ambivalence. She was not unchallenged. The following letter appeared in the *Lady's Pictorial* when the serial came to an end:

> . . . as a late student of Girton College, I write to protest against the caricature of Girton students contained in the story you have been publishing, called *The One Too Many*. I left Girton ten years ago, and since then I have kept closely in touch with college life and college students, and I state without any hesitation and without any reservation, that such women as are described in your story are unknown at Girton. I have never met such characters, I have never heard such conversation, as theirs, either in college or out of it, and I firmly believe you will never find any one who has.
>
> It is evident, of course, that the writer of the story can have had little or no acquaintance with Girton or Cambridge women-students. . . . the author's statements as to the language and habits (I refer to the smoking and constant taking of stimulants indulged in by these 'Girton B.A.'s') are calculated to create very great and unjust prejudice in the minds of those who read your paper, and who, knowing nothing of the manner and life of university women, cannot

judge for themselves of the truth or falsehood of the descriptions.

... To justify the language I have used, I have only to remind you that of the 'Girton B.A.'s' in the story, one marries a policeman, having first nursed him through an illness and then proposed to him; one flirts outrageously with a married man in the presence of his wife, the intimate friend of her 'pal' who marries the policeman; the third constantly advocates suicide, and is consequently the indirect cause of the heroine's death by her own hand. All drink, smoke, swear, use vulgar language, and are represented as knowing and talking about unfitting subjects.

And the writer does not merely indulge in generalities, and say, 'These *will be* the results of the higher education of women.' ...

There is a great deal more in the same vein. A temperate enough letter, to which Eliza replied:

I am sorry that you should have been in any way troubled through me or my work; sorry, too, that I have offended others by what I have written. I am afraid, though, that the students at Girton, etc., will not be able to find a law that shall prevent their coming into the sphere of fiction and its uses. As the old Laura Matildas, the Blue-stockings, the fine ladies with spleen and vapours, the dull drudges who 'suckled fools and chronicled small beer', the flirts, hoydens, gamblers, horsey women – in short, the whole list of foils to the idea – have been used in fiction, so will the newer developments of womanhood, whether the setting be Girton or Newnham, a London newspaper office or a political platform.

I wanted a link between four girls, and the best that occurred to me was a collegiate friendship. And I wanted to show that intellectual training may exist with (1) absence of womanliness, though in this character are many of the more virile virtues, as in Effie; with (2) want of charm, as in Carrie; with (3) want of mental health and common sense, as in Laura; with (4) want of right feeling, as in Julia. If your correspondent maintains that the higher education changes the elemental qualities of character, and that, given such natures and temperaments as I have described, a knowledge of classics and mathematics will alter them, I think she is wrong. If she maintains that no girl-graduate smokes, drinks more than is good for her, talks slang, swears, or knows more of the darker secrets of human life than is fitting, I *know* she is wrong. If she thinks that no girl of this higher education would come between husband and wife, on the plea of her own greater fitness to understand and companion him, I *know* there, too, that she is wrong. And if she hopes to make the very name of Girton sacred, so that it shall not be employed as a background in fiction, save under conditions of commendation, I fear she will miss her mark as completely as she has done in her belief that the moral nature of women is, or can be, changed by intellectual acquirement.

But really, is not your correspondent a little too hasty in thus taking up the cudgels for the honour of a place which is only named as a locality and is not attempted to be described? . . .

At the end of a letter to another critic, she wrote: 'I am not hard to girls – only to the new woman I am implacable. All the girls I know like me and I love them.'[16]

# 17
# Beatrice Harraden

During Eliza's last years one of her close women friends was Beatrice Harraden, a novelist now forgotten but for her second book, *Ships That Pass in the Night* (1893).* Their friendship was close but not so cosy that Beatrice was afraid to criticise Eliza, and this certainly happened when *The One Too Many* was published.

Beatrice told Layard, 'My blood was up and I was much tempted to write a letter to the *Lady's Pictorial*.' But she restrained herself when she realised how upset Eliza would have been. So she contented herself with writing a letter to Eliza herself. She usually called Eliza 'Viking' whilst Eliza named her 'the B.A.' (Beatrice had a B.A. degree from London University). The letter, however, caused a distinct coolness between them.

> Of course you know how I should be likely to feel on the subject; indeed, I don't remember ever having been so hurt. We are all smarting, we young women of the day, of whom you think so badly, for I range myself on their side naturally, being one of them myself and having had so many of them as comrades and friends. And if any one does know about them, surely I do, having been at three colleges. Well, there it all is, and your book will represent us as we are *not*. I have met some such characters as you describe, but they have been the untrained ones, not those who have been through their facings. I quite think that the modern young woman who has had no particular training loses her balance and goes off at a tangent; *but* steady work and ambition, and

* Eliza mentions this title in *The One Too Many*.

## Eliza Lynn Linton

the desire to work out a career for herself, do not produce the description of modern young woman. That is a separate class having no point of contact with the trained and eager and brave souls whom I call my comrades and friends. I have met such people as you describe, but I have found them amongst the leisured and society-loving, not amongst the workers. To class the workers with them is an injustice.[1]

But the friendship continued, and Beatrice later told Layard:

She was herself so gallant and brave, that it would seem disloyalty to her memory not to make the attempt to be brave and gallant oneself, under any circumstances whatsoever. She was most generous about other people's work, and her praise and encouragement were always bracing. You felt, after reading one of her kind letters, that you must 'pull yourself together' to justify what she had so generously said of you. I think that all her friends must have felt that. She will always remain, to quote her own words to me, 'as a silver trumpet heartening to the strife'. Perhaps I have felt this all the more because she never failed, during my many months of illness, to encourage and stimulate me to get better. 'You will recover your health and do good work, and I shall live to be proud of my little dear', she wrote constantly. She had the tenderest heart imaginable, and I know she had a very special tender love for me. . . .

She took the greatest interest in my accepted and rejected MSS – generally rejected in those days; but she never once offered to help me to place any story, and never once gave me any letter of introduction to any editor. I have since thought this all the more strange, because I hear what immense trouble in that way she took for others. I suppose she thought that it was better if possible to fight one's battle alone. But she sent me out to it full of hope and courage, and buoyed up with the consciousness that she believed in me. And that is the healthiest kind of help. Looking back now I realise how much I owe to her in so many ways quite apart from love and friendship. Herself a veteran writer, she took myself, a young beginner, into her life on equal terms. . . . She opened her home to me at once, and I was free to come and go and take my part in her Saturday afternoons, where I made many delightful friendships. . . . But the greatest pleasure and interest of those afternoons was when she got into discussion with any one. She would become very angry and emphatic at times, but I never thought she lost her delicate sense of courtesy and fine sensitiveness. I have seen people show signs of incipient rudeness to her over some hot discussion, and then the sound of her singularly sweet voice restored them to themselves. But of course to me the greatest pleasure of all was to get her alone, and when she was in a non-combative mood. . . . Then and then only one learnt to know the real Mrs Lynn Linton. Working diligently at her embroidery, she would speak of her girlhood's troubles and her passionate desire and attempts to educate herself. Then one heard the story of her own emancipation from a close-pressing environment; the story of her hard work and struggles in London; of her successes, disappointments, failures; of her friendships and disillusions; of her strong belief in the good of human nature, and her robust delight in life and everything which life had to offer of its best and truest. . . . So we sat and talked together, now of her past life and present, now of my young life, my past and present; and we spoke of religion and philosophy and languages, and sometimes ended up with an ode from Horace or a passage from Homer. And once or twice she read to me. Her favourite sonnet from Shakespeare was, 'When in disgrace with fortune and men's eyes', and once she told me the story of her unsuitable marriage. The last real talk I had with her was at the Royal Academy Exhibition.

. . . And we sat together hand in hand and renewed old times. She spoke of her projects and asked me about mine, and she drifted on to the subject of religion. I could see that her ideas had undergone a change, and that her tone had become distinctly conventional. . . .

I saw her once again at Queen Anne's Mansions, and she was especially gentle and tender, but I, and others who knew her much better than I did, thought she seemed detached and impersonal. This detachment from her old friends was thought to have been growing on her for some time. . . . But as no one ever realized that she was nearly seventy-seven,

*Eliza Lynn Linton*

no one ever allowed her the advantage or disadvantage of being seventy-seven years of age. To me she always seemed a strong-brained, strong-framed woman of about fifty. . . .[2]

In 1888 Beatrice Harraden had sent her Christmas greetings and Eliza replied to her:

And the lady, sitting alone in her high chamber – alone and sorrowful – sat long into the night, thinking of many things. From the far distant past of her own childhood and her vigorous youth, rose the ghosts of dead hopes, of slain joys, of beautiful illusions murdered by the cruel hands of truth, of lost phantoms, born of time and experience, which replace in age the rosy clouds of youth. The world seemed very silent, very sad, and life looked purposeless and dreary – merely a retrospect now with no foothold on the present – when suddenly there stole on the stagnant air a low and tender melody.

It came from nowhere. It was not from the Christmas waits outside; it was not from any indweller in the high house, it was not here nor there, but everywhere – something that pervaded the whole atmosphere like a subtle perfume, and turned what had been stillness to exquisite harmony. And with the music came a faint light – at first diffused, like the light of the dawn, then gathering into one point like the morning star before the sun has risen. And this light, slowly concentrating itself, took a form and shape, and in it the lady saw the face of a little black-haired, bright-eyed girl . . . Then she knew that her life, though solitary, was not in the past, but still in the present and the future, and that to her had come this new sweet love – this new and golden link – who was to be as her spiritual child, carrying on her own work to nobler and higher issues. She knew that the music was this child's message for this dark Christmas time, and that it was made by the Spirit of Love himself.

Eliza met the ignominies of increasing age with a stoicism that is to be admired, as can be seen in a letter of 10 March 1893 to a new friend, Mrs Gulie Moss, who edited an anthology of excerpts from Eliza's novels.

... It is hard for you to lie like this, unable to use your hands. That would be one of the worst trials to me, for I am a great needleworker, and love it. ... and if I could not use my hands, I am afraid I should be less patient than the angelic person, whose beauty of mind and of body both fills me with admiration and something more. ...

I wonder if you get the grand consolation I get when evil days are on me, of consciousness of law. You are suffering sweet woman, from some probably unknown cause, which yet is as absolute in its effects as that fire would burn your hand if you thrust it inside the bars. If science can find a remedy – counter-agent – well and good. If not, there is no use in knocking your head against a stone wall or praying into the void. Patience is the only dignified attitude. 'Wearying heaven with prayers' that are not answered may comfort some, and it does, but to me it would be more maddening than comforting to ask an Almighty Power to help and not be answered! Then comes in the attitude of submission, unquestioning, un-reasoning, full of faith – 'If I am not answered, God knows best.' Then if He knows best and gives or withholds at His own pleasure, where is the use of asking? Does He need to be *told* what is wanted? It is all such an illogical jumble! and to me the old Stoics' *pride* of endurance in silence and with dignity is so much grander and finer! But, all the same, let us fight our physical enemies inch by inch, and do what we can to overcome. I am in the grasp of that 'foul fiend' rheumatism, with whom I am having a tussle. I am almost lame, and when I get up from the chair, hobble along the first few steps bent half double. Then slowly and by degrees I become less of an ape and more of a human, and by the time I have gone a few hundred yards cease to hobble. But does it not take it out of my pride when, in the coffee-room, I go parrot-like from chairback to chairback, limping and hobbling as I go![3]

In June, Herbert Spencer sent her an advance copy of *Principles of Ethics*, having previously sent her the proofs to vet against the susceptibilities of the public, and, after she had made a commentary for him, he now referred to her as his 'Grundyometer'. Spencer was immediately concerned that she might think that he had sent the book for her to review, but that was far from his mind and he wrote hastily to say the book was for her. She replied from Swanage, where she was staying in a hotel:

> No one who knows anything about you could imagine you doing anything whatever to secure a press notice, still less from one so imperfectly educated as I am. Quite equal to your transcendent mental powers is your moral *straightness*, that lofty independence which contents itself with doing good work and leaving it to fructify by its own vitality. No man could be less of a popularity-hunter than you are. No man could have a higher moral standard. That is one reason why I, among so many, love and reverence you so deeply. For, to my way of thinking, the grandeur of the moral nature, that part of the intellect which deals with man as man, is quite as valuable as even epoch-making thought....[4]

In the following year Eliza met the editor of the *St James's Budget*\* at Sidney Low's house, and agreed to contribute a series of weekly articles. Commenting on her and her work, Penderel-Brodhurst wrote that her articles were

> ... full of the old acuteness and incisiveness; full, too, of that tender kindliness, which shone through everything she wrote, when she was not pouring scorn and contempt upon the things and types she hated, and had taught so many others to hate. There is an idea that, in her later days, Mrs Linton had lost her fire and vigour. But it is the eternal *cliché* of the hasty or ill-informed critic, that practitioners of the art of writing must necessarily grow feeble as they grow old. It assuredly was not so in this case. Since the days of *The Girl of the Period* and *Patricia Kemball*, there had no doubt been time for her point of view and the singularly direct and unmistakable way in which she enforced it to grow familiar. Her work had necessarily lost novelty, but it had not lost vigour. She had established a convention of her own, which educated people admired to the end; but because it was a convention, the easily fatigued modern palate

---

\* An offshoot of the *St James's Gazette*.

was inclined to fancy that she always gave them the same dish. As a matter of fact, the essays she wrote for me – there must have been one hundred and fifty of them – were singularly varied in subject. As a contributor, Mrs Lynn Linton was a delight. Always two articles ahead, her MS. arrived with perfect regularity. Lacking at first sight somewhat of legibility, it was really much more easily read than some handwritings which are apparently clearer. . . .[5]

During 1893 Helen C. Black published a collection of interviews with most of the women writers then living which was called 'Notable Women Authors'. The first of the series was Mrs Lynn Linton, then seventy-one years old. She describes her as being

> . . . tall, upright, and stately in appearance, the keen but kindly bright blue eyes smiling through the gold-rimmed glasses which she always wears. She is clad in a suitable black dress, trimmed with jet, a white lace cap partially covers the thick grey hair, which escapes in a tiny natural curl or two on each side of the smooth, intellectual forehead. The eyebrows – far apart – are straight and level, but shaded off so delicately that they impart a look of benignity and softness to the aristocratic nose, while the curves of the well-cut lips indicate straightforwardness, sincerity of disposition, and power. Can it be possible that you had felt a momentary trepidation before meeting the gifted woman for whose genius you have entertained the greatest reverence? But Mrs Lynn Linton will have none of it! Her kind and friendly greeting puts you at ease at once. . . .[6]

In June 1894 Eliza heard again from Herbert Spencer. It is a long letter, which begins 'I am in the mood of mind of the weather-beaten old tar whose nephew proposes to teach him how to box the compass, and who is prompted to tweak his nose.' He goes on to attack Professor Drummond's then recently published book, *The Ascent of Man*. It seems that in Spencer's view he himself in various writings had already propounded the ideas which Drummond wrote of as his own and claimed as original. Not being able to say so himself Spencer

*Eliza Lynn Linton*

asked Eliza to review Drummond critically in the *Nineteenth Century*. He made very clear the lines along which he wanted Drummond's book to be criticised. As a result Eliza did review the work, virulently attacking Professor Drummond's Lowell Lectures, given at Boston in 1893, and published as *The Ascent of Man*,[7] in an article she sent to the *Fortnightly Review*[8] not the *Nineteenth Century*. But, if Eliza slated Professor Drummond, she equally strongly extolled Spencer:

> No philosopher of our days has insisted more on the importance of this same altruistic result of evolution and its relation to civilization than has Mr Herbert Spencer. In his *The Data of Ethics*, published fifteen years ago, the chapter on 'Altruism *versus* Egoism' sets forth the value and far-reaching results of this quality with that clearness of speech and accuracy of thought which leave no room for doubt or mistake.

On 25 June 1895 the short-lived Rosebery administration fell and Salisbury took office. Eliza's shifting political views and the change of government were recorded by her in an article entitled 'The Philistines' Cunning Triumph', in the *National Review* of September 1895.

# 18

## *In Haste and at Leisure*

*In Haste and at Leisure* was the last but one of Eliza's novels published during her lifetime (her last novel was published posthumously), and was a further attack upon what she called 'Wild Women', who, she explained, were those without 'morality or holiness'. In short, a species of pre-suffragette. Once again she pulled out all the stops to prove that women were far better employed in domestic affairs. Women in clubs, women speaking for Members of Parliament, women in public affairs, she considered made fools of themselves, in spite of the fact that she herself had reiterated time and again in her many novels that the Victorian matron was a stultified and foolish creature. So one is driven to conclude that Eliza was largely exploiting a journalistic line in which she had already achieved success and notoriety and which had paid handsomely. By now she had encountered many pretentious ladies who were enjoying the 'new' fashion of appearing on the public platform and posturing in clubs for women, and they now provided a new outlet for her pen.

*In Haste and at Leisure* is the story of a teenage elopement and marriage which went wrong. The young couple are separated by their parents and the boy sent off to South Africa, while the girl goes back to her mother and has an unwanted baby daughter. She has a yearning for a broader way of life, is drawn into a club and persuaded there to train as a professional speaker. When the husband returns from South Africa he gets a bleak welcome from his transformed wife. Of course he next falls in love with a 'home-loving' and 'pure-hearted' girl of the kind that Eliza would approve of herself, but the estranged wife soon comes on bad times and is forced to return to her husband, who no longer loves her but accepts her. *In Haste and at Leisure* was largely ignored by the press, although some journals, such as the *Queen* (23 March 1895), to which Eliza was a regular contributor, reviewed it favourably:

> *In Haste and at Leisure* is one of the most important contributions to the New Woman question, both because it comes from one who has always given deep attention to the question of how we are going to bring up our daughters and because Mrs Lynn Linton has always looked the advanced woman fairly and squarely in the face, and has not attempted to shirk the issues. . . .

On the other hand, the *Athenaeum* commented a week later: '. . . the zeal of her purpose has eaten up the artistic and literary efforts of Mrs Lynn Linton's latest story, which cannot be deplored when some of its predecessors are recalled.'

Nevertheless, from a technical aspect, this novel ranks higher than many of its predecessors, for her characters are less exaggerated and the situation created does propound her sentiments. Her continued attacks on the modern woman brought her enemies, and some of them were bitter. Thus a Miss Elma Stuart of Wokingham wrote to her friend Mrs Evans on 11 September 1895:

> Many people – friends and the outside public – have appealed to me to answer that most despicable travesty of a woman, calling itself Mrs Lynn Linton – I have always made reply – that neither pen nor boots will be used by me for the reason that I like to keep both clean. Of course this animal *deserves* kicking, but who is to do it? I like clean feet – and *I* won't. . . . My contention is this – her articles will in a short time die – as all foul things die – and be forgotten. . . . Mrs L.L. is an odious pit – leave her in the mire – a diamond rolled over and over and over in it, can't be hurt.

Such violent views were not held by those who recorded meeting her; they nearly all delighted in her company. J. Comyns Carr (1849–1916), critic and playwright, first met Eliza at the height of her notoriety, when she had just pub-

*'In Haste and at Leisure'*

lished her 'The Girl of the Period' essays in the *Saturday Review*. 'Afterwards', he wrote, 'I got to know her well, and learnt to discover in her earnest, enthusiastic nature, qualities that struck much deeper than the superficial satire which she had exercised in this series of papers exploiting the foibles of her sex.'[1]

Mrs Aria met Eliza at Queen Anne's Mansions, and she writes:

> How vividly she comes back to me with her large piercing blue eyes behind highly polished glasses and her grey hair surmounted by a cap with a lace bow . . .
> On that evening when she patted my shoulder and asked where I lived and expressed approval of my articles, I was tongue-tied and awkward, though not blind to her splendid bearing, to her well-made black satin dress with its white satin waistcoat overlaid with black lace and jet, or to her beringed hands and the note of authority in her voice. By me she was respected as headmistress of my craft, and whilst I listened to her she told – how strange it seems now to record it! – that she was the first woman to obtain a fixed salary on a daily newspaper. . . .
> One afternoon I was as gladly and badly as usual writing at my table in my exalted flat in Maida Vale when I found Mrs Linton at my elbow bonneted, cloaked and beaming with benevolence. 'You are surprised to see me, but I have been thinking of you so much, and I hear that your husband is in South Africa; my dear,' she concluded impressively, 'don't make his return impossible; you are young, you are attractive, and you are in the thick of it, be sure you take to yourself no man friend, and be sure that you,' she repeated it, 'do not make it impossible for your husband to come back to you.'
> I reassured the dear old lady that my mother was living with me, that no stricter duenna could be imagined, and that I was really quite safe by myself. . . .
> She stayed with me only a very few moments, but begged me to go and see her on Saturdays, when I knew she held a court of great contemporaries and smiled upon all young seekers after fame. Many years later I did hazard a proposition to interview her, and I felt so guilty of my tactlessness

201

when she wrote to me from Malvern where she had gone to rest from her strenuous town labours.

'What have I ever done to you in this life or a former that you should want to open the door of a mental torture chamber?' . . . I gave her a mile of my repentance at having dared to disturb her badly wanted peace.[2]

Edward Clodd (1840–1930), the anthropologist, wrote of her:

A warmer-hearted, braver, more chivalrous, and candour must add, less discreet woman never lived. She loved and hated 'not at all or all in all', and in those unsubdued emotions lay the cause of misconceptions about her, begotten among those who knew her only as a writer saying in plain English what she meant. By such persons this dear woman, who was more heart than head when pouring out what grieved her soul; this dear woman who looked, what she was, all tenderness, winning you by the softness of her voice and the sweetness of her smile, was denounced as a virago and a scold. True champion of freer life for her sex, she brought on herself torrents of misrepresentation and abuse by her articles. . . .[3]

# 19
# Malvern

On 1 January 1896 Eliza had gone to live at Brougham House, Malvern. She wrote to the Hon. Mrs Nash:

> I have taken a pretty little house, which I have furnished and made home, and here I am with my books, two servants, a garden, a greenhouse, a vine, a table for the birds, domestic worries of coal and oil that go as if they were snow that melts or water that runs away, and good health in this lovely air and perfect quiet. . . .[1]

The year also began with her being elected a member of the Society of Authors; soon afterwards she received the honour of being the first woman to be asked to serve on its committee.

As to her work, she was as busy as ever, though her best was passed. She wrote an article on sex relationships in the January *Woman at Home*, called 'The Propaganda of Platonism', in which she made clear her firm opinion that a platonic relationship between men and women was impossible, despite the fact that time and again in her novels she had made reference to instances when either sex 'longed' for a 'brother and sister' relationship. In another essay, 'The Tyrannies of Private Life',[2] she voiced the opinion that there were impossible ties preventing freedom, absolute freedom being more a man's prerogative than a woman's. A further matter she touched upon concerned the position of the professional 'anonymous' writer, the recognition of whose work would be scant. She expressed this in a long letter written from Malvern to Sidney Low:

203

*Eliza Lynn Linton*

> Mrs Lynn Linton sends her love, respect, and admiration to the writer of the leaders in the *St James's Gazette*, who is, she imagines, a certain person called Sidney Low. She does not want that writer to feel that she is patting him on the back . . . she just wants to clasp his hand across space for his manly, wise, and far-seeing articles, which express all the very best traditions and sentiments of Englishmen. . . .[3]

*Dulcie Everton*, the last of Eliza's novels to be published during her lifetime, was one of her weakest. A short novel, issued in two volumes, it had been written some four years previous to publication. A melodramatic story, it concerns a girl

> good-tempered and unselfish, contented with home and not longing for change; with a conscience kept scrupulously bright, yet not morbidly introspective nor afraid of spiritual shadows; knowing little of the sorrows of life and less of its perplexities and sins; not dabbling in filth on the pretence of searching for an impossible purity; not a propagandist of any half-crazy faith whatsoever; neither the travesty of a young man in dress, nor his panting imitator in pursuits; neither a 'Soul' nor a 'good fellow' – neither 'fast' nor 'earnest' – Dulcie Everton was as unlike any of those modern types as her home was unlike a modern home and her upbringing had been different from the loose-handed system in present vogue.

Dulcie marries the cast-off lover of a girl who is her complete antithesis, who eventually comes to suicide when she finds that her new lover is no gentleman. When Dulcie discovers that her husband has had an earlier affair with the now dead girl, she is deeply shocked but forgives him.

*Dulcie Everton* was ignored by the press, and Eliza herself was not surprised, for she thought little of it.

The last letter Eliza wrote in 1896 was to her sister Lucy:

> I have had the feeling you speak of, Loo, with Ernest,* as if the beloved was there in the room. The mind creates its own world, and imagination is as powerful a fact as reality

---

\* Lucy Gedge's son.

of sense. We see and know and feel and are, by the brain alone, acted on by the sense organs through the nerves. If you act on the brain independently of the sense organs, you bring about the same result, but weaker, as dreams are not so vivid as realities, and waking dreams do not satisfy like the touch and sight and moving – still the brain works and this (weaker) result is produced, and you felt the presence of the son you love so fondly though you could not see him. 'This earth is full of messages that Love sends to and fro', and we know very little yet of the possibilities of spiritual communication.

Who knows? He might have been thinking of you very intently then, for he loves you *dearly*, and you might have met in the spirit if not in the body. No one knows, Loo, what life really is – what are its possibilities. We know a little but not all! . . . One must have one of two things to get on in this life – buoyant cheerfulness that cannot be 'submerged', and that always rises to the surface like a cork, or grim and dogged determination *not* to be conquered.[4]

In August 1897 she heard from her old friend Lady Paget, who herself recorded in *In My Tower*,[5] 'She [Eliza] had always shown me real friendship and when I heard that she was settled in Malvern, close to Hewell, I wrote to ask her advice about some literary business.' Eliza replied:

It was a pleasure of pleasures to receive your letter. What a flood of memories it let loose! Your ball! Ouida, and the Storys' evening when the Marchese della Stufa was there, poor Mr Cook, the Earls, your sweet daughter and your dear good husband, yourself, your house, young Tzikow and his attempt to swindle me, my own rapturous enthusiasm for Italy! and now! The contrast with my quiet life in this little cottage, growing old in peace and silence and with some not too poignant regret for all the vigour and vitality of the dead past! No, I never go to Rome or Sicily or lovely Florence now. In all probability I shall never cross the silver strip again, for I have lost my strength and health and have to fight off death in the shape of 'lung trouble', as the Americans say, having had two hand-to-hand struggles with the, in the end, inevitable Conqueror. . . .

Lady Paget then wrote to ask Eliza to come and visit them at Hewell, to which she replied:

Ten thousand thanks for your kind letter and invitation. If the fates are kind and the sky is clear I shall be delighted to go over and see you and Lady Windsor. It will be a joy, and joys are precious. I fear I am too old for the air treatment. It would be kill or cure, but the 'kill' would win the day. I have had one attack of double pneumonia, which very nearly killed me; I was dying for some little time, and then I had an attack of single pneumonia, one long suffering, and I have had two 'influenzas', and bronchitis is my constant companion, more or less pronounced. I am seventy-five years old now, and take the ailments as they come as the tribute to be paid to Time, before Time passes into Death. . . .

I know that the dear mind has turned to Hygiene and 'Therapeutics', as well as that beloved Art, but the converts must have some elasticity of body left to them. Radical changes are impossible for old people, and for one thing the night air is simply illness – I will not say death and destruction – but illness and distress untold to me. Your open-air beds, dearest lady, would be the gateway to the grave. . . .

Lady Paget says, 'It was her [Eliza's] straightness which always attracted me to her. She despised shams and hated falseness.' Despite a further letter from Lady Paget, Eliza had to decline visiting her, for her health would not permit it.

Earlier in the year Eliza heard from the editor of the *St James's Gazette* that he would prefer a fortnightly article from her instead of a weekly contribution, but that they would continue to pay her the same. But she would accept from him 'no charity'. On another occasion when she was corresponding with Mr Chambers, editor of *Chambers' Journal*, she said, '. . . no money until it is fairly earned. I might die one day in your debt and then my poor ghost would have to take to wandering and gibbering, perhaps to knocking its empty head against tables, and beseeching incredulous executors to pay you back.'[6]

She was still furiously busy and one of her major essays was a contribution to *Women Novelists of Queen Victoria's Reign*.[7] She wrote to Lucy about this on 17 January 1897:

> I have had a letter from Hurst & Blackett asking me to contribute to a Queen's Jubilee kind of volume they are going to bring out, of reviews of dead authoresses by the living. They have given me my choice, of all the chief; but I have set aside George Eliot and Charlotte Brontë, Mrs Craik (Dinah Mulock) and Harriet Martineau, and if I do any at all, have chosen Mrs Gaskell. Not that I *know* anything of her and I have not read her books since I was a young woman, but my impression of her is sweet. She was such an unaffected woman – to my memory, at least. I saw her once, and she seemed to me such a dear, and not as affected as either George Eliot or Mrs Craik. I should have to read all her books again if I did her. . . . I always feel I owe a debt of gratitude to Mrs Gaskell, for, when I was quite young and was being acrimoniously discussed at Harriet Martineau's, she upped and defended me, though she knew nothing of me. So, if I *do* her, she cast her bread upon the waters then, and will find it to her memory after long years. I never forget a kindness – nor an injury – Lucy, and if I am tenaciously grateful, I am also tenaciously resentful.

But Mrs Gaskell had already been bespoke by Edna Lyall. Eliza's contribution – a detailed appreciation of George Eliot's works.

She also began work on what was to be her last novel, *The Second Youth of Theodora Desanges*, which was published posthumously by Hutchinson in 1900. It is undoubtedly autobiographical: Eliza wistfully reminisces, seeing herself when she was young in the role of the heroine – a womanly woman. She had had a beautiful figure, and doubtless in looking back she wished she had had an ardent admirer. Her heroine was just such a woman but a firm opponent of women's emancipation who dominated her admirer and forced him to vote against women's suffrage. But she became, despite her beauty and her chances, a bitterly disillusioned woman. She was re-

*Eliza Lynn Linton*

buffed by her adopted daughter, and when she met her first lover again she found him unattractive, miserable and henpecked. Thwarted throughout her life, she is a tragic heroine who welcomes death. This was a bitter and sad book.

Regardless of the deterioration of her sight, the last months of Eliza's life were still tremendously active. Layard tells us she wrote, during 1897, no fewer than 2,124 letters. Moreover, she was far from being neglected by friends and acquaintances; they were continually asking her to functions and begging her to come to London. But she knew how frail she had become and how easily she was subject to pneumonia and its complications. When Mrs Kelly had asked her to visit London to hear Nansen lecture, she replied:

> I should like to go to the Nansen lecture immensely, and I should love to go and stay with you. The spirit is willing all through – but the poor old flesh? Am I fit to go and stay with any one in the winter? I want so much warmth! – a fire to go to bed by, and a fire to get up by, and a hot bath in the morning – not a decent, cool, tepid fellow, but water as hot as can be borne without inconvenience – and is not all this a nuisance beyond words to any mistress? – not to speak of servants!
>
> I scarcely know what to say. I shall have to write to the Society to-day, yes or no, and of course to you I must say yes or no before I finish the letter. I wish it had been later! What a worry indecision is, darling! That shuttlecock of the mind, 'back and forth', is far worse than doing the most painful thing possible. To hesitate over a pleasure – shall I? shall I not? – is in itself a pain. . . . Still – still – the temptation is too great! Selfish or not, 'here goes!' – Yes, darling, on the 8th I will go up, and I will go up by a train that will get me into London by daylight.[8]

In June Herbert Spencer wrote:

> Let me suggest to you a work which might fitly be the crowning work of your life – a work on *Good and Bad Women*. You have rather obtained for yourself the reputation of

holding a brief for Men *versus* Women, whereas I rather think the fact is that you simply aim to check that over-exaltation of women which has long been dominant, and which is receiving an *éclatante* illustration in a recent essay by Mrs J. R. Green, which is commented upon in this week's *Spectator*. The flattering of women has been, one might almost say, a chief business of poets, and women have most of them very readily accepted the incense with little qualification; and this has been so perpetual and has been so habitually accepted by men, as to have caused a perverted opinion.

I think you might, at the same time that you duly dealt with that side of the question, which you have done frequently, deal with the other side by emphasising the goodness of women in many illustrations and in many cases, and you would thus re-habilitate yourself in the matter at the same time that you would be doing an extremely serviceable thing.

The natures of men and women are topics of continual discussion, but entirely of random discussion, with no analysis and no collection of evidence and balancing of results.

If you entertain my proposal, I should like very well by and by to make some suggestions as to modes of inquiry and modes of comparison.[9]

Her reply to this suggestion is not to be found, but she was undoubtedly too old to embark on it.

Eliza had boiled over with indignation at Lady Burton's egregious 'Life' of her husband, and welcomed the prospect of *The True Life of Captain Sir R. F. Burton*, upon which Miss G. M. Stisted was now engaged.[10] Eliza wrote to her:

> ... I am very glad indeed to hear that there is to be a truthful and rational life of dear Sir Richard Burton. I have always resented Lady Burton's false and affected endeavour to claim for her husband the profession of a faith which, if he did hold, proved him the falsest and most cowardly of men. She and I crossed swords on that point, and I said to her roundly that Sir Richard belonged to the world, not only to her, and that she had degraded his memory by her

assumptions of this and that principle we all know he did not hold. I said, and have ever said, a man must stand or fall by his own life, and that the greatest indignity that can be done to his memory is to interfere with the integrity of his principles expressed and acknowledged during his lifetime. It was only her intense vanity that made Lady Burton take the attitude she did. Had she really loved and respected her husband as she professed, she would have been content to *leave him to himself*, and not have placed herself on the throne of the superior and on the seat of the judge. She would have somehow reconciled it to herself that he was an 'infidel' yet 'saved'. Love has no better toga than this of divine partiality. 'God will save him (or her) for his goodness, for all his want of faith.' So Lady Burton would have said, and would have carried out to the letter every wish of her dead husband, and would have respected his integrity.[11]

Also among Eliza's friends was the then successful novelist, Jean Middlemas, who had written her most popular novel, *Dandy*, in 1881. Like Eliza, she was a tall, handsome woman, and short-sighted. Politically, however, she was a strong Conservative. Eliza wrote to her on 27 December 1897:

I do not think any one realises more vividly than I the contraction of time – the gradual lessening to nothingness of that *peau de chagrin* in which is inscribed our term of life – but without dread, without repining – with a *little* regret that the day has to come when I shall not see the sky and the clouds and the fields and the flowers, and shall not hear the song of birds or the voice of friends. Still it is the charter on which we have held our life and enjoyed our days! I find old age has infinite compensations. If we have lost the grand activities and glorious personal possessions of youth, we have lost its disturbing passions and turbulent unrest. We have peace, and we can give so much happiness to others! I feel like a cornucopia, whence I can pour out small good gifts to the poor, and the greater gifts of sympathy, wise advice, and affection for my friends. I feel a kind of pride in saying to myself, 'No one shall be made unhappy by me. All shall be made happier for the brief moment of contact. All shall

*Malvern*

feel the warmth of human love and sympathy, and the ice of selfishness shall never form round my heart.'[12]

On the same day she wrote to her sister:

I was thinking last night when I went to bed what a lot of pleasure is still left to us old people! When we are tired and sleepy to go up to that warm, comfortable bedroom and warm, comfortable bed and sleep – what a pleasure it is! and then to wake up in the morning and be ALIVE – to see the sky and the hill and the laurels and the road and the trees, and to be still ONE with this divine nature, and to have yet on one's plate some of the *banquet de la vie* we have enjoyed so long – what a joy that is – and then to do good and kindly to one's fellows – to make one's servants and surroundings happy by one's geniality and consideration, to help the cheerfulness of one's companions by one's own, mellowed as it is by the consciousness of the smallness of little worries and the nearness of the great things – all this is the joy of old age, Lucy – to taste with lingering love the few drops left us, and to do good and kindly by our fellows, and to be sweet-tempered and genial and cheerful for their sakes. *I* have lost much. In early youth and maturity my great joy was in long walks, in the putting out of my strength, and in seeing new places. Later, when that physical strength left me, I was a social personage. If I went into a public place, I heard people whisper my name and stare; and if I went into private society, I was always the main centre of the company – always – and now I am here quite alone, without being able to go even on the Wyche Road on my feet . . . And I am as happy as possible. . . .[13]

There is one remarkable letter, written probably in December 1897, to a friend, showing Eliza to be hardly the anti-religious person many thought her:

. . . At the risk of boring, perhaps of vexing you, I must write out my thoughts on this late craze of yours, for it is nothing else, against your children's religious life. You are doing what I should not have moral strength to do – taking on yourself the responsibility of those young souls, and destroying one of the strongest incentives that man has to be virtuous and to abstain from vice. *I* would as soon tell ―― the whole mysteries of life and vice and maternity, etc., and fling her into the society of fast women. Also with the boys. Yet I am not a moral coward, as I think my life has proved. But the responsibility one accepts for one's own soul I certainly would not dare to accept for the souls of others – my own children above all. You talk of reason being our guide – reason of what period? of what school? Have we in the nineteenth century the fee simple of Truth any more than any other age has had? What do we know of the grand mystery of life and death and pain, and the why and wherefore of things – of the whence and whither? Can reason tell us any more than an (even so-called) revelation? Reason is silent. Reason leads us to absolute agnosticism; but do you want your children to be without a guide to good living? without a God in the world? What reason have they got? When the time of youthful passions comes for your boys, will reason keep them out of the haunts of evil, or may you not hope something from the belief of the purity demanded by God for acceptance, and taught by Christ as the model for humanity? Why throw open the doors to them to every kind of sinful excess by taking from them all the restraints of religion? and why stultify yourself as you will do? You had them baptized – you have had ―― confirmed – you take them to church – and now, suddenly, because you have heard a man of whom you know nothing, whose apparent record is *bad*, but of whom you choose to assume all holiness and purity of motive and faithfulness to truth, you are inclined to make your children all 'rationalists' – to destroy the only real authority you have over them, and to open to them the way to corruption of morals and undutifulness of life. You have not thought out the matter. You have neither studied nor been instructed. You have given yourself *tête baissée* to this man, and are now going to inflict the very worst injury you *can* on your children for the craze you have suddenly taken against religion. All this is not the sign of a well-balanced mind, as little as your restlessness about ――, and your fidgeting about her companions, her *pleasure* – and she still under instruction! – and her future. All ——'s bodily restlessness is repeating itself in your mental instability. You can let nothing go on quietly – your house – your children – your life – all must be in a perpetual state of change, and of placid contentment you do not seem to me to have a trace. I don't think I have ever known so restless a mind as yours, one always so seeking for change of condition. But nothing is of the same importance as this new departure of yours – so superficially come at! of desire to destroy your children's faith in Christianity, when you have nothing better to give them. Far rather than that you should do this, cultivate your vicar, and let *him* talk to the children. If your own sense of truth is so strong that you cannot conceal your denial for the sake of their supreme good, get someone who has no doubts to strengthen that which to young people is their only safeguard. To the young and ignorant some kind of positive faith is an *absolute necessity*, and the best philosophers who have thought out the matter with long and anxious care, will say the same thing. You call me 'mad' and all sorts of injurious things, because I recognize this and do all that I can to strengthen the faith – and with the faith – the practising my ignorant servants in the Christian religion – concealing from them my own unbelief as a thing with which they have nothing to do – a thing which concerns my own self only. As a member of the community I feel bound to support so far openly the Established Church. All my intelligent friends here know the real truth, and some of them are in exactly the same state as myself – unbelievers in the *mythology*, but conformists outwardly for the sake of the weaker brethren – and those who have children for the sake of the children. I remember hearing ——, brought up an atheist, say it was the most cruel thing that could be done to a child to bring him up without a definite religion. Give him the chance of a choice, and when he is old enough to reason and judge, *then* let him do so.[14]

On the last day of the year she again wrote to her sister Lucy. She knew the end of her life was approaching, but she was no coward about death:

## Eliza Lynn Linton

... It is a comfort that we have held together so strongly and closely, and that we are still of the old family and with the old family memories to look back to in concert. I am glad you like *Julia*. I have read it, for Mr Stead sent me two copies, one for myself and one to give away. It does not matter what *I* think of it. I knew it would comfort and soothe you. But I do not think it well or wise, sweet Loot [sic], to dwell on that which we can never know till we experience. Nor can we in the present state, with all the limitation of our senses and bodily experience, rightly conceive what the future will be. It is all unprofitable speculation; and the vague undesignated hope and trust that it will be all well – and so leave it – is better. While we live, our duty is plain and clear – to live for others and to be thoughtful of others, considerate to them in all ways, and unselfish in our endeavour to make them happy. No one can realise the nearness of death more vividly than I do – and for that very cause I *live* every hour of the day that I can. I should think a day terribly lost where I had not done something kind, or said or written, or in some way felt, that I had cast a ray of sunshine, however pale and weak, over some one's life. It is a joy to me to see how intensely happy my servants are, and how happy even the kitten is! Now no one who comes in contact with me leaves me without a smile and a glow of pleasure somehow created. This I take as my duty, and I fulfil it, no matter what I am suffering in my own person. For I am never out of pain. I never know a moment's cessation from pain. ...

20

# The last year

The end of 1897 brought to Eliza the news, by telegraph, of her husband's death in America on 29 December. Eliza was to survive him by seven months.

Writing to Lady Wardle, she says:

> I do not know if you have seen in the paper the announcement of poor dear Mr Linton's death. He was eighty-five, and quite worn out. Life had no more to give him now but pain and sorrow, and existence had become a burden. It is best so. He is at peace and rest, and anyhow he is better off than when he was groaning in that weariness which is *worse* than pain! He either knows no more of suffering or of joy – or he is free from the one and is full in the sunshine of the other!

It is fitting that from this last year of her life are some remarkable letters which show her as a skilled devotee of epistolary art. Many were to her sister Lucy, like this one, written on 3 January 1898.

> We follow the law of our physical being so closely, and when we are well things all look bright, and when we are not well they look dark. But also we have a *certain* amount of free will and a *certain* amount of power over ourselves, and as we resolutely set ourselves to *be* and to *think* and to live, so we can, up to a certain point. Hopelessness has always been your cross. . . . Only remember, dear, that life is exactly as it was when we were children. It is *we* who have changed, not humanity. That remains constant with a different dress, but the thing underneath is the same. The want of respect and

215

discipline among the children is unpleasant to us who were brought up under a different régime – but it is perhaps better than the deceit and slyness and suppressed lives and crushed individuality of the older, sterner rule.

All things have *two* sides, and hopeless ruin does not stare us in the face yet. As I told you, sweetheart, I find my happiness in activities of small kindnesses. I cannot do big things for any one, but I do all sorts of little things, and the first thought I have is, what can I do to help so and so? What can I say? What can I give? Life to me is life and has to be lived, and the preparation for the hereafter is the now. When we grow old the *imperiousness* of passion and our own individuality burns low and sinks, and then the others are the first consideration. To live in others and for others – to be eager to utilize the fast-fleeting time for all good that may come in our way – to feel that 'he prayeth best who loveth best' – that to me is the one great law and rule of life. Social and even literary ambitions have fallen from me – but not the love of my kind – not the desire to help, to solace, to brighten the lives of others. In doing so one finds one's own happiness – and all that one *can* have, with one's weakened energies and absolutely nil future for good fortune. Prince Charming, who used to live round the corner, is dead and buried – there are no fortunes to be made and no legacies to come. The past and present have determined the future for ourselves, save in the possibility of sorrow; but love remains – love of our own – love of one's kind, love of nature and beauty and art and goodness – and *only* when love dies, then does the meaning of life die too![1]

As a postscript to a letter to Lucy the next day, she added: 'I hate women as a race, Lucy. I think we are demons. Individually we are all right, but as a race we are monkeyish, cruel, irresponsible, superficial.'

When Layard was collecting his material for his biography of Eliza, he received from her friend, John Stafford, the following assessment of her:

> It was not so much against individuals that her lance was levelled, as against the literary, artistic, and moral iniquities

*The last year*

she conceived they represented. The very name of one of these arch-offenders would act as a sudden squall on a placid lake: it seemed in other words, to hit her like a violent blow. The hot blood would rush to her face; her dilated eyes would blaze through her glasses; her hands (she had beautiful hands) would clench to veritable fists; and for some moments she would sit trembling and speechless. After that one's ears buzzed. At times it was terrible; but it was quickly over, and as often as not the storm would find its end in one of her charming little laughs, and she would turn, not without a *soupçon* of shame in her comely face, to another subject. No living men, I hope, ever dared to continue the previous one.[2]

Eliza had never liked the French as a nation, and as a republican she had hated Louis Napoleon. The Dreyfus case had sparked off this hatred anew: 'Of all the nations now living on the face of the earth, the French are the most contemptible – the most detestable, vain, hysterical, emotional, unreasonable, and always posing – entirely without spontaneity or self-forgetfulness.'[3]

A further letter to Lucy gives Eliza's opinion on a variety of subjects:

The weather is certainly freezing. . . . Cold or warm, damp or dry, it hurts us in this best of all possible worlds! this in reality *loveliest* of all worlds! – Everything hurts us – the weather and the elements – wild beasts, insects, hidden causes of disease, drought, deluge – we are the mere footballs of matter, and we can make only our good out of it – the necessity of endeavour – endeavour being supposed to be a finer thing than enjoyment – the fight with unfriendly conditions, a nobler exercise of power than the more placid and contented use of surplus energies. But we are here, Lucy, and *have* to make the best of it. . . . We are making such wonderful discoveries in the whole region of physiology as well as in other things that we can place no limits. We have already such apparent miracles among us – the Röntgen rays, the new telegraphy, the photography of unseen stars, the limitation of the universe (unthinkable, but still seeming to be a fact), that we cannot say, No farther. We shall find out more and more as time goes on, and, as I believe will be, we get deeper convolutions of the brain, more of them, and more grey matter to work with.

I grant the absolute need of religion as a system visible and imperative, and I acknowledge the existence of the spiritual life, but I think the forms we give the unseen divine are the necessities of our own human nature, which cannot jump off its own shadow nor travel beyond its own experience. But I think that conscience is the sense of duty and of right and wrong – apart from the conventional forms which obtain according to race, faith, time, and even latitude and longitude. I think that this is part of the scheme of human life, just as an advanced taste in art or dressing or manners. *Morals are integral to society*, and are part of the condition of humanity. . . . We should have them whether or not after a certain period of civilization, and so, Loo, I stand and *wait*. Death will soon solve the mystery one way or the other. Meanwhile, in all the multiplying of faiths I cannot see which is the Absolute. Here is the R.C. who will not let his 'penitent' join in the family worship of a Protestant – here is the Protestant who will not use the symbols or join in the worship of an R.C. – a Churchman who will not dance with the Salvationist – a Plymouth Brother who thinks all the world save a very small remnant is to be damned – a Mohammedan who does the same by all but the Faithful – a Thug who worships his black goddess Kali by murder – a Zoroaster who prays to the sun – and so on, and so on; and then above us all is the Great Incommunicable First Cause to whom one is as dear a child as the other – who never made an elder branch . . . and never gave the Christian a charter of greater blessedness than the heathen. We are all, all, all His children, and He does not speak to us apart, but to us all in our own language, equally according to our age, that is our knowledge and our civilization.

To Him I live, and in Him I believe – but all the rest is dark.[4]

Eliza still kept up a political correspondence with her friend William Woodall:

*The last year*

... Would going down on my knees prevail on you and your wicked comrades not to hamper the Government at this critical time, and not to preach the doctrine of Scuttle and Knuckle Under? Oh, let us have the war and be done with it! Lop off one at least of the arms of the Russian Octopus;* strike back at that insolent stout-boy Germany;† spurn, as she deserves, France, the most contemptible nation of ancient or modern times. Be once more Englishmen whom nations feared to affront, when they were united, and before this cursed system of governing by party had killed all patriotism on both sides alike. . . .

We have to go through the phase in which we are at present. We shall come to manhood suffrage and womanhood as well. We shall have mob rule heightened by the hysteria of the feminine element, and then – the saviour of society will appear with his 'mailed fist', and we shall swing back to despotism and oppression.

Human nature is a constant quantity, my dear W.W., M.P.! You nineteenth century men and women have not got a new charter, nor are you exempt from the logic of consequences. What has been will be again, and – 'the mirror of the prophet hangs behind him.'[5]

In replying to this letter, Woodall asked Eliza to say what Lord Salisbury and his colleagues had done in their conduct of foreign affairs, and especially in safeguarding British interests, to entitle them to the exceptional confidence and abstention from criticism she demanded for them. A few days later came the rejoinder:

I am broken-hearted! *Delenda est Carthage!* Ichabod! Ichabod! Who is to be trusted with the honour of England? no one! This cursed spirit of party government has killed all independent patriotism. The 'party' comes before the country, and a man is a Tory or a Liberal before he is an Englishman.

* Lord Salisbury had in January submitted to Tsar Nicholas I a settlement for the partition of Turkey; meantime Russia had seized Port Arthur. The prime minister protested.

† Admiral von Tirpitz had recently become Minister of Marine and announced that the German Navy would become the most powerful in the world and would dispute English naval supremacy.

*Eliza Lynn Linton*

It is not so close a system as the papacy, but it has the same essential defect. Depose Lord Salisbury, and where to find a stronger man on either side? Lord Rosebery? Sir William?* Chamberlain† might do. He is not afraid of responsibility as those others are, and I do not think would be afraid of war as every one else is. I know the next war will be the battle of Armageddon, and I know that we are not sure of how our new ships will behave; still, to recede as we do, step by step, inch by inch, to submit to the insults of Germany and America, and to the crafty encroachments of Russia – surely this is far worse than one supreme trial – a death struggle if you will – for the old supremacy under new conditions! We are all so afraid of death! What does it signify if we die to-day or to-morrow – if the individual goes for the sake of the nation? The *things* of life are before and beyond the individual, and national honour is of more value than a battalion of even our finest and most lovely men. Woman as I am, old and timid, I would give my life in torture to save the honour and majesty and dominion of England! Oh for some strong statesman! Some one with the wide vision of a Caesar and the resolution of a Napoleon! Turn where we will, we have no one. Your party is riddled through and through with unworkable fads and unpatriotic formulae – the Conservatives are wooden sticks painted to look like iron – the curse of weakness masked as humanitarianism is upon us, and the folly of an impracticable morality has eaten into our statesmanship. . . .

Four days later, Eliza was again writing to Lucy:

I *have* read *Tennyson's Life*, Lucy, and I told you so, and recommend it to you. It is a very sweet picture of a very lovely life, but of course it is imperfect because of what it *does not* say. No man's character is so entirely without shade, without even the hint of minor faults. A son could scarcely have chronicled the defects – but the result is like Queen

---

* Sir William Harcourt (1827–1904), who, when Gladstone resigned in 1894, was expected to be nominated prime minister. The Queen chose Rosebery. Harcourt was hated by his colleagues in the Cabinet for his overbearing conduct.
† Chamberlain was then much in the news. He was the prime mover, along with the Duke of Devonshire, in the endeavour to break down our isolated position.

*The last year*

Elizabeth's face, when she refused to let the painter put a shadow on her nose. The whole is a lovely, lovely outline – lovely – and is as good as a sermon. I do not agree with your dislike of biographies, Loo. I love them, and history too. We do not read half enough history. If we read more we should have a truer sense of the continuity of human life, and how time never causes the break of power, nature, and habits which it has pleased people to imagine. Man has been always man, as he is now, with improved mental and mechanical powers, improved morals and social instincts in excess of egotistical desires, and improved *international* ideas of common rights, so that one strong nature has no right to swallow up a weaker for the mere lust of conquest, as in the old days before international law established itself as the police of correction; but beyond all this man is man as he was in the days of Pericles and Julius Caesar, of Xerxes and Scipio.[6]

On 6 February she again refers to Tennyson, evidently in answer to something her sister has remarked about the portraits:

... I do not think Tennyson's face is discontented, Loo, so much as thoughtful. A thoughtful face is never a jocund one. It is always grave and sad. He was a striver after better work and still better, but though deeply thoughtful and keenly alive to the moral and mental difficulties of life, he had made the whole thing so far clear to himself that he could say, All is for the best. Well for those who can double down the blood-red edges and say this, Lucy! who can with one breath say benevolence and love and fatherhood, with the next recount the massacres and horrors of the past, the cruelty of nature all through, and recognize the dominion of pain and sorrow, suffering and death. I prefer the riddle unsolved and insoluble, but I could not say, All is for the best. I can only say the mystery of life, as we have it, is a mystery I, for one, cannot solve nor explain away into the rule of mercy and love.[7]

Eliza was reading as voraciously as ever. Layard was helpful

*Eliza Lynn Linton*

to her in providing her with the books she desired. It was hardly 'light reading', nor cursory, for she was annotating many of the works, such as Polybius's *History of the Roman War with Carthage and Sicily*, Procopius's *Secret History of the Time of Justinian and Theodora*, Gregorovius's *History of Rome in the Middle Ages*, and Romanes's *Animal Intelligence*. She was an extraordinarily rapid reader, and, like Lord Macaulay, seemed to grasp the meaning of a page without differentiating the words.[8]

Layard then sent her *The Ballad of Reading Gaol*, just published anonymously, and had suggested to her the author was Oscar Wilde. Having read it, she immediately wrote to Layard:

> It does not read like Oscar Wilde in method – only one word, 'wine-red', seems to point at him. The diction is simpler and less sensuous – more direct and more manly – than his in general, though of course the subject is as perverted as ever. It is all pity for the man who murdered the 'thing he loved' – who took from her love of the sunlight and the glory of the free breath of heaven – all excuse for crime, and pity for the criminal, but none for the victim – like Pater's moan over 'those two poor young boys' whose brief lives had been chronicles of crime, but for the respectable man – husband, father, master, citizen, and they so cruelly murdered, let them go! It *may* be Oscar's – but I do not recognize the affected, artificial, Assyrian-monarch kind of touch he used to affect.[9]

A letter to her sister shows her vigour and her passion for tidiness hardly deflated. She possessed also all her mental faculties to the end:

> I was out in the front garden and on the roadway, Lucy, at 8.30. Our new neighbours opposite had the dustcart early. . . . So the wind was blowing, and it blew off some of the papers, and the Betsey Trotwood woke up in me like a lion on the prowl, and I busked and bounced, and I went downstairs like a flash, and out of the garden stalks I and on to the road and up to the cart, and I says, 'My men, you'll be

*The last year*

very careful, won't you, of all the paper and mess, and pick it all up and sweep the roadway clear?' So they says, says they, 'Yes, m'm; there's a lot of this here mess, and we have to come with another cart.' All the neighbours . . . are so much obliged to me for my Betsey Trotwoodism – for I look after the bits of paper like a tiger![10]

Layard now sent her Burke's *Vicissitudes of Families*, and she replied:

> Thank you for the Burke; I have read the first volume, but I have sundry extracts to make which will take another day. Then will come the second, out of which I shall probably have to extract more marrow – like Rabelais's dog – and then you will have them back. Some of the men who ruined themselves by their brutal extravagance were surely mad – Jack Mytton one of them! The Irish, too, have only themselves to thank for their ruin – that Wm. Wray who made the road over the mountain and horsed his friend's carriage with his own bullocks – and those two dear girls, the laundresses! They were angels. I am always glad when women come out nobly as women, in a womanly way. Then I bend my knee and kiss their hands and gladly own their sweet supremacy. But the New Hussies! No, George – not for this Joseph! Here are two toads celebrated in to-day's paper as having cycled in knickerbockers to the polling booth, to be jeered at by the rabble – and then there is the case of the maidservant and her cigarettes. . . . Your loving subject and grateful . . .[11]

On sending back the book she wrote:

> Herewith I return the Burke with many, many thanks and a few quite unnecessary heartaches over the vicissitudes of the great. It is heart-aching reading! and one feels so thankful for one's own bite and sup and wobbly old roof-tree. As for me, I am cocky-whoopy beyond measure, for my banker wrote to me on Saturday and told me he had invested £200 in Marshall and Snelgrove's 4½ debentures. Now I did not know I had £200 at my back unwanted, and I did not know

*Eliza Lynn Linton*

till to-day that M. and S.'s debentures were scarce to be had for love or money, and that I might hold myself lucky to possess them. So far, you see, I am not on the high road to vicissitudes as per examples cited! . . .

Towards the end of April she journeyed back to London and Malvern never saw her again. Writing to Mrs Layard she says:

> This is just a word to tell you that I am here, and already more than half dead. I think this will be my last visit to London. I know too many people, and they are all too kind to me, and I am torn to pieces – and I cannot stand it, dear! Willing is the spirit, and the old warhorse neighs and pricks up her ears at the familiar sound of the trumpet; but the flesh is very weak, and the poor old limbs fail, and the poor old spirit has to own itself beaten. I am beaten to-day – after the private view of the New Gallery and all the people. . . .[12]

On 3 May she moved from a temporary address back to Queen Anne's Mansions. At the Authors' Dinner of this year she was again given the place of honour, and the spectacle of the authoress of *Under Which Lord?* hobnobbing on the best of terms with the Bishop of London was not without humour and significance. She wrote an account of the affair to Layard.

> . . . My dinner, Authors', went off fine. I looked like the Queen of Sheba. I had another one yesterday. Mr and Mrs Gully, Mr and Mrs Labouchere, and Zangwill. I was between Mr Labouchere and Zangwill, and talked politics to the one and philosophy to the other, and I had a fine time of it. Zangwill is going to *convert me to some form of religion through my intellect.* To-day I have been to see Father K——. *He* would convert me to Romanism if he could. He is a very dear fellow, with the waxen skin of an ascetic.
> 
> The bishop was very nice at the dinner, and so was Lord Welby. I was between both, and the bishop did not seem to think me a pariah. . . .[13]

At this function was her friend Rider Haggard, who later wrote to Layard:

*The last year*

The last time I met her was at the 'Authors' Dinner', I think in the year of her death. After the speeches we sat together in a corner of the room, and I asked her how she was. To this she replied that in health she felt quite well, but that a wonderful change had taken place in her mind, for now she seemed no longer to belong to the world. If I remember right, the metaphor she used was that she felt like one seated on a precipice watching a torrent brawling beneath her – the torrent of humanity, which for her had no longer any meaning, but was a mere confusion of voices and of battling desires, hopes and fears – wherein she had no share.

At this time she seemed to know that she would not live long; to realise with extraordinary distinctness the utter vanity of human life, of success and failure, and all we strive to reach; and to face its ending without fear.

That long and, considering its gay surroundings, curious conversation impressed me much, and when I said goodnight to her it was for the last time.

In my long friendship with her I always found her a most honourable and upright lady, very kind-hearted, though at times she could be bitter with her pen, rather contradictory in her views, or in the expression of them; and somewhat undiscerning in her estimate of acquaintances. She was, in my opinion, one of the very ablest and keenest intellects of her time, and will, I think, be reckoned in its history.[14]

On 13 May she wrote to Mrs Pelly:

All of my own generation are passing into the 'Great Beyond', and a very few years now will see us laid to rest for ever. I do not fear death myself – not the least in the world – but I do not like to see the fine vigorous intellects and bodily powers of my dear friends lose in volume and strength. Still it has to be, if we live long enough; but the dregs come badly after the rich wine![15]

From London she went for a short visit to her friend Mrs Mills at Newbie, Bowdon, Cheshire. On 21 May she wrote to her sister Lucy about Gladstone, who had died on the 19th:

*Eliza Lynn Linton*

> His personality will always remain a national splendour. He was a rarely gifted man intellectually and physically. He got a twist of late years, and he was a very bad patriot, a slack imperialist, but as a man he was magnificent. We have no such masterly intellect left among us now. Better statesmen, better patriots, yes – but finer intellects, No! – I wonder if the family will consent to the Westminster Abbey interment. With all his faults of government he was no snob, and not in the least self-seeking. His hands were emphatically *clean*, and he perpetrated no job nor the shadow of one for his family's sake. He aggrandised no one belonging to him, and made no money by the back stairs. It is all very interesting at present, the war and all that happens about us. Life is lovely to me yet, and full of interest and love.[16]

It had been her intention to return to Malvern and the Layards were to meet her when she arrived, but on 9 June she wrote to them:

> I am sorry to say I shall not be at home till to-morrow week, the 17th. I have been persuaded to stay till the 17th, to go to the dinner given by the New Vagabonds to the Old Stagers. But I have caught a cold, of course, and I have been ill and in bed, and coughing and horrid since Sunday night. It came on all in a minute, and I have been quite ill. But I got up on Tuesday and went out to a dinner made for me, and I had some friends here yesterday to tea. And now I am shut up and not allowed out in a 'kerridge' even. I was asked to the Royal Society Soirée last evening. Sir William and Lady Crookes would have taken me, so I should have been well companioned; but Lord love ye! my dear doctor would have murdered me if I had gone, and I should have died of cold if he had not! But to have heard and seen and realised this new disintegration of the once compacted element, the atmospheric air! It was a cruel temptation.[17]

Late on the 11th she drove out for the last time, and on her return felt so ill that she went straight to bed. She was attended by her friend Dr Kiallmark, who had been her medical adviser for twenty years. The illness had originated with a chill taken at the private view of the Royal Academy and now developed into an attack of bronchial pneumonia. Through this she was devotedly nursed by Mrs Hartley and Mrs Dobie. But the vital powers were exhausted and she succumbed on Thursday 14 July 1898 to a general failure of the system.

From the beginning she seems to have realised that her illness would prove fatal, and she faced the inevitable with admirable stoicism. 'When one has to die', she had once said, 'let it be with decorum. To fight for the reprieve which will not come, to cry out for the mercy which will not be shown, advantages no one. Better the silent acceptance of the blow – and forgiveness of the executioner.'

Her remains were cremated, and on 30 September the ashes were interred in the presence of many of her friends in the churchyard at Crosthwaite at the foot of her father's grave, north-east of the church.

At the conclusion of the service, in which the Reverend Augustus Gedge, Eliza's brother-in-law, took part, Canon Rawnsley gave an address concluding with these words: 'Her desire to get people to work whilst it is called to-day, and to do rather than dream, in some measure made her less firm to believe with a sure and certain hope in the great Beyond. But

> There lives more faith in honest doubt,
> Believe me, than in half the creeds.'

The obituary notices at her death were considerable. Thus the *Academy*:

> Mrs Linton had always something forceable and interesting to say, but an overriding suspicion of the unwomanly woman weakened much of her later work. For what she called the shrieking sisterhood Mrs Linton kept the best of her extraordinary powers of invective, and she pursued her bugbear with admirable if wearisome pertinacity as a writer.[18]

The *Academy* also pointed out that she had been praised by many of her great contemporaries, Dickens, Landor and Swinburne. The last named wrote a poem:

*Eliza Lynn Linton*

> *On the Death of Mrs Lynn Linton*
> Kind, Wise, and true as truth's own heart,
> A soul that here
> Chose and held fast the better part
> And cast out fear . . .[19]

Sir Walter Besant, too, wrote a tribute to her on her lifelong battle, while *The Times*'s notice concluded by saying, 'Mrs Lynn Linton will probably be remembered as a remarkable example of those writers whose sensationalism of expression is more than half-redeemed by their sincerity of conviction and transparent honesty of purpose.'[20]

Studying Eliza Lynn Linton over a number of years, one cannot but feel that few of the harsh things that have been said about her since her death have much justification. She was a woman of immense personality, inflexible as to her own standards, but generous and helpful to those who came to her for help. She attracted many great minds as well as those of lesser calibre. She was a lonely woman, nevertheless, and she knew that she did not possess the talents of her contemporary, George Eliot. She knew that she was a mediocre novelist, but she knew equally that as a controversial journalist she had been successful and effective, and she was determined to stay the course, pursuing to the end the highly topical and controversial subject of the emancipation of women.

# List of Eliza Lynn Linton's works

Linton, Eliza[beth] Lynn (1822 – 1898), novelist and writer of miscellaneous articles: on staff of *Morning Chronicle* 1848 – 1851, and of *Saturday Review* from 1866 to 1877 or later. She contributed 21 articles in 1866 and 10 in 1867 and was in 33 of the 52 numbers in 1868. See Layard, *Mrs Lynn Linton*, pp. 125, 137, 138, 212. She wrote both middles and reviews. Three reviews are identified in Layard, op. cit., pp. 107, 138.
R *Hester's Sacrifice*, XXI, 480, 21 April 1866. This was Mrs Linton's first.
R *A Life's Love*, XXI, 789, 30 June 1866 [Probably *A Lost Love*].
R *Elster's Folly*, XXII, 117, 28 July 1866.
Mrs Linton's *The Girl of the Period and Other Social Essays* reprints one essay from 1867, twenty from 1868 and others as late as 1875. Listed below are those of 1867 and 1868.
M 'Paying One's Shot', XXIV, 720, 7 Dec. 1867.
M 'Modern Mothers', XXV, 268, 29 Feb. 1868.
M 'The Girl of the Period', XXV, 339, 14 March 1868.
M 'Little Women', XXV, 545, 25 April 1868.
M 'Ideal Women', XXV, 609, 9 May 1868.
M 'Pinchbeck', XXV, 676, 23 May 1868.
M 'Affronted Womanhood', XXV, 707, 30 May 1868.
M 'Feminine Affectation', XXV, 776, 13 June 1868.
M 'Interference', XXV, 841, 27 June 1868.
M 'La femme passée', XXVI, 49, 11 July 1868.
M 'Spoilt Women', XXVI, 153, 1 Aug. 1868.
M 'The Fashionable Woman', XXVI, 184, 8 Aug. 1868.
M 'Sleeping Dogs', XXVI, 286, 29 Aug. 1868.
M 'Beauty and Brains', XXVI, 318, 5 Sept. 1868.
M 'Nymphs', XXVI, 353, 12 Sept. 1868.
M 'Mésalliances', XXVI, 419, 26 Sept. 1868.
M 'Weak Sisters', XXVI, 484, 10 Oct. 1868.
M 'Pinching Shoes', XXVI, 516, 17 Oct. 1868.
M 'Superior Beings', XXVI, 677, 21 Nov. 1868.
M 'Feminine Amenities', XXVI, 743, 5 Dec. 1868.
M 'Grim Females', XXVI, 795, 19 Dec. 1868.
*Modern Women and What is Said of Them* (New York 1868) reprints thirty-seven essays from *SR* of 1866–8, of which ten appeared later in Mrs Linton's *The Girl of the Period and Other Social Essays*, and ten were written by J. R. Green. Of the remaining seventeen, Mrs Linton's hand can perhaps be seen in the following at least:

*Eliza Lynn Linton*

M 'Feminine Influence', XXII, 784, 29 Dec. 1866.
M 'Husband Hunting', XXIII, 47, 12 Jan. 1867.
M 'Pigeons', XXIII, 652, 25 May 1867.
M 'Costume and Its Morals', XXIV, 44, 13 July 1867.
M 'Foolish Virgins', XXIV, 211, 17 Aug. 1867.
M 'Plain Girls', XXIV, 495, 19 Oct. 1867.
M 'Mistress and Maid, on Dress and Undress', XXV, 136, 1 Feb. 1868.
M 'Pushing Women', XXV, 578, 2 May 1868.
M 'A Contrast', XXVI, 612, 7 Nov. 1868.

NOVELS AND OTHER WORKS

*About Ireland*, Methuen, 1890.
*About Ulster* (with an Appendix of papers issued by the Irish Unionist Alliance), 1892.
*Amymone: A Romance of the Day of Pericles*, Bentley, 1848.
*At Night in a Hospital*, reprinted from *Belgravia* for July 1879, E. Fisher & Co., 1879.
*Atonement of Leam Dundas, The*, 1876.
*Autobiography of Christopher Kirkland, The*, Bentley, 1885.
*Azeth the Egyptian*, T. C. Newby, 1846.
*Dulcie Everton*, Chatto, 1896.
'George Eliot' in *Women Novelists of Queen Victoria's Reign*, Hurst & Blackett, 1897.
*Girl of the Period, The*, reprinted verbatim from the *Saturday Review*, 1868.
*Girl of the Period and Other Social Essays, The*, Bentley, 1883.
*Grasp Your Nettle*, Smith Elder, 1865.
*In Haste and at Leisure*, Heinemann, 1895.
*Ione*, Chatto, 1883.
*Lake Country, The*, in collaboration with W. J. Linton, 1864.
*Lizzie Lorton of Greyrigg*, 1866.
*Mad Willoughbys and other Tales, The*, Country House Library, No. 1, 1876.
*My Literary Life*, Reminiscences of Dickens, Thackeray, George Eliot, etc., Hodder, 1899.
*My Love*, Chatto, 1881.
*Octave of Friends with other Silhouettes and Stories, An*, Ward & Downey, 1891.
*One Too Many, The*, Chatto, 1894.
'Our Illusions', an essay in the *Fortnightly Review*, 1891.
*Ourselves*, a series of Essays on Women, Routledge, 1869, reprinted Chatto & Windus, 1884.
*Paston Carew, Millionaire and Miser*, Bentley, 1886.
*Patricia Kemball*, 1874.
*Philosophy of Marriage, The*, ('Is Marriage a Failure?'), 1888.
*Realities*, Sanders & Otley, 1851.
*Rebel of the Family, The*, Chatto & Windus, 1880.
*Rift in the Lute, A Tale, The*, Bryce, Glasgow, 1885.
*Second Youth of Theodora Desanges, The*, with an Introduction by Layard, Hutchinson, 1900.

*Sowing the Wind*, Chatto & Windus, 1867.
*Stabbed in the Dark*, F. V. White, 1885.
*Through the Long Night*, Hurst & Blackett, 1889.
*True History of Joshua Davidson, The*, Chatto & Windus, 1872, reprinted Methuen, Two Shilling Series, 1916.
*Twixt Cup and Lip*, Tales, Digby Long, 1896.
*Under Which Lord?*, 1879.
*Was He Wrong?*, serialised only, 1889.
*Witch Stories*, 1861.
*Within a Silken Thread and Other Stories*, Chatto & Windus, 1880.
*World Well Lost, The*, 1877.
*Extracts from the works of Mrs Lynn Linton, selected and arranged by G.F.S. (Mrs Gulie Moss)*, Chatto & Windus, 1892.

# References

Chapter 1 (pp. 3–14)

1. Linton, *Christopher Kirkland*, vol. 1, p. 42.
2. Layard, *The Life of Mrs Lynn Linton*, 1901, p. 4.
3. Linton, *Christopher Kirkland*, vol. 1, p. 43.
4. 'Education was at its lowest possible ebb – though local Grammar-Schools in the North were plentiful, kept up by old-time grants and bequests from former founders and benefactresses.' *Kirkland*, vol. 1, p. 2.
5. id., p. 7.
6. *Kirkland*, vol. 1, pp. 15–16.
7. id., p. 22.
8. id., p. 24.
9. id., p. 25.
10. id., p. 34.
11. ibid.
12. *Kirkland*, vol. 1, p. 47.
13. Layard, *The Life of Mrs Lynn Linton*, 1901, p. 21.
14. ibid.
15. *Kirkland*, vol. 1, p. 75.
16. id., p. 113.
17. id., p. 129.
18. Reprinted in 1972.
19. *Kirkland*, vol. 1, pp. 152–3.
20. id., p. 157.
21. id., p. 188.
22. id., pp. 208–9.

Chapter 2 (pp. 15–19)

1. 'A Retrospect'.

Chapter 3 (pp. 20–33)

1. *Kirkland*, vol. 1, p. 226.
2. id., p. 227.
3. id., p. 239.
4. id., p. 240.
5. id., p. 245.
6. id., vol. 1, pp. 249–50.
7. id., pp. 250 ff.
8. id., p. 261.
9. Mackay, *Forty Years' Recollections of Life, Literature, and Public Affairs from 1830 to 1870*, vol. 1, p. 70.

References

10 Linton, Lynn, *Reminiscences of Dickens, Thackeray, George Eliot*, etc. pp. 47 ff.
11 ibid.
12 id., p. 51.
13 For a full account of this tragic case see Elwin's *Landor*.
14 Linton, Lynn, *Reminiscences of Dickens, Thackeray*, etc., p. 53.
15 Layard, *Mrs Lynn Linton*, p. 162.
16 Linton, *My Literary Life in London*, 1899, p. 92.
17 In a letter to Barbara Leigh Smith, of 24 August 1855, Chapman says, 'I was born in 1821.' The DNB says 1822.
18 Haight, *George Eliot*, p. 81.
19 Linton, *My Literary Life in London*, pp. 94-5.
20 id., p. 96.

Chapter 4 (pp. 34-39)

1 *Kirkland*, vol. 2, p. 12.
2 id., pp. 22-3.
3 ibid.
4 Ashburner was the translator of Reichenbach and author of *Studies in the Philosophy of Animal Magnetism and Spiritualism*.
5 *Kirkland*, vol. 2, pp. 23-4.
6 id., p. 25.
7 Layard, *The Life of Mrs Lynn Linton*, 1901, pp. 176-7.
8 ibid.

Chapter 5 (pp. 40-47)

1 *Kirkland*, vol. 2, pp. 31-2.
2 Layard, p. 80.
3 F. B. Smith, *Radical Artisan*, p. 93.
4 Linton, *Memories*, 1895, p. 123.
5 Layard, p. 82.
6 *Kirkland*, vol. 2, pp. 149-50.
7 Henrietta Cockran, *Celebrities and I*, 1902, p. 171.
8 *Kirkland*, vol. 2, p. 156.
9 id., pp. 183-4.
10 id., p. 200.
11 *Household Words*, April 1854, pp. 158-61.

Chapter 6 (pp. 48-66)

1 Linton, *Memories*, p. 5.
2 id., p. 8.
3 F. B. Smith, *Radical Artisan*, p. 15.
4 F. B. Smith, *Radical Artisan*, p. 18.
5 Julius West, *A History of the Chartist Movement*, p. 49.
7 F. B. Smith, *Radical Artisan*, p. 40.
8 id., pp. 42-3.
9 Linton, *Memories*, pp. 51-2.
10 id., p. 52.
11 id., p. 104.
12 F. B. Smith, *Radical Artisan*, p. 91.

233

## Eliza Lynn Linton

13 id., p. 92.
14 id., p. 106.
15 id., p. 109.
16 Linton, *Memories*, p. 129.
17 Layard, p. 91.
18 Linton, *Memories*, p. 124.
19 Layard, pp. 94-5.
20 id., p. 95.
21 Linton, *Kirkland*, vol. 3, p. 26.
22 id., p. 27.
23 id., p. 29.
24 id., p. 30.
25 F. B. Smith, *Radical Artisan*, p. 132.
26 Layard, p. 100.
27 id., p. 102.
28 *Kirkland*, vol. 3, p. 45.

Chapter 7 (pp. 67-71)

1 *Sowing the Wind*, 1867.
2 Layard, pp. 106-7.
3 *Spectator*, 21 July 1866.
4 *The Times*, Thursday 17 January 1867.

Chapter 8 (pp. 72-94)

1 Bevington, Merle, *The Saturday Review 1855-1868* (New York, 1941), pp. 17-18.
2 Grant, *The Saturday Review. Its Origins and Progress*, pp. 8, 16-17.
3 Bevington, op. cit., p. 23.
4 Lord Bryce, *Studies in Contemporary Biography*, p. 360.
5 Layard, p. 137.
6 *Kirkland*, vol. 3, pp. 2-3.
7 ibid.
8 id., p. 4.
9 Linton, *The Girl of the Period and Other Social Essays*, vol. 1, p. 2.
10 *Kirkland*, vol. 3, p. 3.
11 id., p. 6.
12 Linton, *The Girl of the Period and Other Social Essays*, vol. 1, p. 5.
13 id., pp. 7-8.
14 id., 'Modern Mothers', p. 10.
15 id., p. 16.
16 id., pp. 22-3.
17 id., 'Paying One's Shot', vol. 1, p. 30.
18 id., 'What is Woman's Work?', vol. 1, pp. 38-9.
19 id., 'Little Women', vol. 1, pp. 54-5.
20 id., 'Pinchbeck', vol. 1, p. 73.
21 ibid.
22 ibid.
23 id., 'Saturday Mornings', vol. 1, p. 92.
24 id., 'Feminine Affectations', vol. 1, p. 97.
25 id., 'The Fashionable Woman', vol. 1, p. 117.
26 id., 'Saturday Mornings', vol. 1, p. 120.

*References*

27 id., 'Beauty and Brains', vol. 1, pp. 128–9.
28 id., p. 131.
29 ibid.
30 ibid.
31 id., vol. 1, p. 151.
32 Linton, Preface to collected edition of *The Girl of the Period and Other Social Essays*.
33 Patricia Thomson, *The Victorian Heroine*, p. 86.
34 Layard, *Life of Mrs Lynn Linton*, p. 131.
35 id., p. 152.
36 ibid.
37 id., p. 154.
38 id., p. 155.
39 ibid.
40 id., p. 158.

Chapter 9 (pp. 95–101)

1 *Saturday Review*, 23 March 1867.
2 Cockshut, *Truth to Life*, p. 83.
3 *Kirkland*, vol. 2, p. 76.
4 Bevington, The *Saturday Review, 1855–1868* (New York 1941), p. 87.
5 *The Athenaeum*, 23 July 1898.
6 Layard, pp. 181–2.
7 id., p. 182.
8 id., p. 183.
9 id., p. 183.
10 27 May 1876.
11 24 June 1876.

Chapter 10 (pp. 102–116)

1 Layard, p. 203.
2 id., p. 205.
3 id., p. 206.
4 ibid.
5 id., p. 209.
6 id., p. 210.
7 id., p. 214.
8 See Rev. O. Shipley, *The Church and the World*, and the recently published fine study Rowell, *Hell and the Victorians* (OUP, 1975).
9 Layard, pp. 215–16.
10 Linton, *Kirkland*, vol. 3, pp. 245–6.
11 Layard, pp. 218–19.

Chapter 11 (pp. 117–128)

1 Layard, *Mrs Lynn Linton*, p. 221.
2 See *Our Book of Memories* by Justin McCarthy and Mrs Campbell Praed, 1912.
3 Layard, p. 223.
4 ibid.
5 id., pp. 227–8.
6 Article by Mrs Alec Tweedie in *Temple Bar*.

235

## Eliza Lynn Linton

7  Layard, p. 230.
8  Leon Edel, *Henry James*, vol. 2, pp. 308–9.
9  ibid.
10 Linton, *The Rebel of the Family*.

### Chapter 12 (pp. 129–141)

1  Layard, p. 234.
2  id., p. 235.
3  ibid.
4  id., p. 236.
5  Linton, *The Girl of the Period and Other Social Essays*, 2 vols, 1883, p. viii.
6  R. A. Gettmann, *A Victorian Publisher*, p. 128.
7  M. Elwin, *Landor*, p. 457.
8  ibid.
9  William Cowper's 'Verses Supposed to be Written by Alexander Selkirk', 1, 29.
10 In Dickens's *Nicholas Nickleby*, Chapter 15.
11 Presumably in his *Poems and Ballads*.
12 Pope's 'Moral Essay IV', 1, 149.
13 Acts 10: 28; 11: 8.
14 *The City of Dreadful Night and Other Poems* appeared in 1880.
15 Cymbeline, III, iv, 53.
16 Layard, p. 241.
17 'Wordsworth and Byron' (Bonchurch, 14, 155–244) appeared in the *Nineteenth Century* in April and May 1884 and was reprinted in *Miscellanies*.
18 Layard, p. 244.
19 ibid.
20 Doctor St Claire – the hero in Eliza's novel *Ione*.
21 *Atalanta in Calydon* (Bonchurch 7, 280), echoing Psalm 80: 5.

### Chapter 13 (pp. 142–154)

1  Nancy Anderson, *Eliza Lynn Linton and the Woman Question in Victorian England*, p. 260.
2  id., p. 262.
3  The *Spectator*, 3 October 1885.
4  ibid.
5  Linton, *Kirkland*, vol. 2, pp. 80–1.
6  ibid.
7  id., p. 84.
8  Patricia Thomson, *The Victorian Heroine*, 1956, p. 17.
9  Kirkland, vol. 2, p. 89.
10 id., pp. 92–3.
11 id., p. 95.
12 id., p. 205.
13 id., p. 2.
14 id., p. 4.
15 id., p. 7.
16 *Contemporary Review*, April 1886.
17 *Kirkland*, vol. 3, p. 76.
18 ibid.
19 id., p. 77.

20 id., p. 80.
21 *The Pentateuch and the Book of Joshua Critically Examined.*
22 *Kirkland*, vol. 3, p. 82.
23 id., vol. 3, p. 106.
24 id., p. 110.
25 id., p. 113.
26 ibid.
27 ibid.
28 id., p. 116.
29 ibid.
30 *Kirkland*, vol. 3, p. 123.
31 id., p. 125.
32 Layard, p. 250.
33 *Saturday Review*, 1 August 1855, p. 155.
34 Layard, p. 247.
35 ibid.

Chapter 14 (pp. 155–168)

1 Layard, p. 252.
2 ibid.
3 R. A. Gettmann, *A Victorian Publisher*, p. 116.
4 id., p. 126.
5 N. Anderson, *Eliza Lynn Linton and the Woman Question in Victorian England*, 1973, an unpublished thesis.
6 The *Fortnightly Review*, 1886, pp. 498–510.
7 id., p. 499.
8 The *Fortnightly Review*, 1886, p. 499.
9 ibid.
10 Layard, p. 255.
11 ibid.
12 id., p. 257.
13 id., p. 269.
14 The articles appeared on 17 and 24 August 1889.
15 Layard, p. 266.
16 id., p. 267.
17 id., p. 269.
18 R. B. Smith, *Radical Artisan*, p. 207.
19 Layard, p. 271.
20 Duncan Crow, *The Victorian Woman*, pp. 250–1.

Chapter 15 (pp. 169–177)

1 The *Fortnightly Review*, February 1888.
2 'An Eighteenth-century Abbé', The *Fortnightly Review*, September 1888.
3 The *Fortnightly Review*, September 1888, p. 347.
4 Edited by Lucien Perey and Maugras, 1882–3.
5 The *Fortnightly Review*, September 1888, p. 347.
6 id., p. 348.
7 The *Fortnightly Review*, October 1888.
8 The *Fortnightly Review*, 'The Irresponsibilities of Genius', p. 522 ff.
9 id., p. 525.
10 The *Fortnightly Review*, October 1886, quoted in 'The Higher Education of Women', p. 504.

## Eliza Lynn Linton

11 ibid.
12 ibid.
13 *Universal Review*, September 1888, p. 21.
14 id., p. 24.
15 id., p. 25.
16 id., September 1888, p. 26.
17 id., p. 28.
18 id., p. 30.
19 id., p. 31.
20 id., p. 33.

### Chapter 16 (pp. 178-190)

1 Layard, p. 273.
2 The *Lady's Realm*, 1890, p. 173.
3 id., p. 174.
4 Susan, Countess of Malmesbury, *Lady's Realm*, 1890, p. 178.
5 id., p. 179.
6 Guinevere Griest, *Mudie's Circulating Library and the Victorian Novel*, 1970.
7 Layard, p. 278.
8 *Fortnightly Review*, April 1891, p. 584.
9 ibid.
10 id., p. 586.
11 id., p. 587.
12 id., p. 590.
13 id., p. 591.
14 id., p. 594.
15 The *Athenaeum*, 17 March 1894.
16 Layard, p. 294.

### Chapter 17 (pp. 191-198)

1 Layard, pp. 301-3.
2 id., pp. 299 ff.
3 id., pp. 304-5.
4 id., p. 306.
5 id., p. 309.
6 Helen C. Black, *Notable Women Authors*, pp. 1-2.
7 London, 1894.
8 The *Fortnightly Review*, September 1894, p. 449.

### Chapter 18 (pp. 199-202)

1 J. Comyns Carr, *Some Eminent Victorians*, 1908, p. 265.
2 Eliza Aria, *My Sentimental Self*, pp. 44-6.
3 Edward Clodd, *Memories*, p. 264.

### Chapter 19 (pp. 203-214)

1 Layard, p. 318.
2 The *National Review*, December 1895.
3 Layard, pp. 319-20.
4 id., p. 324.

5  Lady Paget, *In My Tower*, p. 238.
6  Layard, p. 326.
7  Hurst & Blackett, 1897.
8  Layard, p. 328.
9  id., p. 332.
10 Published in 1897.
11 Layard, p. 332.
12 id., p. 333.
13 ibid.
14 id., pp. 334-6.

Chapter 20 (pp. 215-228)

1  Layard, pp. 342-3.
2  id., p. 344.
3  ibid.
4  id., pp. 345-8.
5  id., p. 349.
6  id., p. 353.
7  id., pp. 353-4.
8  id., p. 355.
9  id., p. 356.
10 id., p. 358.
11 id., pp. 360-1.
12 id., p. 364.
13 id., p. 365.
14 id., pp. 365-6.
15 id., p. 366.
16 id., p. 369.
17 id., p. 371.
18 *Academy*, 23 July 1898.
19 Swinburne, *Works*, vol. 6, p. 287.
20 *The Times*, 16 July 1898.

# Bibliography

Printed Sources.
Layard, George Somes, *Mrs Lynn Linton Her Life, Letters and Opinions* (1901).
Anderson, Nancy, *Eliza Lynn Linton and the Woman Question in Victorian England* (University Microfilms, Michigan, U.S.A., 1973).
Bellflower, J., *The Life and Career of Elizabeth Lynn Linton 1822-1898* (University Microfilms, Michigan, U.S.A., 1967).
Aria, Eliza, *My Sentimental Self.*
Bevington, Merle, *The Saturday Review 1855-1868* (1941).
Black, Helen C., *Notable Women Authors of the Day* (1893).
Bullet, Gerald, *George Eliot* (1947).
Carr, J. Comyns, *Some Eminent Victorians* (1908).
Clodd, Edward, *Memories.*
Cockran, Henrietta, *Celebrities and I* (1902).
Crow, Duncan, *The Victorian Woman* (1971).
Edel, Leon, *Henry James: The Conquest of London 1870-1883* (1962).
Elwin, Malcolm, *Landor: A Replevin* (1958).
Gettmann Royal, A., *A Victorian Publisher: A study of the Bentley Papers* (1960).
Granville-Barker, Harley (ed.), *The Eighteen-Seventies* (1929).
Griest, Guinevere L., *Mudie's Circulating Library and the Victorian Novel* (1970).
Haight, Gordon S., *George Eliot* (1968).
Haight, Gordon S., *George Eliot and John Chapman* (1940).
Harris, Frank, *My Life and Loves.*
Hichens, Robert, *The Green Carnation* (1949 edition).
Laski, Marghanita, *George Eliot and her World* (N.D.).
Linton, William, J., *Memories* (1895).
McCarthy, Justin, and Mrs Campbell Praed, *Our Book of Memories* (1912).
Mackenzie, K. A., *Edith Simcox and George Eliot* (1961).
Paget, Lady Walburga, *In My Tower.*
Pearsall, Ronald, *The Worm in the Bud* (1969).
Richards, Grant, *Memories of a Misspent Youth.*
Royle, Edward, *Victorian Infidels* (1974).
Rowell, Geoffrey, *Hell and the Victorians* (1974).
Smith, F. B., *Radical Artisan: William James Linton* (1973).
Spencer, Herbert, *An Autobiography* (1904).
Swinburne, A., *Letters* (Bonchurch edition).
Thomson, Patricia, *The Victorian Heroine* (1956).
Yates, Edmund, *Recollections and Experiences* (1884).

# Index

Aberdeen, Lord 55
*About Ireland* (Linton) 164-5
*Academy, The* 132, 154, 188, 227
Ainsworth, Harrison 40, 173
*All The Year Round* 29, 69
*Amymone* (Linton) 23-4
Anderson, Nancy Bartlett 159
*Angel in the House, The* (Patmore) 93
Anti-Corn-Law League 52
Aria, Mrs 201-2
Ashbourne's Act 165
Ashburner, Dr John 37
Asher, Dr 150, 151, 152
*Athenaeum, The* 95, 97, 101, 154, 162, 188, 200
*Atonement of Leam Dundas, The* (Linton) 83, 100-1, 110
Attwood, Thomas 52
*Australian Heroine, An* (Praed) 117
Authors, Society of 203
*Autobiography of Christopher Kirkland* (Linton) 75, 113, 132, 142-54, 158
*Azeth the Egyptian* (Linton) 23

Babbage, Sir Charles 40
Balfour, A. J. 165, 166
*Ballad of Reading Gaol, The* (Wilde) 222
Ballantyne, James 58
Barrie, Sir James 121
Bell, Robert 36
Benn, Alfred William 104-7
Benn, Reverend William 104
Bentley, George, publishers 24, 87, 142, 143n, 158
Besant, Sir Walter 182, 228
Black, Helen C., *Notable Women Authors* 197
Blackwell, Dr Elizabeth 90-1
Blackwell, Emily 90-1
Blackwood, William, publisher 68, 133
Blanc, Louis 35
Bonner, George Wilmot 48-9
Bowring, Dr 53-4

Brabant, Robert Herbert 26-7
Bradbury and Evans 69
Bradlaugh, Charles 98
Brantwood, Linton's house, 59 60-1, 65-6, 67
Bray, Charles 34
Brewitt, Susanna, *see* Chapman, Mrs John
Bright, John 98
Brontë, Charlotte, 134, 207
Brontës, The 3
Brooks, Charles Shirley 30
Broughton, Rhoda 154
Browning, Elizabeth Barrett 38, 43, 148
Browning, Robert 38, 50
Bryce, Lord 72
Bulwer-Lytton, Edward 35, 173
Burke, T. H. 164
Burton, Lady 134, 209-10
Butler, Josephine 168

*Candour in English Fiction* 182
Carlile, Richard 50
Carlisle, Bishop of 3-4
Carlyle, Thomas 11, 34
Carpenter, Mary 173
Carr, J. Comyns 200-1
*Cause of the People, The* 56
Cavendish, Lord Frederick 164
Chamberlain, Joseph 220
*Chambers' Journal* 206
Chambers, Robert 148, 206
Chapman, Mrs John 30
Chapman, John 30, 31, 32
Chapman and Hall 133-4
Charlotte, Queen, Consort of George III 3
Chartist Movement 51-2
Clairvaux, Mme de 44
Clarke, Mary, *see* Mohl, Madame von
Clodd, Edward 202
Cockburn, Sir Alexander 35

241

# Eliza Lynn Linton

Cockman, Henrietta 43
Coleridge, S. T. 11, 26, 170, 172
*Conservative, The* 51
*Contemporary Review, The* 147
Cook, John Douglas (Editor, *Morning Chronicle*) 24, 25, 26, 72, 95
Cowen, Joseph 58, 59
Craik, Mrs (Dinah Mulock) 207
Crawford, John 91–2, 148
Crookes, Sir William and Lady 226
Crosthwaite, Fisher 161, 162
Crosthwaite, living of 3, 6, 7

*Daily Graphic* 88, 101
*Daisy Miller* (James) 122, 123, 124, 125, 126
*Dandy* (Middlemas) 210
Davies, Emily 187
*Dear Davie* (Linton) 127
Delane, J. T. 24
Dickens, Charles, 15, 16n, 29, 37–8, 42, 63, 68, 69, 85, 227
Drummond, Prof. 197–8
Duffy, Sir Charles Gavin 56
*Dulcie Everton* (Linton) 204
Duncombe, Thomas 54

*East Lynne* (Wood) 182
Edel, Leon 122–3
Eliot, George 26, 30–1, 32, 33, 68, 69, 148, 155, 156, 207, 228
*Elster's Folly* (Wood) 67
Emerson, R. W. 34
Empson, Bookshop in Bath 26
*English Republic, The* 58, 59
*Eöthen* (Kinglake) 148
*Examiner, The.* 24, 101

*Family at Fenhouse, The* (Linton) 127
*Fate of Madame Cabanel, The* (Linton) 127
Fletcher, Mrs 53–4
Forman, Buxton 49
Forster, John 29
*Fortnightly Review,* 169–70, 183, 198
Foster, W. E. 41
Fox, W. J. 50
Froude, J. A. 34
Fry, Elizabeth 173
Fuller, J. F. 163–4

*G. P. Almanack* 87
*Galloping Dick* (Linton) 127
Gaskell, Mrs 34, 207

Gedge, Ernest (nephew) 112, 204
Gedge, Lizzie and Ada (nieces) 107
Gedge, Mrs Lucy (Eliza's sister) 9, 102, 103, 109–10, 111, 112, 121, 122, 129, 139, 157, 160, 161, 183, 186, 204, 207, 211, 213, 214, 215, 216, 217, 220–1, 222, 225
*Gentleman's Magazine* 111
Gibson, Milner 34, 35–6
Gibson, Mrs Milner 34–5
*Girl of the Period* (Essay) 74, 75, 76, 79, 87, 88, 131–2, 141, 147, 196
Girton College 187–8, 190
Gladstone, Wm. E. 225–6
Goodenough, Charlotte Alicia, *see* Lynn, Mrs James
Goodenough, Samuel, Dean of Rochester, *see* Carlisle, Bishop of
Graham, Sir James 54, 55
*Grasp Your Nettle* (Linton) 68, 70, 76
Grattan, Thomas Colley 172
Green, Mrs J. R. 209
Greg, William Rathbone 45–6
Grote, Mrs 25

Haggard, Sir H. Rider 121, 224
Harcourt, Sir William 220
Hardy, Thomas 87, 182, 183
Harraden, Beatrice 191–4
Harrison, Frederic 98
Harte, Bret 184
Hartley (Mrs), née Sichel, Beatrice 103–4, 107, 108, 109, 111, 112, 114
Harvey, George Julian 58
Hemans, Felicia Dorothea 8
Henderson, Sir James 187
Hennell, Caroline 26, 31
Herzen, Alexander 57, 58
Hetherington, Henry 51, 52
*History of England* (Macaulay) 181
*History of Greece* (Grote) 148
Hodgson, Dr 34
Holyoake, G. J. 56
Home, Daniel Dunglas 12, 35, 36, 38
Home Rule Act 165–6
Horne, A. H. 49
Houghton, Lord 30, 35, 133
*Household Words* 46, 69
Hugo, Victor 139
Hunt, Thornton 34, 40, 41, 56, 57, 58

*Illustrated London News* 52, 53, 56
*In Haste and at Leisure* (Linton) 199–200

242

*Index*

Ione (Linton) 134, 138, 140, 141
Israel, Mrs Ben 149

James, Henry 122, 123, 131
Jerrold, Douglas 40, 50, 173
Jex-Blake, Sophia 91

Keats, J. 136
Kemble, Charles 49
Kemble, Fanny 43, 49
Kiallmark, Dr 226
Kipling, Rudyard 121
Kingsley, Charles 41

Labouchere, Mr and Mrs 224
*Lady's Pictorial* 191
*Lady's Realm, The* 179
*Lake Country, The* (Linton) 65
Lamennais, Abbé 55-6, 57
Landor, Miss 102
Landor, Mrs 102
Landor, Walter Savage 24, 27, 28, 29, 33, 58, 62, 63, 102, 133, 134, 135, 136, 170, 171, 184, 227
Larken, Reverend Edmund 41
*Last Tenants of Hangman's House, The* (Linton) 126
Layard, George Somes 38, 88, 154, 187, 191, 192, 208, 216, 221-2, 223, 224-5, 226
Layard, Mrs 224
*Leader, The* 34, 41, 56, 57, 58
Leitch, Dr, of Keswick 59
*L'Enfant Prodigue* (Wormser) 186
Lewes, George Henry 32, 34, 41, 56, 58, 69, 155, 156
*Life of Landor* (Forster) 29
Linton, Eliza Lynn: birthplace, 3; on her father 4-5; childhood 6-8; and her youthful reading 9; and youthful difficulties 10-11; early religious concepts 12-13; and an emotional event 13-14; at Gadshill 15-19; determined on a career 20-1; goes to London 22; her first novel 23; meets John Douglas Cook 24-5; meets Dr Brabant 26; meets Landor 27-8; and reviewing Forster's *Landor* 29; boarder with Chapman 30; meets George Eliot 31; ends relationship with Chapman 32; meets notabilities 34-5; meets Home 35-6; and occultism 37-9; in Paris 40-7, 59; nurses Emily Wade 60; and the Linton family 61; marries Linton 62; life in Bayswater 63; helps in husband's work 64; split in her marriage 65; working on a new book 67; her separation 68; her novels 70; Lizzie Linton 70-1; contributions to *Saturday Review* 72-89; important friendships 91-4; and religion 96-7; and Rev. Charles Voysey 98-9; travels 102; A. W. Benn and Eliza 104-5; in Italy 106-11; visiting friends 112-14; meeting with Mrs Campbell Praed 117-18; interviewed by Mrs Tweedie 119-20; controversy over James's *Daisy Miller* 122-5; her short stories 126-8; essays published 131; and Swinburne 133-6; in Sicily 137-8; at Queen Anne's Mansions 139; sees Swinburne 140; autobiography of Christopher Kirkland 142-54; correspondence with Herbert Spencer 155-7, 183-5; return to Keswick 161; and Irish affairs 163-5; contributions to the *Fortnightly Review* 169-70; and 'The Higher Education of Women' 173-4; and sport 179-81; criticisms of *The One Too Many* 187-90; and Beatrice Harraden 191-4; recalled by some contemporaries 200-2; last years at Malvern 203; religious beliefs 211-13; final months in London 215-28
Linton, W. J. 41, 48, 49, 50, 52, 53, 54, 55, 56, 57, 58, 59, 60, 61, 62, 63, 64, 65, 66, 67, 73, 156, 167, 215
Linton, Mrs W. J. 50
*Lizzie Lorton* (Linton) 70-1, 95
Loaden, William, family solicitor 21, 23
Longfellow, W. 52
Low, Sir Sidney 196, 203-4
Lyall, Edna 207
Lyell, Sir Charles 148
Lynn, Arthur Thomas 4, 9
Lynn, Charlotte Elizabeth 4
Lynn, George Goodenough 4
Lynn, Reverend James 3, 4, 5, 8, 9, 10, 13, 15, 16, 20, 21, 63
Lynn, Mrs James 3, 4, 5
Lynn, James Narborough 4
Lynn, Lucy, *see* Gedge, Mrs
Lynn, Samuel 5

243

## Eliza Lynn Linton

Malmesbury, Susan, Countess of 179, 180, 181
Marlowe, Christopher 136
Martineau, Harriet 25, 59, 144, 207
Maurice, Frederick 41
Mazzini 35, 53, 54, 55, 56, 57, 58
Meredith, George 133
Meyrick, Sir Samuel 28
Middlemas, Jean 210
*Mildred's Lovers* (Linton) 126
Milner, Lady 181
Milnes, Monckton, see under Houghton, Lord
Mohl, Julius von 42, 43
Mohl, Madame von 42
Moir, Mrs 67
Montague, Lord Robert 97
Moore, George 182
Moore, Thomas 26, 172
Morgan, John Minter 41
Morgan, Matthew 87
*Morning Chronicle, The* 24, 30
Moss, Gulie, Mrs 187, 19₁
Mudie's Circulating Library 71, 181-2
Muller, Max 148
Murchison, Sir Roderick 148
Murray, Amy (her niece) 130
Murray, Rose Caroline, see Praed, Mrs Campbell
*My Love* (Linton) 122
Myers, the Reverend 11, 12

Nansen Lecture 208
*National, The* 51
*National Review, The* 175, 198
*New Review, The* 164
Newby, T. C. 23
Nietzsche 105
Nightingale, Florence 173
*Nineteenth Century and After* 198
Norton, Andrew 149
Norton, Caroline 25, 89
Nugent, Lady 28

O'Brien, William 166
O'Connell, Daniel 19
*Odd Fellow, The* 52
*Once A Week* 69
*Ourselves* (Linton) 68, 132
Owen, Robert 145
Oxford Movement 96

Paget, Lady 205-6

*Pall Mall Gazette* 178
Panizzi, Sir Antonio 22
Pardoe, Julia 40
*Paston Carew, Millionaire and Miser* (Linton) 139, 157, 158
Patmore, Coventry 94
*Patricia Kemball* (Linton) 196
Pelly, Mrs Raymond 225
*Peuple Constituant, Le* 55
Piggott, Edward 34
*Poor Man's Guardian, The* 51
Praed, Mrs Campbell 117, 118, 119
*Present Age* 58
Priestley, Lady 112
*Punch* 55, 181
Puseyism 96

*Queen, The* 178, 200

Raffles, Sir Stamford 91
*Realities* (Linton) 30, 32, 33, 43, 68
*Rebel of the Family, The* (Linton) 114-16, 122, 136-7, 160
*Red Republican, The* 58
Reform Club 58
*Republican, The* 50
Rochester Grammar School 3
Rosebery, Lord 220
Rosebery, Lord, Administration 198
Ruskin, John 186-7

*St James's Budget* 196
*St James's Gazette* 157, 206
Saintsbury, George 188
Salisbury, Lord 219, 220
Sand, George 53, 148
Sanders & Otley, publishers 33
*Saturday Review, The* 72-89, 95-6, 97, 117, 131, 154, 201
*Second Youth of Theodora Desanges* (Linton) 207-8
Shelley, P. B. 171
*Ships That Pass in the Night* (Harraden) 191
Sibson, Thomas 53
Sinnett, A. P. 38, 39
Smith, Harvey Orrin 64
Smith, John Orrin 53, 64
Smith, Dr Southwood 50
Smith, William 34
Southey, Robert 170-1, 172
*Sowing the Wind* (Linton) 89, 93
*Spectator, The* 209

244

*Spectator, The* 34, 55, 143
Spedding, James 92–3
Spencer, Herbert 148, 155, 156, 157' 183–4, 195, 197–8, 208
Spottiswoode, William 92
*Stabbed in the Dark* (Linton) 155, 157
Stafford, John 216–17
Stisted, G. M. *True Life of Captain Sir R. F. Burton* 209
Swinburne, A. C. 133, 134, 136–7, 138, 139, 140, 227–8

Talfourd Bill 74
*Temple Bar* 119, 155
Tennyson, Lord 92, 220, 221
Thackeray, W. M. 35
*The One Too Many* (Linton) 187–8, 191
Thompson, Colonel Perronet 58
Thomson, James 135
*Through the Long Night* (Linton) 158, 162, 175
*Times, The* 24, 71, 72, 228
Toynbee, Joseph 54
Trollope, Anthony 182
Trollope, Thomas Adolphus 104
*True History of Joshua Davidson, The* (Linton) 93, 97–8, 100, 111, 134, 158
Tweedie, Mrs Alec 23, 119, 120

*Under Which Lord?* (Linton) 110, 111, 224

Vizetelly, Henry 87
Voysey, Reverend Charles 98–9, 100 165, 166

Wade, Emily 52, 53, 57, 58, 59, 61
Wade, Laura, *see* Linton, Mrs
Wade, Thomas 49, 53
Wadham College, Oxford 3
Walker, Dr Mary 90
Walter, A. F. 166
Walter, John 24
Wardle, Lady 215
*Was He Wrong?* (Linton) 178
Watson, Ellen 58
Watson, James 50, 51
Watts-Dunston, Theodore 137
Wedgwood, Julia 147
Weller, Mr 16
*Westminster Review, The* 31
Wette, Wilhelm De 149
*What-not or Ladies' Handy Book, The* 89
Wilde, Oscar 222
Wills, Henry 15, 41, 42, 122
Wills, Mrs 139
*Witch Stories* (Linton) 12, 68
Withers-Moore, Dr 173
*Within a Silken Thread* (Linton) 125–6
Wollstonecraft, Mary 46
*Woman at Home* 203
*Women Novelists of Queen Victoria's Reign* 207
Women's Property Bill (1870) 89, 168
Wood, Mrs Henry 67
Woodall, William 218, 219
Wordsworth, William 11, 138, 143, 171
*World Well Lost* (Linton) 103, 110

Zangwill, I 224